Study Guide

for

EDUCATIONAL PSYCHOLOGY

Study Guide

for

Woolfolk
EDUCATIONAL PSYCHOLOGY
SIXTH EDITION

by

Lynne Díaz-Rico
University of California, San Bernardino

and

Ruth Sandlin
University of California, San Bernardino

Allyn and Bacon
Boston · London · Toronto · Sydney · Tokyo · Singapore

ISBN 0-205-16210-X

Printed in the United States of America

10 9 8 7 6 5 4 3 2 1 99 98 97 96 95 94

Contents

Preface

The decision to become a teacher is not made lightly. The course of preparation to become a teacher requires many years of undergraduate study, combined with specific professional education coursework, on-site observation and participation in local schools, and practice teaching or beginning teaching supervised by experienced colleagues. Despite this prolonged process, many new teachers leave the profession during their first years of employment. What does it take to prosper in this demanding profession?

A commitment and dedication to young people…a desire to "make a difference"… a life involved in learning… a joyful participation in the lives of children… the motives that attract and bind teachers to this career are as varied as the styles of teaching that fill our classrooms. However, one outstanding trait that good teachers share is the mastery of the fundamentals of education: The knowledge of human development, learning theories, teaching practices, student motivation, and communication skills that the best teachers exemplify. This knowledge lies at the core of educational psychology.

The Study Guide functions as a valuable adjunct to the text, highlighting the key points and offering applications which make these ideas come alive in the context of the classroom. The final goal: That the new teacher has experienced these central concepts in depth, and these ideas have penetrated to a level which will shape effective instruction and give spirit and inspiration to the life of the classroom.

No preliminary instruction in teaching is ever vital enough to reflect the actual experience of the classroom, with its daily challenges and triumphs, setbacks and breakthroughs, vexations and victories. No training can fully prepare a new teacher for the joy and terror of facing the first day of the first school year. And no illumination is ever so rewarding as the insight that comes from-- at last-- beginning to master the psychology of instruction, in class, in touch with a student who is learning because a teacher knows how to teach. This is the essence of our goal in providing this tool for the study of educational psychology.

Study Guide

for

EDUCATIONAL PSYCHOLOGY

1

Teachers, Teaching, and Educational Psychology

Teaching Outline

I. What Do You Think?
II. What is good teaching?
    A. Inside five classrooms
        1. A bilingual first grade
        2. A suburban sixth grade
        3. An inner-city middle school
        4. Two advanced math classes
    B. Expert teachers
        1. Have richer and more elaborate categories for understanding problems in teaching
        2. Work from integrated sets of principles instead of dealing with each new event as a new problem
        3. Have a sense of what is typical in classrooms
        4. Have knowledge that is solid and thoroughly developed
        5. Have mastered a number of moves/routines without thinking
    C. Expert knowledge as defined by Lee Shulman (1987)
        1. Academic subjects taught
        2. General teaching strategies
        3. Curriculum materials/programs for their subject area and grade level
        4. Subject-specific knowledge for teaching
        5. Characteristics of learners and their cultural background
        6. Settings in which students learn
        7. Goals and purposes of education
III. Teaching: Artistry, technique, and a lot of work
    Point/Counterpoint: Whose Classroom Is It Anyway?
    A. Concerns of beginning teachers
        1. Developing confidence in their teaching skills
        2. Maintaining class discipline, motivating and accommodating differences among students
        3. Surviving the real-life situation of the classroom: "reality shock"
    B. What about the students?
IV. The role of educational psychology
    A. Is educational psychology just common sense?
        1. Example: Taking turns
        2. Example: Classroom management
        3. Example: Skipping grades
    B. Using research to understand and improve teaching
        1. Descriptive research: Describes what is happening in class
            a. Ethnography: Descriptive research about naturally occurring events
            b. Participant observation: The researcher is a part of the action
            c. Case study: In-depth investigation
        2. Correlation: Indicates the strength and direction of a relationship between two events/measurements (negative or positive)

        3. Experimentation: Changes are introduced and results are noted

        4. Theories for teaching

V. The contents of this book

    A. A quick tour of this book

        1. Part 1: Human Development

        2. Part 2: Individual Variations

        3. Part 3: Learning: Theory and Practice

        4. Part 4: Motivation and Management

        5. Part 5: Teaching

        6. Part 6: Assessment

    B. How this book can help you

        1. Helps build professional knowledge base for teaching

        2. Enables reader to think critically about teaching

        3. Helps develop a repertoire of effective principles and practices for first years of teaching

VI.   Summary

VII.   Key terms and concepts

VIII. What would you do?

IX.   Cooperative learning activity

Key Points

See if you understand the main points which are covered in this chapter:

What is good teaching?

- Classroom examples of good teaching

  - High expectations for student success

  - Constant encouragement of students

  - Pace is brisk

  - Instructional delivery is varied

  - Teacher respects students' culture and takes time for home visits

  - Instruction may include innovative use of technology

  - Teacher takes an interest in social and emotional development of students

  - Hands-on experience augments formal instruction

  - Attention is devoted to students' concept formation and development

  - Smooth and efficient classroom procedures

- **Expert versus novice teachers**

  - <u>Expert teacher</u>: Experienced, effective teacher who has developed solutions for common classroom problems

- Novice teacher: Inexperienced teachers just beginning their careers

- Teachers can elaborate knowledge and have a variety of teaching methods

- Expert teachers understand why students make mistakes; this guides reteaching

- Expert teachers look for patterns, and teach from sets of principles

- Problem-solving, information-seeking, and alternative solutions enrich subject matter teaching

- Teaching routines are smooth and automatic, leaving time for creativity

- Experts can improvise explanations and create new examples spontaneously

- Most experts continually upgrade their knowledge by continuing education

- Expert knowledge: What teachers know

  - They have mastered the academic subject they teach

  - They can apply general teaching strategies (non-subject-specific)

  - They use curriculum materials and programs appropriate for their subject and grade level

  - They can adapt their subject-specific teaching knowledge to meet student needs

  - They are aware of characteristics of learners and their cultural backgrounds

  - They understand the various settings for student learning

  - They recognize the goals and purposes of teaching

Teaching: An art, a science, and a lot of work

- The practice of teaching is based upon research, combined with teachers' judgment, intuition, commitment and creativity

- Reflective teaching: Analyzing situations to improve learning for students

- Concerns of beginning teachers

  - Maintaining classroom discipline, motivating students, accommodating individual differences, evaluating student performance, dealing with parents

- There is usually no break-in period; new teachers face full responsibilities from the first day

- Seasoned teachers can focus on students' needs and successes

The role of educational psychology

- <u>Educational psychology</u>: Discipline concerned with the teaching and learning processes

  - Educational psychology forms the scientific basis for the art of teaching

  - Studies involve controlled laboratory experiments and field testing in the classroom

The value of research and theory

- Research versus common sense approaches to teaching

- Research can examine common-sense practices for their scientific validity

- Theories present a unifying view of methods and practices

- Using research to understand and improve teaching

- <u>Descriptive research</u>: Studies that collect detailed information about a specific situation, often using observation, surveys, interviews, recordings, or a combination of these methods.

  - <u>Ethnography</u>: A descriptive approach to research that focuses on life within a group and tries to understand the meaning of events to the people involved.

  - <u>Participant observation</u>: A method for conducting descriptive research in which the researcher becomes a participant in the situation in order to better understand life in that group.

  - <u>Case study</u>: Intensive study of one person or one situation.

  - <u>Correlational research</u>: Research that describes statistically how closely two variables are related.

  - <u>Positive correlation</u>: A relationship between two variables in which the two increase or decrease together.

  - <u>Negative correlation</u>: A relationship between two variables in which a high value on one is associated with a low value on the other.

  - <u>Experimentation</u>: Research method in which variables are manipulated and the effects are recorded

- <u>Subjects</u>: People or animals studied

- <u>Random procedure</u>: Each subject has an equal chance to be in any group

- <u>Statistically significant</u>: The effect observed is not likely to be a chance occurrence.

- <u>Theory</u>: An integrated statement of principles and laws that attempts to explain a phenomenon and make predictions

- <u>Principle</u>: Established relationship between factors

Concept Map: Expert Teachers

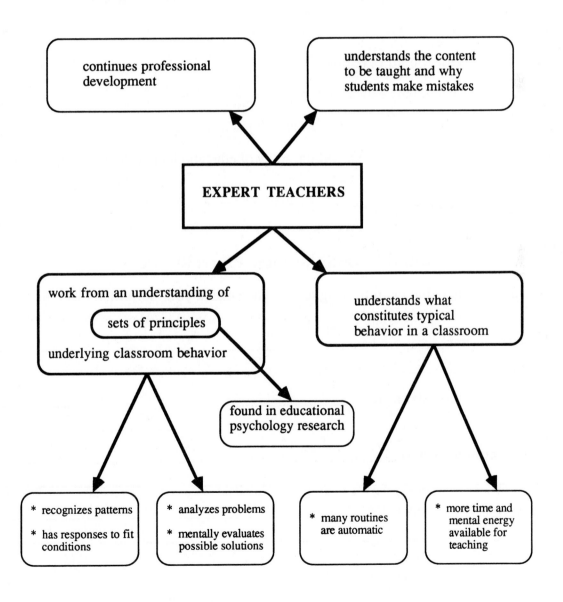

Do You Know This?

Answering these questions will help you to check yourself on your mastery of the chapter objectives.

What is Good Teaching?

Compare your perception of teaching with the classroom examples given in this chapter.

Give your reasons for wanting to be a teacher.

What are Shulman's seven areas of professional knowledge?

Teaching: Artistry, Technique, and a Lot of Work

Describe the differences between expert and beginning (novice) teachers.

What are the greatest concerns of beginning teachers?

The Role of Educational Psychology

Give reasons for studying educational psychology.

Give examples of how theory and research can make an impact in education .

What specific kinds of problems will the study of educational psychology help to solve?

Key Terms and Concepts

DEFINITIONS: Teachers' Expert Knowledge

See if you can define the following terms. Then check your definitions with those in the text.

Expert teacher _____

_____

General teaching strategies _____

_____

Curriculum materials _____

_____

Subject-specific knowledge _____

_____

Cultural background of learners _____

_____

Settings for student learning _____

_____

IDENTIFICATION: Expert Versus Novice Teachers

Distinguish expert teaching behaviors from those of novices. Choose Expert (E) or
Novice (N) for each blank. To check your answers, see Answer Key.

_____ 1. Recognizes the misconceptions behind students' wrong answers

_____ 2. Much time is consumed with classroom organization

_____ 3. Limited ability to elaborate subject area knowledge

_____ 4. Can analyze situations to diagnose the source of a problem

_____ 5. Works with integrated sets of principles

_____ 6. Has difficulty generating spontaneous examples when explaining

_____ 7. Efficient in time management

COMPLETION QUESTIONS: Theory and Research in Educational Psychology

Fill in the blanks below with the following concepts. Each term is used only once. To
check your answers, see Answer Key.

Descriptive	**Ethnography**
Participant observation	**Case study**
Correlational	**Experimental**
Positive correlation	**Negative correlation**
Subjects	**Random procedure**
Statistically significant	**Theory**

1. A school psychologist evaluates a child's adjustment to a recent parental divorce.
   This research involves a _____ method.

2. The researcher is collecting detailed information about beginning teachers'
   classrooms concerns by interviewing teachers who have taught less than two years.
   This is an example of _____ research.

3. The students in a classroom who are being studied by an educational psychologist
   become the _____ of the research.

4. Researchers trying to determine whether superior performance on an intelligence test is related to subsequent vocational success would use a _____ study.

5. A psychologist who becomes a substitute teacher in a school in order to study the discipline challenges in a junior high school to more fully understand life in that setting is using _____ .

6. According to experimental results, one method is definitely superior to another. In order to be sure that these results did not happen by random chance, these results must be demonstrated to be _____.

7. The higher the summer temperature, the higher the electrical bill. This is an example of _____ .

8. A set of related principles can be called a _____ .

9. A researcher studying the perception of school from a Cambodian immigrant's point of view must use a type of research called _____.

10. The students in a classroom are being divided into two groups for test a new teaching method. They are divided into these groups by drawing numbers from a hat. This is considered a _____ .

11. As the amount of rainfall increases, the attendance at a football game goes down. This is an example of a _____.

12. Bringing children into a mobile laboratory set up next to their school, researchers measure their learning as they are taught with different materials. This study uses _____ research .

DEFINITIONS: Theory and Research

Write explanations for the following pairs of terms. Your explanation should clearly distinguish the two from one another. Check the Glossary to see if your explanations are equivalent.

Ethnography/Participant Observation _____

_____

Negative/Positive Correlation _____

_____

Descriptive/Experimental Research _____

_____

IDENTIFICATION: Positive, Negative, and Zero Correlation

Distinguish positive, negative, and zero correlation. Choose positive (+), negative (-), or zero (0) correlation to label the most probable correlation for each relationship described. To check your answers, see Answer Key .

_____ 1. Miles over speed limit / Cost of moving violation ticket

_____ 2. Number of times a students arrives late to school / Number of tardy notices sent home

_____ 3. Temperature of day / Amount of clothes worn

_____ 4. Shoe size / Grade on mathematics test

_____ 5. Cost of automobile / Cost of automobile insurance

_____ 6. A child's height / Grades achieved in school

_____ 7. Teacher's musical ability / Students' spelling performance

_____ 8. Number of students in class / Teacher attention available for each student

_____ 9. Reduction of caloric intake / Reduction of weight

_____ 10. Absences from school / Time spent on class activities

APPLICATION: Experimental versus Descriptive Research

A teacher of a seventh-grade class is concerned that her students have difficulty writing a two-paragraph summary of their science laboratory activities. She wishes to design a study so that the results can improve the students' writing in this area. What would a descriptive study of the writing behavior include? What form would the results take? Contrast this with an experimental study. What procedures would she follow? What form would these results take?

APPLICATION: Expert Teacher Knowledge

Expert teachers can use student errors to diagnose the misunderstanding or lack of information behind several types of student mistakes, so that they can reteach and correct the misunderstanding. Practice this expert knowledge in the domain of subtraction. Suppose you are the teacher of a second grade mathematics class. Below are several problems with wrong answers. For each of the problems, suggest what the student misunderstands about subtraction with regrouping (carrying a digit to the next column), and what specific reteaching may be necessary.

```
    17              17
    19              19
  + 18            + 18
    72              44
```

CASE STUDY: Maintaining Student Focus

Mr. Barlow, a first-year teacher, is conducting a third-grade social studies lesson. The following is a partial transcript of this lesson. What would you suggest to improve student-teacher interaction?

Barlow: …And who can tell me how the earliest settlers found drinking water? (pause) Billy, pick up the pencil on the floor. No yelling out, raise your hands. I'm still waiting… Louise, stop talking. Yes. José?

José: They brought water with them in the covered wagons.

Barlow: No. I said the <u>earliest</u> settlers. They didn't come in a covered wagon. Jennifer?

Jennifer: Daniel's making funny noises.

Barlow: Daniel, I've told you 100 times to stop the noises. Next time you do it, you'll go to the office. OK, who can answer the question?

PRACTICE TEST: Multiple Choice

Select the <u>best</u> answer for each of the following items. For answers, see Answer Key.

1.   Current conceptions of educational psychology view it as being concerned with
   a.   teaching.
   b.   learning.
   c.   improvement of classroom methods.
   d.   all of the above.

2.   Which of the following terms does not fit the category of descriptive research?
   a.   Observational
   b.   Correlation
   c.   Manipulative
   d.   Classroom-based

3. The most likely correlation between height and shoe size of adults is
    a. positive.
    b. negative.
    c. close to zero.
    d. 0 to 100.

4. Correlations range in value from.
    a. -1.00 to +1.00.
    b. 0 to +1.00.
    c. 0 to 100.
    d. 1 to 10.

5. Which of the following correlation coefficients indicates the strongest relationship?
    a. -.03
    b. +.56
    c. -.78
    d. +.70

6. A person who is tested in a research study as a part of a treatment group is called a
    a. case.
    b. participant observer.
    c. guinea pig.
    d. subject.

7. Random assignments would be most critical in _____ research.
    a. case study
    b. correlational
    c. descriptive
    d. experimental

8. Which one of the following is usually established prior to the other three?
    a. Principle
    b. Theory
    c. Valid scientific explanation
    d. Consistent findings

9. A theory is expected to
    a. explain and predict perfectly.
    b. provide solutions to specific problems.
    c. provide an explanatory framework for understanding a variety of problems.
    d. represent a causal relationship between environmental variables and behavior.

PRACTICE TEST: Essay

A. What do beginning teachers need to learn in their first year of teaching? Give three areas in which they must focus.

B. Explain how ethnographic knowledge can be helpful to a classroom teacher. For example, suppose a teacher's students are predominantly of a certain ethnic group. How would ethnographic research about that group be helpful in the classroom?

Answer Key

IDENTIFICATION: Expert Versus Novice Teachers

1.	E	5.	E
2.	N	6.	N
3.	N	7.	E
4.	E		

COMPLETION QUESTIONS: Theory and Research in Educational Psychology

1. Case study
2. Descriptive
3. Subjects
4. Correlational
5. Participant observation
6. Statistically significant
7. Positive correlation
8. Theory
9. Ethnography
10. Random procedure
11. Negative correlation
12. Experimental

IDENTIFICATION: Positive, Negative, and Zero Correlation

1.	+	5.	+
2.	+	6.	0
3.	-	7.	0
4.	0	8.	-
5.	+	9.	+
6.	0	10.	-

CASE STUDY: Maintaining Student Focus

There are several ways in which Mr. Barlow could improve the students' focus. USING PREVIOUS KNOWLEDGE: He could set the stage for learning by reviewing previous learning regarding the earliest settlers. This could minimize the confusion when he asked a question about the earliest settlers. ASKING OPEN-ENDED QUESTIONS: He could ask the same question in a manner which would generate a variety of correct answers, such as "Let's think of all the ways that settlers could find water." SETTING CONSISTENT CONSEQUENCES FOR BEHAVIOR: Mr. Barlow could praise positive behavior (raising hands appropriately), while misbehaviors should result in an immediate negative consequence.

APPLICATION: Expert Teacher Knowledge

	17		17
	19		19
+	18	+	18
	72		44

(The student has added 7 + 9 + 8 and obtained 24; however, has entered 2 instead of 4 in the one's column and entered 4 in the ten's column)
REVERSING THE DIGITS

(The student has added 7 + 9 + 8, entered 1 instead of 2 in the ten's column, thinking that 1 is always entered when regrouping occurs)

CARRYING THE WRONG DIGIT

PRACTICE TEST: Multiple Choice

1. d Although educational psychology makes a distinction between teaching and learning, it is concerned with both areas as well as classroom methods. Specifically, it attempts to increase understanding of the processes of teaching and learning and of how to improve these processes.

2. c A correlational study is descriptive research, because it provides information on an existing relationship between two variables. Observational research and classroom-based research are also descriptive. In contrast, manipulative or experimental type research is not descriptive because it purposely changes normal conditions to evaluate or test a treatment.

3. a Height and weight are positively correlated. As height increases, weight tends to increase; that is, taller people tend to weigh more and vice versa.

4. a Correlations range from -1.00, which represents a perfect (very strong) negative correlation, to +1.00, which represents a perfect positive correlation.

5. c The strongest correlation of the four choices is represented by -.78. It is not the sign (direction) that determines strength; it is the closeness of the correlation to either +1.00 or -1.00. A correlation of -.78 represents a fairly strong negative relationship.

6. d The common term used to describe a participant in a research study is subject.

7. d Random assignments are critical in experimental research. If such assignments are not employed, the researcher will be unable to determine whether treatment differences are caused by the treatments themselves or by the treatment groups being different in some important way that is related to the outcome being studied.

8. d Consistent findings form the basis for establishing principles. Theories are explanations of why different outcomes occur.

9. c A theory provides a general explanatory framework for understanding problems. Principles are more specific explanations of given problems.

PRACTICE TEST: Essay

A. Beginning teachers develop routines for making assignments, checking work, and setting rules. They experiment with new methods and materials. They focus on students' needs.

B. Ethnographic methods can describe the recurring patterns of behavior that typify the groups' daily life, and what those behaviors mean to the group members from their point of view. This can benefit the teacher by making it easier to adjust to the groups' behavior and adapt that behavior to desired classroom patterns.

2

Cognitive Development and Language

Teaching Outline

I. What Do You Think?

II. A definition of development
- A. Orderly, adaptive changes by human and animals between conception and death: Physical, personal, social, and cognitive
- B. Influential factors
  1. Maturation--genetically programmed, naturally occurring changes
  2. Environmental interaction
- C. Principles of development
  1. Occurs at different rates
  2. Is relatively orderly
  3. Takes place gradually
- D. The brain and cognitive development
  1. Various parts of the brain are involved with various functions
  2. Two hemispheres of the brain show lateralized development
  3. Contemporary research connects learning to brain functioning

III. Piaget's theory of cognitive development
- A. Piaget's basic assumption: Development as "making sense of the world"
- B. Influences on development: Maturation, activity, social transmission, equilibration
- C. Basic tendencies in thinking
  1. Organization: Tendency to organize thinking processes into psychological structures/schemes
  2. Adaptation: Tendency to adapt to the environment through complementary processes of assimilation and accommodation
  3. Equilibration: A balance among organization, assimilation and accommodation
  4. Disequilibration: Failure of a scheme to produce satisfying a result, so search continues through assimilation and accommodation
- D. Four stages of cognitive development
  1. Stage theory broadly defines the unvarying sequence of steps in the development of thinking abilities
  2. Infancy: The sensorimotor stage (approximate ages 0-2)
     a. Development based upon information obtained through the senses or body movements
     b. Development of understanding of object permanence
     c. Development of goal-directed actions and reversible actions
  3. Early childhood to the early elementary years: The preoperational stage (approximate ages 2-7)
     a. Beginning of logical mental actions (operations)
     b. Difficulty with two principles: Decentering and conservation
     c. Egocentrism: Tendency to see world from own view
     d. Collective monologue characterizes children's speech (no real interaction takes place)
     e. Guidelines: Teaching the Preoperational Child

4. Later elementary to middle school years: The concrete operational stage (approximate ages 7-11)
   a. "Hands-on thinking" stage: Recognizes stability of physical world, realizes elements can be changed and retain original characteristics (identity), and is capable of reversible thinking
   b. Operations mastered at this stage: Conservation, classification and Seriation
   c. Guidelines: Teaching the Concrete Operational Child
5. Junior and senior high: Formal operations (approximate ages 11-15)
   a. "Scientific" reasoning stage: Hypothetico-deductive and inductive reasoning
   b. This stage not necessary for survival; achieved in areas of interest and experience
   c. Do we all reach the fourth stage?
   d. Guidelines: Helping Students to Use Formal Operations

IV. Implications of Piaget's theory for teachers
   A. Understanding students' thinking
      1. Determine students' logic/solutions as they solve problems
      2. Look for repeated mistakes or problems
   B. Matching strategies to abilities
      1. Keep disequilibrium "just right" to encourage growth
      2. Ensure students active engagement in learning process
      3. Apply and test principles learned in one situation to a new situation
   Point/Counterpoint: Can Cognitive Development Be Accelerated?
   C. Some limitations of Piaget's theory
      1. Children's development does not fit consistently into stages
      2. Theory may have underestimated younger children's cognitive ability
      3. Piaget's theory overlooks the effects of children's cultural and social group

V. Vygotsky's alternative to Piaget: Cognitive development through interaction with more capable people
   A. The role of language and private speech
      1. Allows younger children to guide behavior and thinking
      2. Transitions to inner speech--helps solve problems
   B. Comparison of Vygotsky and Piaget's views
   C. Self-talk and learning: Teaches students to use cognitive self-instruction
   D. Assisted learning: Provides categories and concepts for thinking
      1. "Scaffolding" provides mediation in order to structure help
   E. The zone of proximal development
      1. Area where child cannot solve problem alone, but can with "scaffolding"
      2. Optimal for teaching and learning
   F. Instructional conversations
      1. Designed to promote complex language and cognition
      2. Alternative to the dominance of teacher talk

VI. The development of language
   A. How do we learn language?
      1. Universal grammar : A set of specifications and rules that limit the range of language created
      2. Language is learned like other cognitive activity" by active pattern-seeking
      3. Care-givers may use reward to shape language
   B. Stages in the process of language acquisition
      1. First words
         a. Holophrases: Single words to express complex ideas

           b. Overextension: Use of one word to cover a range of concepts

           c. Underextension: Use of words too specifically

      2. First sentences

           a. Telegraphic speech: Nonessentials omitted, as in a telegram

           b. Sentences are short, but semantics are complex

      3. Learning grammar

           a. Overregularization uses rules too extensively

           b. The order of words in a sentence is simplistically understood

      4. Learning vocabulary

           a. Between ages 2 and 4, vocabulary doubles every six months

           b. By age 5-6: Child masters basics of language; still egocentric with meanings

   C. Language development in the school years

      1. Pronunciation: The distinctive sounds of a language

           a. By first grade most phonemes mastered

           b. Intonation: Word emphasis may still cause problems

      2. Syntax

           a. Early elementary -school years: Passive sentences understood but not generally used

           b. Elementary school--Complex grammatical structures first understood, then used

      3. Vocabulary and meaning

           a. Average six year old has a vocabulary of 8,000-14,000 words

           b. From 9-11, 5000 new words added

           c. Abstract words, justice or economy still difficult in early years

      4. Pragmatics: Appropriate use of language in context

           a. Use of simpler sentences to talk to younger children

           b. Ability to argue or contribute to conversations on the same topic

           c. Interest in understanding the perspective of other speakers

  D Teaching and language

      1. Metalinguistic awareness: explicit understanding of language and how it works

      2. Teachers can help students develop language abilities and knowledge by:

           a. Enriching students' language by focusing on idea expressed, not usage

           b. Probing and extending students' ideas

           c. Planning interactions and conversations with adults to promote word meaning

           d. Reading aloud to promote language

           e. Interacting one-to-one

VII.   Summary

VIII.   Key terms and concepts

IX.   What would you do?

X.   Teacher's casebook

Key Points

See if you understand the main points which are covered in this chapter:

A definition of development

- Development: The orderly, adaptive change we go through from conception to death

- <u>Physical development</u>: Changes in body structure over time

- <u>Personal development</u>: Changes in personality that take place as one grows

- <u>Social development</u>: Changes over time in the ways we relate to others

- <u>Cognitive development</u>: Gradual, orderly changes by which mental processes become more complex and sophisticated

- <u>Maturation</u>: Genetically programmed, naturally occurring changes over time

Piaget's Theory of Cognitive Development

- Provides an explanation of thinking from infancy to adulthood

- Underlying assumption that individuals strive to make sense of the world

- There are three factors that influence changes in thinking:

    - <u>Maturation</u> is the unfolding of biological changes that are genetically programmed

    - <u>Activity</u> involves the individual's ability to act in the environment

        - Through social transmission, people learn from others

    - <u>Equilibration</u> is the search for balance between cognitive schemes and information from the environment

        - <u>Schemes</u> are the structures that are the basic building blocks of thinking

- Piaget believed that all species inherit two basic tendencies:

    - <u>Organization</u> is the ongoing process of arranging information and experience into mental systems or categories

    - <u>Adaptation</u> is the tendency to adjust to the environment in one of two ways:

        - <u>Assimilation</u> is fitting new information into existing cognitive structures

        - <u>Accommodation</u> is altering existing cognitive structures (schemes) or creating new ones in response to new information

            - <u>Disequilibration</u> occurs when a person's current ways of thinking are not working

- Piaget's four stages of cognitive development

    - Sensorimotor stage: Development involves the senses and motor activity

        - Object permanence: During the sensorimotor stage, a child realizes that an object that is hidden from view still exists; objects have a separate permanent existence

        - Goal-directed actions: Actions that are a result of deliberate planning are the chief accomplishment of the sensorimotor period

    - Preoperational stage: The child has not yet mastered mental operations but is moving toward mastery

        - Operations: Actions carried out by thinking them through rather than actually performing the actions

        - Reversible thinking: The child learns to think backward from the end to the beginning

        - Decentering: The child can focus on more than one aspect or dimension at a time

        - Egocentric: Children assume that others experience the world the way they do

        - Collective monologue: Form of speech in which children in a group talk, but do not really interact or communicate

    - Concrete Operations stage: Mental tasks are tied to concrete objects and situations

        - Identity: The child learns that a person or object remains the same over time

        - Compensation: Changes in one dimension can be offset by changes in another

        - Classification: Grouping objects into categories

        - Seriation: Arranging objects in sequential order according to one aspect or dimension like size, weight, or volume

        - Conservation: A child learns that some characteristics of an object remain the same despite changes in appearance or changes in other aspects

    - Formal Operations stage: Mental tasks involving abstract thinking and coordination of a number of variables

        - Hypothetico-deductive reasoning: Thinking about a "what-if" situation and deducing the possible outcomes

- Adolescent egocentrism: The assumption that everyone else shares one's thoughts, feelings, and concerns

Implications of Piaget's theories for teachers

- Theory helps teachers understand students' thinking

- Theory helps teachers match strategies to abilities

- Piaget's theory has limitations:

    - The stages are inconsistent; similar operations actually occur many years apart

    - Children's abilities are underestimated; they can be very expert in some areas

    - The child's cultural group may have an important effect on the thinking produced

Vygotsky's alternative to Piaget

- Children's knowledge, ideas, and values develop through social interactions

- Vygotsky viewed children's private speech not as egocentric, but as internalizing what the child learns from others, and using self-talk to guide thought

- The transition from private speech to thought is a fundamental process in development; children learn "self-talk"

- Scaffolding: Adult help that provides information and support to children

    - Adults provide verbal prompts, structuring, and cooperative groups as help through process of assisted learning

- Zone of Proximal Development: The difference between the child's ability to solve a problem alone and the ability to solve the problem with adult help

- Instructional conversation is designed to promote complex language and cognition

The development of language

- Language has three aspects: pronunciation, grammar, and meaning

    - Phonemes: The distinctive sounds of a language (ex. "sh")

    - Morphemes: The smallest unit of meaning in a language (ex. plural = "-

s" or "-en")

- Syntax: The order of words in phrases or sentences (ex. "Joan comes home," not "Home Joan comes.")

- Semantics: The meanings of words and combinations of words (ex. "homely" means "physically unattractive" but is a gentler word than "ugly.")

- Pragmatics: Area of language involving the effects of contexts on meaning,
including when to speak and what to say in various situations

- Transformational grammar: A theory that suggests that humans have an inborn ability to use and make sense of language by transforming the surface structure of phrases and sentences into a deep structure of meaning

- Some characteristics of children's early language development:

    - Holophrases: In children's speech, one word can mean a whole phrase

    - Overextension: Children may use one word to cover a range of concepts

    - Telegraphic speech: Children use "important" words and leave out prepositions and other less important aspects of sentence structure

    - Overregularization: Once children learn a rule, they apply it in inappropriate instances (ex. Rule: "Past tense is formed using '=ed'" --> "goed")

    - Metalinguistic awareness: Children gradually become adept at examining language and understanding how it is best used; they can think about language rather than merely using it

- Language development plays a large role in cognitive development

- Teachers can enrich children's language environment by focusing on the children's ideas

- The key to language development is to encourage reading, writing, talking, and listening

- The whole-language teaching approach encourages teaching and learning in a reciprocal and collaborative relationship

    - Classroom learning focuses on authentic, real-life tasks

    - The emphasis is on the integration of reading, writing, speaking, and listening

- Teachers strive to impart to children a love of literature

Concept Map: PIAGET'S THEORY OF COGNITIVE DEVELOPMENT

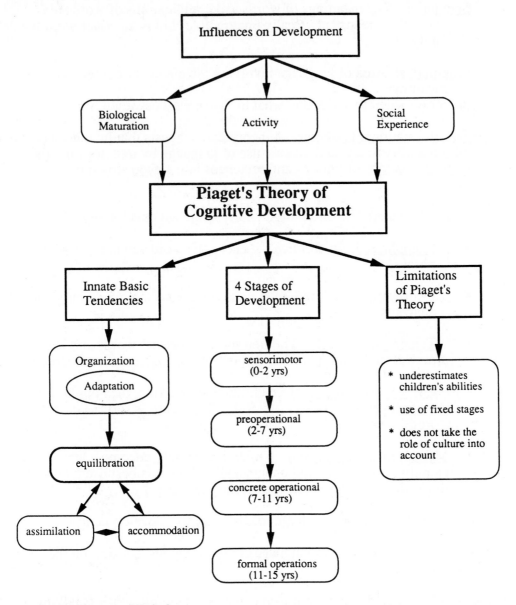

Do You Know This?

Answering these questions will help you to check yourself on your mastery of the chapter objectives.

A Definition of Development

Can you give three general principles of human development? Can you give an example of each principle?

Piaget's Theory of Cognitive Development

What are the four stages of cognitive development, according to Piaget? Approximately what ages are children in each stage?

Can you explain how children's thinking differs at each stage of development? What are some of the characteristics of thinking that children display at each stage?

Implications of Piaget's Theory for Teachers

Describe some ways that Piaget's theory is helpful to teachers. How do teachers use their knowledge of a child's cognitive stage as they teach children of different ages?

Vygotsky's Alternative to Piaget

Can you explain what Vygotsky's theory implies about teaching children?

Compare the main points of Piaget's theory with Vygotsky's. Use the chart below.

	Piaget	Vygotsky
Some key concepts		
Role of teacher in the child's development		
Can development be accelerated?		
How does the child's thinking change with age?		
How does social interaction affect cognitive level?		

The Development of Language

Can you describe the stages by which children learn language?

Can you suggest ways that the teacher can help children expand their language use and comprehension?

Key Terms and Concepts

DEFINITIONS: General Developmental Concepts

Write the definitions for the following terms. Then check the text to see if your definition is appropriate.

Development _____

_____

Physical development _____

_____

Personal development _____

_____

Social development _____

_____

Cognitive development _____

_____

Maturation _____

_____

MATCHING: Concepts in Cognitive Development

Match the numbers of the descriptions on the right to the corresponding items on the left. Use each definition only once. For answers, check Answer Key.

_____ 1. Organization	a.	Altering existing schemes or creating new ones
_____ 2. Adaptation	b.	Fitting new information into existing schemes
_____ 3. Schemes	c.	Sense of "out-of-balance" when current thinking
_____ 4. Disequilibrium		is not adequate
_____ 5. Assimilation	d.	Mental systems of perception and experience
_____ 6. Accommodation	e.	Arranging information into mental systems
_____ 7. Equilibration	f.	Adjustment to the environment
	g.	Search for mental balance between cognitive schemes and environment

COMPLETION QUESTIONS: Piagetian Concepts

Fill in the blanks below with the following concepts. Each term is used only once. For answers, see Answer Key.

Adolescent egocentrism	**Goal-directed actions**
Classification	**Hypothetico-deductive reasoning**
Collective monologue	**Identity**
Compensation	**Object permanence**
Concrete operations	**Operations**
Conservation	**Preoperational**
Decentering	**Reversible thinking**
Egocentric	**Semiotic function**
Equilibration	**Sensorimotor**
Formal operations	**Seriation**

1.   Infants explore the world by using their senses and motor skills during the _____ stage of development.

2.   When babies understand that a toy which is hidden from view still exists, they have mastered _____.

3.   When infants have the ability to try deliberately to accomplish something, they are demonstrating _____.

4.   When children can carry out processes using logical thought rather than having to manipulate objects physically, they are using _____.

5.   Young children begin to represent things mentally and use language during the _____ stage of development.

6.   Using symbols, signs, or gestures to represent actions or objects is called the

_____.

7.   Thinking   backward   from   the   end   to   the   beginning   is   called

_____.

8.   The principle of _____ states that changing an object's shape does not change its quantity.

9.   When a child can focus on both width and length of two rectangles in order to compare their areas, we say that the child is capable of _____.

10.   Preschoolers' inability to take someone else's perspective illustrates their _____ thought.

11.   When children are playing together and seem to be conversing, but are not actually interacting, they are engaged in _____.

25

12.   As children develop logical reasoning skills and can understand increasingly complex conservation problems, they are mastering _____.

13.   In order to master concrete operations, children must learn that an object or person remains the same over time. This is called _____.

14.   Change in one dimension can offset changes in another.   This is _____.

15.   When a child realizes that "roses" and "violets" are both in a category called "flowers," this shows a knowledge of _____.

16.   A child who arranges circles in sizes from small to large can perform _____

17.   Being able to coordinate a number of variables during abstract thinking shows the capacity for _____.

18.   Suppose you are a teenager and have borrowed your parents' car; then run out of gas on a deserted highway. Using _____, you can generate some possible solutions to your problem, and evaluate the possible consequences of each alternative.

19.   A young girl who believes that "everyone" is watching what she wears may be demonstrating _____.

20.   The search for mental balance between cognitive schemes and information from the environment is called _____.

DEFINITIONS: Vygotsky's Theory

Describe what the following terms mean in your own words. Discuss with a friend if your definitions are equivalent to those in the Glossary.

Private speech _____

_____

Scaffolding _____

_____

Zone of Proximal Development _____

_____

MATCHING: Concepts in Language Acquisition

Match the numbers of the descriptions on the right to the corresponding items on the left. Use each definition only once. For answers, see Answer Key.

_____ 1. Syntax
_____ 2. Pragmatics
_____ 3. Holophrases
_____ 4. Overextension
_____ 5. Underextension
_____ 6. Telegraphic speech
_____ 7. Overregularization
_____ 8. Metalinguistic awareness

a. The same words are used for various objects
b. Narrowly limiting the meaning of a word
c. The order of words in a sentence
d. Inappropriate use of a grammatical rule
e. A single word means a whole sentence
f. An understanding of the use of language
g. Effects of context on language meaning
h. Children's abbreviated sentences

APPLICATION: General Developmental Concepts

The kindergarten teacher is responsible for a child's growth in a variety of ways: physical development, personal development, social development, and cognitive development. For each of these developmental areas, describe two activities which a teacher could include in a daily plan.

Physical development _____

_____

Personal development _____

_____

Social development _____

_____

Cognitive development _____

_____

APPLICATION: Piaget's Stages of Cognitive Development

Read each behavior description below. On the preceding blank, write which stage of cognitive development in which this behavior would first be evident. For answers, see Answer Key.

Sensorimotor   **Concrete Operations**
Preoperational   **Formal Operations**

_____ 1. Connects voices with faces.

_____ 2. Experiments on objects with preplanning.

_____ 3. Child can think simultaneously about several aspects of a situation.

_____ 4. Ordering is systematic.

_____ 5. Judges others' behavior by general principles.

_____ 6. Ideas are related by cause and effect.

_____ 7. Visually anticipates future positions of objects.

_____ 8. Sounds can express a feeling.

_____ 9. Spontaneously practices bringing hand to mouth.

_____ 10. Reproduces behavior that has an interesting effect.

_____ 11. Words can explain events.

_____ 12. Can represent an object mentally that is not present physically.

_____ 13. Pursues an action which has been interrupted.

_____ 14. Generates alternatives before choosing a plan of action.

_____ 15. Can generate experimental alternatives in a logical manner.

APPLICATION: Vygotsky's Theory

Imagine you are a first grade teacher. Pedro talks to himself in Spanish as he works, and you are concerned that this may be interfering with his learning ability. What would Vygotsky say about this issue?

_____

_____

_____

CASE STUDY: Piaget's Stage of Concrete Operations

Mr. Evans teaches world geography to a ninth grade class. When he discusses the effect of a city's geographical characteristics on its climate, industry, and trade, the students seem to lack comprehension. By studying Piaget, Mr. Evans has suspected that most of his students are still in the stage of concrete operations and are not ready for formal operations thinking. What are some activities which Mr. Evans could incorporate into his lesson plans to help the students learn to use the following:

Classification _____

_____

Seriation _____

_____

Decentering _____

_____

Compensation _____

_____

PRACTICE TEST: Multiple Choice

Select the best answer for each of the following items. For answers, see Answer Key.

1. Which of the following statements about development is false?
   a. People tend to develop at different rates.
   b. People tend to develop abilities in different orders.
   c. Maturation is largely genetically determined.
   d. Development applies to mental as well as physical growth.

2. Which of the following is an example of maturation?
   a. Losing weight during a brief illness
   b. Losing weight due to exercise
   c. Gaining weight from age 2 to age 3
   d. Learning which foods produce the most weight gain

3. The statement "knowledge is based on bodily activity" refers to what stage?
   a. concrete operational
   b. formal operational
   c. preoperational
   d. sensorimotor

4. A child is shown two balls of clay which she identifies as being equal in quantity. When one of the balls is then rolled into a sausage, the child says that piece (i.e. sausage) now has more clay. The child is probably in the _____ stage.
   a. concrete operational
   b. formal operational
   c. preoperational
   d. sensorimotor

5. Ms. Brown entered her classroom to find all the children chattering, but no one seemed to be talking to or interacting with anyone else. Ms. Brown was observing _____ in her classroom.

    a. holophrastic speech
    b. collective monologue
    c. metalinguistic awareness
    d. telegraphic speech

6. The acquisition of which of the following is not associated with the formal operations stage?

    a. Abstract thought
    b. Hypothetical reasoning
    c. Seriation
    d. Adolescent egocentrism

7. Research indicates that children can conserve number a year or two before they can conserve weight. Such results are generally interpreted as

    a. supportive of Piaget's stage idea since they indicate that development is invariant.
    b. supportive of Piaget's stage idea since they show conservation to become more difficult with increasing task complexity.
    c. non-supportive of Piaget's stage idea since they suggest a lack of consistency in children's thinking.
    d. non-supportive of Piaget's stage idea since the stage theory predicts the opposite ordering of task difficulty.

8. Research has shown that when children mispronounce words, their parents are likely to

    a. correct their mistakes.
    b. ask the child to repeat the statement.
    c. ignore the statement until the child says it correctly on her own.
    d. respond to the content of the statement and ignore the error.

9. Children's speech that contains only essential words, such as "go store" or "want cookie" is called

    a. dialectic
    b. holophrastic.
    c. metalinguistic.
    d. telegraphic.

PRACTICE TEST: Essay

A. Describe what kinds of reasoning a child must develop in the preoperational and early concrete operations stages in order to understand that water does not change in amount when poured from a tall beaker to a short one.

B. How might a teacher determine the range of a student's Zone of Proximal Development on the task of multiplying fractions? Describe how a teacher could then use instructional strategies to help a child master this task in a step-by-step manner.

Answer Key

MATCHING: Concepts in Cognitive Development

1. e
2. f
3. d
4. c
5. b
6. a
7. g

COMPLETION QUESTIONS: Piagetian Concepts

1. sensorimotor
2. object permanence
3. goal-directed actions
4. operations
5. pre-operational
6. semiotic function
7. reversible thinking
8. conservation
9. decentering
10. egocentric
11. collective monologue
12. concrete operations
13. identity
14. compensation
15. classification
16. seriation
17. formal operations
18. hypothetico-deductive reasoning
19. adolescent egocentrism
20. equilibration

MATCHING: Concepts in Language Acquisition

1. c
2. g
3. e
4. a
5. b
6. h
7. d
8. f

APPLICATION: Piaget's Stages of Cognitive Development

1. Sensorimotor
2. Sensorimotor
3. Concrete Operations
4. Concrete Operations
5. Formal Operations
6. Sensorimotor
7. Sensorimotor
8. Sensorimotor
9. Sensorimotor
10. Sensorimotor
11. Preoperational
12. Concrete Operations
13. Sensorimotor
14. Formal Operations
15. Formal Operations

PRACTICE TEST: Multiple Choice

1. b   Although people develop at different rates, their development occurs in <u>an orderly fashion</u>. That is, certain abilities tend universally to be developed before others (e.g., crawling before walking).

2. c   Maturation refers to changes that occur naturally and spontaneously, rather than as a result of environmental circumstances. An example would be <u>gaining weight from age 2 to age 3</u>. (Note: losing weight due to illness or exercise is not a natural occurrence, but one that is caused by particular environmental events.)

3. d   During the <u>sensorimotor</u> period, development is based on information obtained from the senses and from actions or body movements. During the next stage, preoperational thinking, which involves the use of language to represent concepts, will develop.

4. c   The child is probably in the <u>preoperational</u> stage because he is failing to demonstrate conservation. If he were in the concrete operations or formal operations stage, he would indicate that both pieces contain the same amount of clay because the quantity of the sausage-like piece has not changed.

5. b   Mrs. Brown was observing a <u>collective monologue</u>, a behavior of preoperational children in which they talk aloud in a group, but mainly to themselves rather than to others.

6. c   The formal operations stage is not associated with the development of <u>seriation</u>, the ability to order things in a logical sequence. That ability is acquired during the concrete operations stage, which precedes formal operations.

7. c   Some critics of Piaget argue that children should acquire similar types of conservation abilities (e.g., weight and number) about the same time. The fact that this does not occur is thus viewed as <u>non-supportive of Piaget's stage idea.</u>

<u>since it contains a lack of consistency in children's thinking</u>.

8.   d   Researchers studying the interactions between children and their parents have found that parents rarely correct pronunciation and grammar during the early stages of language development. <u>They respond to the content and ignore the error</u>.

9.   d   <u>Telegraphic speech</u>, which develops at about 18 months, contains only essential words, as in a telegram. An example would be "go store." Holophrases, which are used earlier, are one-word communications that imply a whole phrase of meaning.

PRACTICE TEST: Essay

A.   In order to understand that water does not change in amount when poured from a tall beaker to a short one, a child must develop the following reasoning in the preoperational and early concrete operations stages: reversible thinking, compensation, decentration, and conservation.

B.   To determine the range of a student's Zone of Proximal Development on the task of multiplying fractions, first determine a step-by-step procedure for completing the multiplication task. To understand what the student is capable of doing during independent work, analyze which steps the student is using independently. Teach the steps the student is not yet using. Sample instructional strategies might be the following: Use the student's mistakes to diagnose erroneous approaches; have the student explain in his or her own words what procedure is being used to solve the problems; and build on what the student already knows.

3

Personal, Social, and Emotional Development

Teaching Outline

I. What Do You Think?
II. The work of Erikson
   A. Framework for understanding needs of students in relation to society
      1. Emergence of self, the search for identity, and individual's relationship with others
      2. Psychosocial: All humans have same basic developmental needs; society must provide for needs
      3. Stages: Eight developmental crises/conflicts need a positive resolution for healthy future development (Table 3.1)
   B. The preschool years: Trust, autonomy and initiative
      1. Infant develops sense of trust when needs for food and care satisfied; trusting more important as realization of separateness from the world grows
      2. Autonomy versus same and doubt--development of confidence and control ; calls for protective but not overprotective parents
      3. Initiative versus guilt: Zest for initiating activities balanced against need for restraint; learning about adult roles through pretend games and increased ability to perform grown-up tasks
      4. Guidelines: Encouraging Initiative in the Preschool Child
   C. Elementary and middle school years: Industry versus inferiority
      1. Industry: Desire to do productive work with a growing sense of competence; difficulty can results in feeling of inferiority
      2. Industrious childhood leads to well-adjusted adulthood
      3. Guidelines: Encouraging Industry
   D. Adolescence: The search for identity
      1. Identity versus role confusion: Answer to the question Who am I? Is based on earlier resolutions
      2. Identity: The organization of person's drives, abilities, beliefs, and history into a structure of self
      3. Marcia's four alternatives for adolescents (Table 3.2)
      4. Identity and the role of the school
         a. Teachers are often the most appropriate adult to help adolescents
         b. Rejection of authority may be involved
         c. Identity formation may be an extended process
      5. Ethnic pride and identity
      6. Guidelines: Encouraging Identity Formation
   E. Beyond the school years: Human relations in adulthood
      1. Intimacy versus isolation: Ability to have a close personal relationship
      2. Generativity versus self-absorption: Caring for the needs for future generations
      3. Integrity versus despair: Sense of having led a satisfied life
III. Understanding ourselves and others
   A. Self-concept and self-esteem: The composite of ideas, feelings, and attitudes people have about themselves
      1. Children's understandings of themselves moves from concrete to abstract
         a. Early views of self based on immediate behaviors and appearances;

thinking rule-bound, segmented, not flexible
    b. In later years, children think abstractly about internal processes--beliefs
  2. Self-esteem is the evaluation of one's own self-concept
  3. Self-concept continues to evolve, influenced by parents/family in early years, friends/peers in later years
  4. Self-concept becomes differentiated over time
    a. Top level is general view of self
    b. Middle level includes the nonacademic self-concept as well as self-concept in English and mathematics
    c. Third level consists of perceptions of physical ability, appearance, relations with peers and family
 B. Self-concept and school life
  1. Higher self-esteem relates to more positive attitudes and success in school
  2. Student self-esteem influenced by teachers' caring, feedback, and evaluation
  3. Suggestions for Encouraging Self-Esteem (Table 3.3)
 C. The self and others
  1. Intention: Differentiates accidental and proposed actions
  2. Taking the perspective of others develops over time
  3. Selman's five stages of perspective-taking (Table 3.4)
IV. Moral development
 A. Kohlberg's stages of moral development
  1. Preconventional (Stages 1, 2): Judgment based on person's own needs and perceptions
  2. Conventional (Stages 3, 4): Taking into account expectations of society and law
  3. Postconventional (Stages 5, 6): Judgments based on principles that go beyond specific laws
  4. Moral dilemmas: hypothetical situations in which no choice is absolutely right-- used to evaluate moral reasoning
  5. Level of moral reasoning related to both cognitive and emotional development
  6.. Stages of morality: Problems and criticisms
    a. In real life, stages not separate, sequenced and consistent
    b. Ordering of stages indicates a sex and cultural bias
 B. Alternatives to Kolhberg's theory
  1. Social conventions versus moral issues
  2. Cultural differences in moral reasoning
  3. The morality of caring-- empathy (feeling emotion as experienced by others)
 C. Moral behavior
  1. Cheating: Involves specific situations; not just beliefs about right and wrong
  2. Aggression: Role models often seem to condone violent behavior
  3. Guidelines: Dealing with Aggression and Encouraging Cooperation
V. Socialization: The home and the school as influences on development
 A. American families today
  1. Growing up too fast
  2. Children of divorce
    a. Single-parent family may be stressed economically and socially
    b. Guidelines: Helping Children of Divorce
  3. Child abuse (see Table 3.6)
 B. New roles for teachers
  1. What do teachers think about affective education?

  2. How do teachers encourage personal growth?
   a. A predictable, stable world where children can succeed and learn
   b. Teacher versus availability to talk about personal problems
  3. Guidelines: Affective Education Programs
VI. The preschool years
 A. Physical development
  1. Physical growth steady and predictable for both boys and girls
  2. Control increases in gross-motor skills
  3. Fine motor skills develop greatly
 B. The impact of day care
  1. Effects of good day-care generally positive
  2. Children in programs are more assertive, self-confident, socially mature and outgoing
  3. Day care not disruptive to child's emotional bonds with parents
  4. Children tend to interact with peers in both positive and negative ways
  5. Day care children of low-income families seem to be more successful than those who do not attend day care
 C. Developmentally-appropriate preschools
  1. Several ages may be grouped together
  2. Materials should be nongraded
  3. Teachers should match the child and materials
VII. The elementary school years
 A. Physical development: Increase in height and weight; awareness of physical differences
 B. Friendships in childhood
  1. Level one: Friends are whoever a child plays with; friendship is based on moment-to-moment actions
  2. Level two: Friendship defined by willingness to help when help is needed
  3. Level three: Friendships based on more personal qualities and less tied to behavior
VIII. Issues affecting adolescents
 A. Early and late maturers
  1. Puberty: Type of change and duration variable
  2. Early maturation brings academic advantage
  3. Boys: Early-maturers more likely to be popular, late-maturers less well adjusted; may be come compensation later in life
  4. Girls: Early-maturing may be a disadvantage
  5. Guidelines: Dealing with Differences in Growth and Development
 B. Adolescents at risk
  1. Teenage sexuality and pregnancy
   a. Majority of American teens 15 and up have had intercourse
   b. Rate of teenage pregnancy higher in United States than similar developing countries
   c. Many teenagers are uninformed about birth control: Research suggests providing facts to teenagers decreases unwanted pregnancies
  2. Eating disorders
   a. Bulimia: Binge eating
   b. Anorexia nervosa: Self-starvation
  3. Drug abuse
   a. Nearly all high school seniors report experience with alcohol; 20% of seniors are smokers; 30% have used an illegal drug
   b. Teachers should not overreact to casual experimentation; but students need

to be given alternatives to drug use
4. AIDS: Students must be educated and informed about risk
5. Suicide
   a. Teachers need to look for warning signs
   b. Common myths and facts about suicide (Table 3.6)
IX.   Summary
X.   Key terms and concepts
XI.   What would you do?
XII. Teachers' casebook

Key Points

See if you can understand the main points which are covered in this chapter:

The work of Erikson

- Psychosocial development: The relationship of the individual's emotional needs to the social environment

- Developmental crisis: A specific conflict whose resolution prepares the way for the next developmental stage

- Crisis resolution is continuous; an individual resolves each crisis somewhere along a continuum of positive vs. potentially unhealthy alternatives

- Unresolved crises can affect the personality qualities that a person carries into adulthood

- Trust: In the first year of life, the infant must feel assured that a loving person will provide caregiving

- Autonomy: Being able to do things for yourself as sensorimotor skills develop

- Initiative: Willingness to begin new activities and explore new directions

- Industry: Eagerness to engage in productive work

- Identity: The complex answer to the question "Who Am I?"

  - Identity achievement: Strong sense of commitment to life choices after free consideration of alternatives

  - Identity foreclosure: Accepting parental life choices without considering options

  - Identity diffusion: Uncenteredness; confusion about who one is and what one wants

  - Moratorium: Identity crisis; suspension of choices because of struggle

- Generativity: Sense of concern for future generations

- Integrity: Sense of self-acceptance and fulfillment

Understanding ourselves and others

- Self-concept: Our perceptions of ourselves

- Self-esteem: The value individuals place on their own characteristics, abilities and behaviors

- Self-concept and self-esteem develop from concrete perceptions to more abstract perceptions with maturity; the process is influenced by friends and family

- A person's self-concept in school can involve both academic and non-academic factors

- Self-concept evolves through constant self-evaluation in different situations

- Ethnic pride: A positive self-concept about one's racial or ethnic heritage

- Social cognition: How children conceptualize other people; how they come to understand thoughts, emotions, tensions, and viewpoints of others

- Empathy: Ability to feel emotion as experienced by others

Moral development

- Moral reasoning: The thinking process involved in making judgments about questions of right and wrong

- Piaget conceived of two stages of moral development: Moral realism (belief that rules are absolute and unchangeable) and morality of cooperation (belief that people make rules and people can change them).

- Kohlberg's Stages of Moral Development

  - Preconventional: A judgment is based solely on a person's own needs and perceptions

  - Conventional: The expectations of society and law are taken into account

  - Postconventional: Judgments are based on abstract, more personal principles that are not necessarily defined by society's laws

  - Moral dilemmas: Situations in which no choice is absolutely right

  - Moral reasoning is related both to cognitive and emotional development
  - Kohlberg's theory has been criticized because stages do not seem to be separate, sequenced, and consistent; because the theory does not

differentiate between social conventions and true moral issues; and because stages are biased in favor of males

- Alternatives to Kohlberg's theory: An ethic of caring

    - Gilligan demonstrated that men and women reason about moral issues differently

    - According to Gilligan, women operate using a framework that values concerns for others, which Kohlberg did not consider

- There is not a strong relationship between moral reasoning and moral behavior

- Moral behavior is influenced by direct instruction and modeling

    - Cheating has more to do with particular situations than with personality traits of honesty or dishonesty

    - Aggression: A bold, direct action that is intended to hurt someone else or take property; an unprovoked attack

    - Modeling plays an important role in the expression of aggression

Socialization: The home and the school

- Socialization: The ways that members of a society encourage positive development for the immature individuals of the group

    - Families differ in child-rearing styles and basic structure

        - Non-traditional families have other than mother, father, and children

        - Blended families are parents, children, and stepchildren merged into families through remarriages

- Teachers' roles are changing as family structures change, and children are affected by such factors as divorce and child abuse

The preschool years

- Physical development: Maturational changes in the body with increasing age

    - Gross motor skills: Voluntary movements of the body that involve large muscles

    - Fine motor skills: Voluntary movements of the body that involve small muscles throughout the body

    - Teachers should address both of these developmental skills in their curriculum

- The need for day care is increasing as more parents work

- Research has shown that children who participate in formal Head Start programs repeat fewer grades, were less often assigned to special education classes, were arrested less frequently and had fewer illegitimate children, graduated from high school more often, went on to advanced schooling, depended less on welfare, and worked more

- Good preschool programs like Head Start can benefit children from low-income families and have positive effects on social development

- Developmentally appropriate preschools: Educational programs and activities designed to meet the cognitive, emotional, social, and physical needs of students

The elementary school years

- Physical development is fairly steady through the elementary school years

- Friendships play a significant role in healthy personal and social development; these can be flexible and change frequently during the elementary years

Issues affecting adolescents

- Adolescents undergo rapid physical changes and face multiple social and physical challenges as they mature

- Puberty: The period in early adolescence when individual reach physical, social maturity

- Boys who mature early physically have a social and academic advantage; girls who mature early can be somewhat disadvantaged

- Teenage sexual development involves emotional and psychological adjustment; unwanted pregnancy and promiscuity are emotional and social risks

- Eating disorders can be cause by excessive concern about the body

  - Bulimia: Overeating, with subsequent self-induced vomiting or laxative use

  - Anorexia nervosa: Eating disorder characterized by very limited food intake

- Drug abuse is an increasing societal problem and therefore increasingly impacts teenagers

- AIDS (Acquired Immune Deficiency Syndrome) is a growing health risk

- Suicide is the third most common cause of death for people aged 15 to 24

  - Teachers need to be aware of suicide warning signs

Concept Map: **ERIKSON'S THEORY OF PSYCHOSOCIAL DEVELOPMENT**

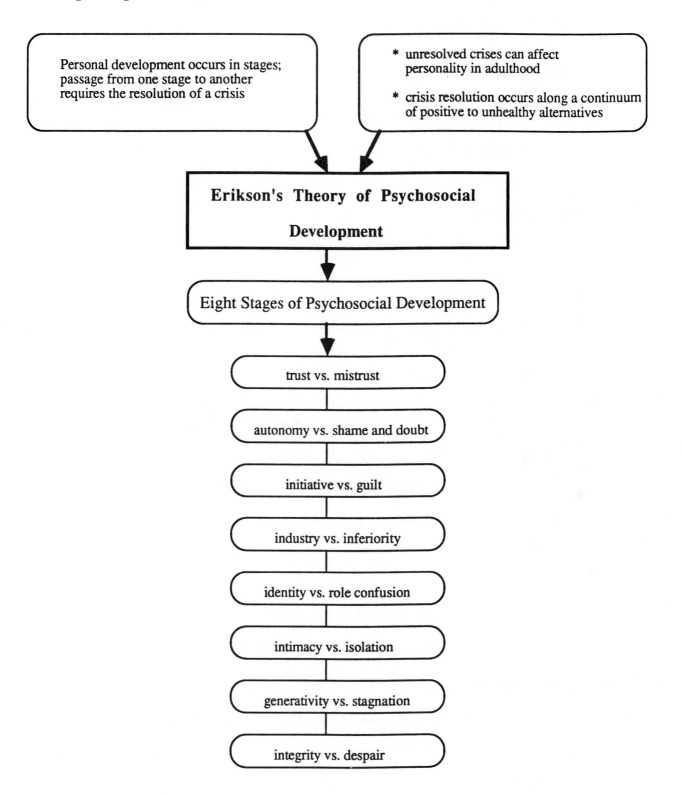

Do You Know This?

Answering these questions will help you to check yourself on your mastery of the chapter objectives.

The Work of Erickson'

Can you describe the Ericksons's stages of psychosocial development? Give examples of the potential implication of this theory for teaching.

Understanding Ourselves and Others

Can you suggest how teachers can promote self-esteem in their students?

Moral Development

Can you illustrate each of Kohlberg's stages of moral development with an example?

Explain the factors that encourage cheating and aggression in classrooms and discuss possible responses to each.

Do you think that teachers need to teach children moral and affective values? Does this usurp the family's role in this area?

Socialization: The Home and the School

Describe how children's friendships change during the elementary school years. Why are friendships important to the social and emotional growth of children?

The Preschool Years

Can you describe a developmentally appropriate preschool?

The Elementary School Years

Can you explain the importance of childhood friendships?

Adolescence

How does early and late maturation affect teenagers?

How can teachers help teenagers make responsible decisions about sex and drugs?

Key Terms and Concepts

MATCHING: Erikson's Theory of Psychosocial Development

Each set of terms below represents healthy and unhealthy resolutions of the developmental crises with which we are presented at each stage of life. Put one of the words in each of the blanks below. To check answers, see Answer Key.

Trust vs. Mistrust   **Identity vs. Role Confusion**

Autonomy vs. Shame/Doubt   **Intimacy vs. Isolation**

Initiative vs. Guilt   **Generativity vs. Stagnation**

Industry vs. Inferiority   **Ego Integrity vs. Despair**

1. _____   Contributing to the community to build a better world

2. _____   Staying alone without a partner

3. _____   Being able to do things for yourself

4. _____   Making your own decisions and then carrying them out

5. _____   Learning that people can be counted upon to satisfy our needs

6. _____   Feeling satisfied over having lived a good life

7. _____   Staying wrapped up in oneself or one's family

8. _____   Feeling bad about something we did or did not do

9. _____   Experiencing that a caretaker is willing to let us suffer

10. _____   Feeling less able than others to perform work

11. _____   Being able to love and let another person love you

12. _____   Feeling disgusted with ourselves for getting old

13. _____   Being eager and able to carry out work

14. _____   Knowing ourselves deeply

15. _____   Feeling that others think we are basically bad

16. _____   Being uncertain of your vocational or gender identity

DEFINITIONS: Possible Resolutions of the Identity Crisis

Write the definitions for the following terms. Then check the Glossary of your textbook to see if your definition is appropriate.

Identity achievement _____

_____

Identity foreclosure _____

_____

Identity diffusion _____

_____

Moratorium _____

_____

IDENTIFICATION: Kohlberg's Stages of Moral Development

For each anecdote below, choose the stage of moral development which best describes the reasoning that is displayed.

Preconventional   **Conventional**   **Postconventional**

_____ 1.   Sally brought a package of colorful pencil erasers to school. Ingrid liked them, so she asked Sally to give her one. Sally refused. When Sally's back was turned, Ingrid took one anyway. When confronted, Ingrid saw nothing wrong with taking what she wanted. What level of moral development was Ingrid demonstrating?

_____ 2.   The social studies class was discussing the Vietnam War and the use of the draft to supply troops for the United States military. Anita and Juan took the position that a country has no right to compel its citizens to kill. What level of moral development were Anita and Juan demonstrating?

_____ 3.   Mr. Taylor observed Bill copying an answer from another student during an exam. He called Bill in after class. "Cheating is not allowed in this school," he told Bill. "It's against the rules." What level of moral development was Mr. Taylor demonstrating?

APPLICATION: Alternatives to Kohlberg's Theory

Read each description of a moral stage. On the preceding blank, write which theorist/level that would characterize this description. To check answers, see Answer Key.

Kohlberg/Level 1 (Preconventional)   **Gilligan/Level 1**
Kohlberg/Level 2 (Conventional)   **Gilligan/Level 2**
Kohlberg/Level 3 (Postconventional)   **Gilligan/Level 3**

_____   1.   Fear of punishment

_____   2.   Commitment to specific individuals, relationships

_____   3.   Focus on self-interest

_____   4.   Emphasis on rational, personal choice

_____   5.   Laws and rules are considered absolute

_____   6.   Concern for the responsibility and care of all people

CHARTING: Developmental Milestones of the Young Child

From the list given, fill in sample skills which a young child can perform at each age on the chart below.   An example has been provided for you.

Gross motor skills	Fine motor skills
Balances on one foot	Copies a circle
Walks well	Buttons with large buttons
Throws and catches large ball	Uses scissors
Jumps in air with both feet	Draws people
Swims in water a short distance	Stacks a few small blocks
Runs in a straight line	Makes simple representational drawings

Approx Age->

2.5	3.5	4.5	5.5
Walks well	_____	_____	_____
_____	_____	_____	_____
_____	_____	_____	_____
_____	_____	_____	_____

APPLICATION: Cheating

Many teachers discourage cheating in their classes by making sure that students are well prepared for tests, by giving tests on which students can perform adequately, making extra help available, and enforcing rules against cheating. What additional teaching suggestions help build a climate in which each child performs without needing to "cheat"?

APPLICATION: Developmentally Appropriate Preschools

Elkind states that a day care program that features excessive academic and didactic teaching has many disadvantages. What activities would you include that would be consistent with a developmentally appropriate day care program, according to Elkind?

CASE STUDY: Adolescent Socialization

Joyce began her ninth grade year in your class as a competent, responsive student who consistently completed her homework and participated willingly in class activities. Shortly after the winter break, you notice that Joyce has become withdrawn and moody in class. She misses school often, turns in her homework inconsistently, and rarely participates in class discussion. What steps might you take to understand the source of Joyce's problem(s)? Suggest an intervention program that will help Joyce return to her former academic behavior.

CASE STUDY: Aggression

Tony, a bright, verbal ten-year-old in the fifth grade, has come to school wearing clothing which suggests that he is identifying with a local teenage gang. His behavior has become increasingly aggressive towards other students, with several pushing and shoving incidents on the playground. The other students often complain about his belligerent taunts and combative behavior. One Monday morning he wrote an entry in his daily journal which graphically depicted a violent gang fight. How would you respond to this journal entry?

PRACTICE TEST: Multiple Choice

Select the best answer for each of the following items. To check answers, see Answer Key.

1. A conflict such as *initiative v. guilt* represents _____ in Erikson's theory.

    a. equilibration
    b. a developmental crisis
    c. cognitive dissonance
    d. disequilibration

2. Children experiencing the Eriksonian conflict of *trust v. mistrust* are also in Piaget's _____ stage.

    a. sensorimotor
    b. preoperational
    c. concrete operations
    d. formal operations

3. The way that children resolve the *autonomy v. shame* crisis influences their later sense of

    a. attachment to the family.
    b. confidence in their own abilities.
    c. cooperation in groups.
    d. evaluation of new ideas.

4. In Erikson's stage theory, when adolescents fail to develop a strong identity, they are likely to experience

    a. role confusion.
    b. moratorium.
    c. diffusion.
    d. achievement.

5. When a person's moral development is at the preconventional level, the most important moral criteria are

    a. statements of law.
    b. intuitive feelings of right and wrong.
    c. the direct, personal results of action.
    d. the principles underlying an action.

6. Kohlberg evaluated moral reasoning by studying responses to

    a. actual recorded events.
    b. moral dilemmas.
    c. rules and regulations.
    d. threats of punishment.

7. According to your text, one result of middle-class couples waiting longer to have children is

    a. less time for parents and children to spend together.
    b. more limited resources for the children.
    c. greater class sizes in schools.
    d. poor academic performance by children.

8. The basic philosophy conveyed in your textbook regarding teacher's responses to students' personal problems is that

    a. such problems should be left to families to resolve.
    b. such problems are more the domain of principals and guidance counselors than of teachers.
    c. teachers should actively try to help with these problems.
    d. attempts by teachers to help will most likely be rejected by the student or his/her family.

9. Elkind's ideas for preschool education directly support

    a. accelerated academic programs.
    b. heterogeneous age groupings.
    c. use of age-specific materials.
    d. all of the above.

10. Which of the following is <u>true</u> regarding friendships in childhood?

   a. Adults who had very close friends as children are generally more insecure as adults.
   b. Boys are more likely than girls to have one "best" friend.
   c. Friendships rapidly change in early childhood.
   d. Friendships do not play a significant role in development as the child matures.

PRACTICE TEST: Essay

A. What personal conflicts are most likely to be experienced by individuals in Erikson's stage of *industry v. inferiority* ? What can teachers do to help the individual achieve a healthy resolution?

Answer Key

MATCHING: Erikson's Theory of Psychosocial Development

1. Generativity	6. Integrity	11. Intimacy	16. Role Confusion
2. Isolation	7. Stagnation	12. Despair	
3. Autonomy	8. Guilt	13. Industry	
4. Initiative	9. Mistrust	14. Identity	
5. Trust	10. Inferiority	15. Shame/Doubt	

IDENTIFICATION: Kohlberg's Theory of Moral Development

1. Preconventional
2. Postconventional
3. Conventional

APPLICATION: Alternatives to Kohlberg's Theory

1. Kohlberg/Level 1 (Preconventional)
2. Gilligan/Level 2
3. Gilligan/Level 1
4. Kohlberg/Level 3 (Postconventional)
5. Kohlberg/Level 2 (Conventional)
6. Gilligan/Level 3

PRACTICE TEST: Multiple Choice

1. b According to Erikson, people face a <u>developmental crisis</u> at each stage (such as initiative v. guilt). The crisis involves conflict between a positive alternative and a potentially unhealthy alternative. (Note: equilibration is a process described by Piaget in which the individual obtains a state of balance.)

2. a Erikson's trust v. mistrust stage, which takes place during a child's first year, corresponds to the beginning of Piaget's <u>sensorimotor stage</u>, which occurs from ages 0 to 2.

3. b   During the autonomy v. shame/doubt period, the child begins to assume responsibilities for self-care (dressing, feeding, etc.). If these activities are not reinforced by parents, children may begin to <u>lose confidence in their abilities</u> to do things for themselves.

4. a   According to Erikson, the key focus for adolescents is developing an identity. Should they fail in that process, the unhealthy alternative is <u>role confusion</u> or being uncertain about who one is and what to become as an adult.

5. c   According to Kohlberg, the most important moral criteria for children at the preconventional level is the <u>direct, personal results of an action</u>. A behavior is considered wrong if you might get caught doing it. Later, children will judge behaviors more on the basis of how they affect other people and of the conditions that prompted the behaviors.

6. b   Kohlberg evaluated moral reasoning by studying responses to <u>moral dilemmas</u>. These are hypothetical situations in which a person is confronted with a difficult moral decision. How the child reacts to that particular decision provides an indication of his/her moral reasoning level.

7. a   One result of middle class parents waiting longer to have children is <u>less time for parents and children to spend together</u>.

8. c   Your textbook conveys the philosophy that teachers can provide valuable support to students who are experiencing problems. Teachers should therefore <u>actively try to help students with their problems</u>.

9. b   Elkind suggests that preschool education should establish <u>heterogeneous age groupings</u> so that advanced younger children can <u>interact</u> with older children. The idea is that the abilities of young children are so variable that age-specific materials and groupings are bound to be overly restrictive.

10. c   Due to the situational nature of selecting friends in early childhood (based largely on who is "nice" on a particular day), <u>friendships rapidly change in early childhood</u>.

PRACTICE TEST: Essay

A. Individuals in Erikson's stage of *industry v. inferiority* are most likely to experience personal conflicts about being competent and about being able to produce work of which they can be proud. Teachers can help the individual to achieve a healthy resolution in the following ways: By helping individuals to set goals that are achievable; by encouraging the class as a whole to be productive and hard-working; by offering students constructive feedback and praise when appropriate; by working with individuals to develop internal standards of worth and judgment; and by communicating with parents to help students to develop good homework habits.

4

Learning Abilities and Learning Problems

Teaching Outline

I. What Do You Think?
II. Language and labeling
    A. Some children are exceptional because they need special education/services
    B. Labeling or "diagnosis" of exceptionalities is controversial
        1. Expectations and assumptions may be self-fulfilling prophecies
        2. Labels may, however, protect students and/or open doors to special help
III. Individual differences in intelligence
    A. What does intelligence mean?
        1. Intelligence: One ability or many?
            a. Spearman: There is one general intelligence factor that different tests assess to a greater or lesser extent
            b. Thurstone: There are several "primary mental abilities", but one ability is correlated with ability in others
        2. Multiple intelligences
            a. Guilford: Three faces of intellect (mental operations, contents, and products) with each divided into multiple subcategories
            b. Gardner: There are at least seven separate intelligences
        3. Intelligence as a process: Sternberg's Triarchic Theory
    B. How is intelligence measured?
        1. Binet's dilemma
            a. Binet's mission: To identify students needing special teaching by measuring intellectual skills necessary for success in school
            b. Mental age: A score based on average abilities for an age group
            c. IQ: Comparison of mental age and chronological age
            d. Deviation IQ: Score identifying where a person's score lies in the distribution of scores for that person's age group
        2. Group versus individual IQ tests
            a. Group test is much less accurate than individual test
            b. Group tests require reading and writing skills more than individual tests
    C. What does an IQ score mean?
        1. Intelligence and achievement: IQ scores strongly predict school achievement, but not good predictors of success in life
        2. Heredity and environment both affect intelligence
        3. Guidelines: Interpreting IQ scores
IV. Ability differences and teaching
    A. Ability grouping: Grouping students based on ability
        1. Between-class ability grouping: Formation of separate ability-based classes
            a. For low-ability students, does not improve learning and may cause problems
            b. High-ability or cross-grade groupings are effective

2. Within-class grouping based on ability
   a. Common with reading and math in elementary schools
   b. Offers positive results when based on current performance and sensitively tailored to student needs.

B. Mental retardation
   1. Student should never be classified as mentally retarded only on the basis of IQ scores alone
   2. Definition and prevalence
      a. Low IQ score: Below 70 to 75
      b. Deficient adaptive behavior, social inadequacy (Table 4.3)
      c. Deficiencies apparent before age 18
   3. Causes of retardation: Biological weakness interacts with environmental factors
      a. Down syndrome range from severely retarded to near normal
      b. Other causes include maternal infections, premature birth, PKU
   4. Teaching retarded learners
      a. Goals for mildly retarded: Basic reading, writing, and arithmetic, the environment, social behavior, and personal interests
      b. Transition programming: Preparing the retarded student to live and work in the community
      c. Help with making friends and personal interests, to promote acceptance in the classroom
      d. Guidelines: Teaching retarded students

C. Gifted and talented
   1. Who are the gifted?
      a. Academic gifts versus "creative/productive giftedness": Success in later life predicted for later group
      b. Gifted students have above average ability, high level of creativity, high level of task commitment
   2. The Terman study
      a. Gifted tend to be larger, stronger, and healthier than the norm
      b. Some gifted students are more emotionally stable and become better adjusted adults
   3. Problems of gifted students
      a. In school: Boredom, isolation from peers, difficulty in facing emotions, impatience with friends & peers
      b. Terman follow-up: Popular gifted children less likely to pursue intellectual pursuits; more-accomplished adults may have preferred adult company as children
   4. Recognizing students' special abilities
      a. Teacher observation successful in identifying 10 to 50 percent of the time
      b. Individual IQ tests imperfect best single predictor of academic giftedness
      c. Other sources of information
   5. Giftedness and formal testing
   6. Teaching gifted students
      a. Enrichment and acceleration both may be appropriate
      b. Teachers need to encourage abstract thinking, creativity, independence;

  must be imaginative, flexible, and non threatening
 V. Cognitive and learning styles
  A. Cognitive styles: Patterns of behavior and performance by which an individual approaches learning; composite of cognition, affect, and physiology
   1. Field dependence and field independence
    a. Field-dependent style: Tendency to see pattern as a whole; orientation toward people and relationships
    b. Field-independent style: Tendency to perceive separate parts of a pattern; ability to analyze its components; greater task orientation
   2. Impulsive and reflective cognitive styles
    a. Impulsive student works very quickly but makes many mistakes
    b. Reflective student works slowly with few errors
    c. Students tend to becomes more reflective with age and can be taught to be more reflective through self-instruction
  B. Learning style preferences: Individual preferences for particular approaches and environments
   1. Several instruments available to assess students' learning preferences
    a. Instruments have been criticized for lack of reliability and validity
    b. Learning may be enhanced if students study in preferred settings
 VI. Students with learning challenges
  A. Disability (specific inability) distinct from handicap (disadvantage in specific situation)
  B. Physically challenged students
   1. Epilepsy: Seizures that result from uncontrolled firing of neurons in the brain
   2. Cerebral palsy: Characterized by spasticity
   3. Hearing impairment: Results from multiple factors
   4. Vision impairment: Mild problem requires only glasses; severe impairment may require specialized materials and strategies
  C. Communication disorders
   1. Speech impairments: Articulation disorder, stuttering or voicing problems
   2. Oral language disorders: Absence, difference, delay, or interruption of language development
  D. Emotional/behavioral disorders: Behavior that deviates enough to interfere with growth and development or the lives of others
   1. Six dimensions
    a. Conduct disorders: Aggressiveness, destructiveness, disobedience
    b. Anxiety-withdrawal disorder: Anxiety, shyness, and depression
    c. Attentional-problems-immaturity: Short attention span, frequent daydreaming, little initiative, messiness, poor coordination
    d. Motor excess: Restlessness, tension, inability to sit still or stop talking
    e. Socialized aggression: Members of gangs; may steal or vandalize
    f. Psychotic behavior: Extremely bizarre behavior
  E. Hyperactivity and attention disorders
   1. Characteristically children are physically overactive, inattentive; have difficulty in responding appropriately and little control of behavior
   2. Many possible causes of hyperactivity; could be minimal brain damage
   3. Certain stimulants bring manageable behavior but can cause negative side

effects
    4. Most successful ways to improve academic learning and social skills are based on behavioral principles
  F. Specific learning disabilities: What's wrong when nothing is wrong?
    1. Learning disabled students have problem with acquisition and use of language; may have difficulty with reading, writing, reasoning or math
    2. May manifest a wide variety of behaviors; causes inherent as well as environmental and early diagnosis important to keep students from becoming victims of learned helplessness
    3. Teaching learning disabled students includes training in information processing and emphasis of study skills

VII. Mainstreaming
  A. Public Law 94-142, 99-457, and IDEA: Free public education for all disabled children
    1. Least restrictive placement: Educating as much in the mainstream as possible Point/Counterpoint: Full Inclusion
    2. Individualized Education Plan (IEP): Written plan and objectives, updated each year
    3. Rights of students and parents, including confidentiality, right to see all records and right to challenge program
  B. Effective teaching in mainstreamed classrooms
    1. Smooth management, planning
    2. Questioning at right level of difficulty
    3. Supportive, corrective feedback
    4. Integration of disabled students into daily life of classroom
    5. Resource rooms and collaborative consultation, and cooperative teaching
    6. Careful preparation before making referral (Table 4.6)
  C. Computers and exceptional students
    1. Computer programs help record keeping and program planning
    2. Programs for students
      a. Can be designed to require small, repetitive steps which are helpful to children with learning problems
      b. Can be engaging and interactive; helpful for students who have problems paying attention
      c. Often do not include sound; helpful for hearing impaired
      d. Can enable students to write when handwriting is a problem
      e. For gifted students, can offer connections with data bases, and computers in universities, museums, and research labs
VIII. Summary
IX. Key terms and concepts
X. What would you do?
XI. Teachers' casebook

Key Points

See if you understand the main points that are covered in this chapter:

Describing individual differences

- Exceptional children may include mentally retarded, gifted, physically challenged, behaviorally disordered, learning disabled, communication disordered, visually or hearing impaired

- Some exceptionalities are inborn; some are relative to task demands

- Difficulties may result from categorizing and labeling students

    - When children are identified, they may benefit from special teaching

    - Labels may be harmful to children and result in low expectations for performance

Concepts of intelligence

- Intelligence has been defined differently by various researchers

- Spearman: Intelligence consists of a "general" ability plus specific abilities

- Guilford: Intelligence has three dimensions (operations, contents, products)

- Garner: Seven kinds of abilities comprise intelligence (linguistic/verbal, logical/mathematical, spatial, musical, bodily, interpersonal, intrapersonal)

- Sternberg: Intelligence has three elements (contextual, componential, and experiential)

    - Triarchic theory: Three-part description of mental processes of individual that lead to more or less intelligent behavior

    - Components of intelligence: In an information-processing view, basic problem-solving processes that underlie intelligence

The measurement of intelligence

- First intelligence tests were 58 activities created by Binet and Simon to estimate the ability or "mental age" of mildly retarded individuals in the schools of Paris

- The Stanford-Binet test represented ability as a ratio of mental age and chronological age (MA/CA) or "Intelligence Quotient" (IQ)

- A more recent form of expressing mental ability is a comparison of the individual against the normal curve of persons who are the same age ("Deviation IQ")

- What does an IQ score mean?

    - IQ tests are normed using a population which represents a realistic distribution of abilities, racial, and cultural backgrounds

    - IQ scores may range from about 50 to 180; the average IQ is defined as 100 and about 68% of the population falls between 85 and 115

- High IQ test scores are a good predictor of success in school

- High IQ does not predict subsequent vocational success or income level

- Differences in intelligence are due to both heredity and environment

Ability differences and teaching

- Between-class grouping ("tracking") often creates differential success opportunity

- Within-class ability grouping should be flexible; teaching methods and pace should be appropriate to needs of groups

- Various teaching methods can promote different types of thinking

    - Divergent thinking: Coming up with many possible solutions

    - Convergent thinking: Narrowing possibilities to the single answer

- Low achievement in school may be due to mild mental retardation

    - Mental retardation: Significantly below average intellectual and adaptive social behavior, evident before age 18

    - Down Syndrome: Retardation caused by presence of extra chromosome

    - Other possible causes of mental retardation: rubella or other diseases, maternal alcohol or drug abuse, lead poisoning, premature birth, or inherited disorders

    - Transition programming: Designing a plan to gradually prepare exceptional students to move from high school into further education or training, employment or community involvement

- Gifted and talented students also have special educational needs

  - Gifted: Very bright, creative, and talented students

  - Many gifted are not served by special academic programs

  - School may cause problems for the gifted such as boredom, isolation, or frustration

  - Alternative instruction may feature acceleration or enrichment

Cognitive and learning styles

- Cognitive styles: Different ways of perceiving and organizing information

  - Field-dependent: Cognitive style in which patterns are perceived as wholes

  - Field-independent: Cognitive style in which separate parts of a pattern are perceived and analyzed

  - Impulsive: Cognitive style of responding quickly, but often inaccurately

  - Reflective: Cognitive style of responding slowly, carefully, and accurately

- Learning styles: Individual differences that affect classroom learning

- Learning preferences: Preferred ways of studying and learning

Students with learning challenges

- Physically challenged students must overcome impairments of physical dysfunction

  - Students using orthopedic devices, who have epilepsy, cerebral palsy, hearing or visual impairment

  - Epilepsy: Disorder marked by suffering partial or generalized seizures, caused by abnormal electrical discharges in the brain

  - Cerebral palsy : Condition involving a range of motor or coordination difficulties due to brain damage; causes spasticity (overly tight muscles)

  - There are many levels and types of hearing and visual impairment

- Hearing impairment may be due to genetic factors, maternal infections, complications during birth, or early childhood diseases

- Signs of hearing impairment: Favoring one ear or misunderstanding speech

- Approaches to teaching the hearing impaired:

  - Speech Reading: Using visual cues to understanding language

  - Sign Language: Communication system of hand movements that symbolize words and concepts

  - Finger spelling: Communication system that spells out each letter with a hand position

- Vision problems that are mild may be overcome with corrective lenses

  - Low vision: Vision limited to close objects

  - Educationally blind: Needing Braille materials in order to learn

- Communication disorders may involve many types of language processing difficulties

  - Speech impairment: Inability to produce sounds effectively for speaking

    - Articulation disorder: Any pronunciation difficulty such as substitution, distortion, or omission of sounds

    - Stuttering: Repetitions, prolongation, and hesitations that block flow of speech

    - Voicing problems: Inappropriate pitch, quality, loudness, or intonation

  - Oral language disorders: Inability, delay, differences, or disrupted development

- Students with emotional/behavioral disorders are the most difficult to teach

  - Conduct disorders may include aggressive, destructive, disobedient, uncooperative, distractible, disruptive behavior

- Anxiety-withdrawal disorders may be associated with hypersensitivity, depression, low confidence

- Attentional problems/immaturity may include short attention span, frequent daydreaming, little initiative, messiness, poor coordination

- Motor excess causes restlessness, tension, and inability to sit still

- Socialized aggression characterized by membership in gangs

- Psychotic behavior is bizarre behavior

- Hyperactivity: Behavior disorder marked by atypical, excessive restlessness and inatttentiveness

- Attention deficit/hyperactive disorder: Current term for behavior disorders marked by overactivity, excessive difficulties sustaining attention, or impulsiveness

- Specific learning disabilities: Problem with acquisition and use of language; may show up as difficulty with reading, writing, reasoning, or math

  - There is no agreement about the cause of learning disabilities

  - Learned helplessness: The expectation based on previous experiences with a lack of control, that all your efforts will lead to failure

Educating exceptional children

- Mainstreaming: Teaching disabled students in regular classes for all or part of regular school day

  - Public law 94-142 (Education for All Handicapped Children Act) : Federal law which mandates that a free and appropriate public education be provided for every child, with provision for the following:

    - Least restrictive environment: Placement of each child in as normal an educational setting as possible

    - Individualized educational plan (IEP): Annually revised program for an exceptional student, detailing present achivement level, goals, and strategies, drawn up by teachers, parents, specialists, and student (if possible)

    - Parents have a right to see all student records and protest a placement with due process of law

- Public law 99-457: Federal law that extended the requirement of a free and appropriate public education to handicapped children ages 3-5

- IDEA: Federal law that replaced the word "handicapped" with "disabled" and expanded services for disabled students

- <u>Regular education initiative</u>: A philosphy of education that assumes that regular education teachers, not special education teachers, should be responsible for teaching mildly handicapped students

- Americans with Disabilities Act (1990): Civil rights extended to people with disabilities

- Effective teaching in mainstreamed classes involves effective management, appropriate direct teaching, and delivery of supportive feedback to mainstreamed students

  - Individualized Education Program (IEP) is written by a school teaching team to individualize instruction

  - Resource room programs are often available to give students individual attention

  - Teachers need to know how to make appropriate referrals for evaluation and to cooperate and collaborate to teach special needs students

- Computers can be used effectively to individualize instruction for exceptional students, including the gifted

Concept Map: ADAPTING INSTRUCTION FOR LEARNER DIFFRENCES

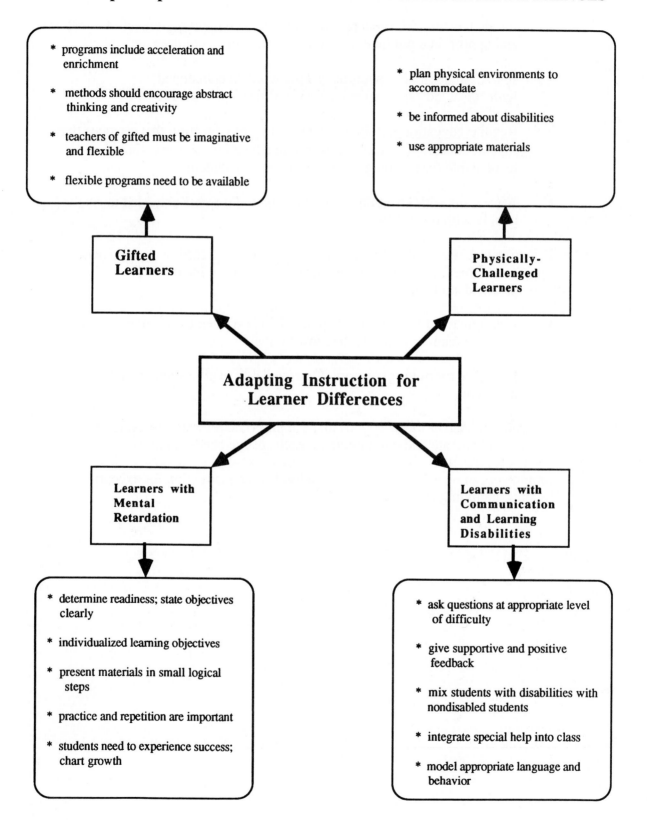

* programs include acceleration and enrichment

* methods should encourage abstract thinking and creativity

* teachers of gifted must be imaginative and flexible

* flexible programs need to be available

Gifted Learners

* plan physical environments to accommodate

* be informed about disabilities

* use appropriate materials

Physically-Challenged Learners

Adapting Instruction for Learner Differences

Learners with Mental Retardation

Learners with Communication and Learning Disabilities

* determine readiness; state objectives clearly

* individualized learning objectives

* present materials in small logical steps

* practice and repetition are important

* students need to experience success; chart growth

* ask questions at appropriate level of difficulty

* give supportive and positive feedback

* mix students with disabilities with nondisabled students

* integrate special help into class

* model appropriate language and behavior

Do You Know This?

Answering these questions will help you to check yourself on your mastery of the chapter objectives.

Language and labeling: What does it mean it be exceptional?

Can you discuss the potential problems in categorizing and labeling students?

Individual Differences in Intelligence

Can you develop your own concept of intelligence to aid you in your teaching?

Ability Differences and Teaching

Explain how you might recognize and teach students who are mildly retarded or who are gifted.

Cognitive and Learning Styles

How can you adapt lessons to make them appropriate for students with varying learning styles?

Students with Learning Challenges

List indicators of hearing, vision, language, and behavioral problems, as well as indicators of specific learning disabilities.

Educating Exceptional Children

Can you adapt your teaching methods to meet the needs of exceptional students?

Mainstreaming

What implications does the Individuals with Disabilities Act have for your teaching?

Key Terms and Concepts

DEFINITIONS: Intelligence

Write the definitions for the following terms. Then check the text to see if your definition is appropriate.

Intelligence _____

Triarchic theory _____

Component _____

Mental Age_____

Intelligence Quotient _____

Deviation IQ _____

MATCHING: Measurement of Intelligence

Match the letters of the descriptions on the right to the corresponding items on the left. Use each definition only once. To check answers, see Answer Key.

_____ 1. Products
_____ 2. Musical
_____ 3. Mental operation
_____ 4. Components
_____ 5. Contents
_____ 6. Logical/ mathematical
_____ 7. Linguistic/verbal
_____ 8. Spatial
_____ 9. Intrapersonal
_____ 10. Adapting to context
_____ 11. Interpersonal
_____ 12. Bodily/kinesthetic

a. Capacity to discern numerical patterns
b. Access to one's own feelings
c. Choosing an environment in which you can succeed, adapting it if necessary
d. Capacity to discern and respond to desires, needs of others
e. The end result of our thinking
f. Processes of thinking
g. Ability to control one's body movement
h. Ability to produce and appreciate rhythm, pitch, and timbre
i. Sensitivity to sounds, rhythms and meanings of words
j. Capacity to perceive visual/spatial world accurately
k. Information-processing elements of thinking
l. What we think about

COMPLETION QUESTIONS: Exceptionalities

Fill in the blanks below with the following concepts. Each term is used only once. To check answers, see Answer Key.

Mental retardation
Down Syndrome
Cerebral palsy
Articulation disorder
Attention deficit-hyperactive disorder

Educationally blind
Specific learning disorder
Learned helplessness
Hearing impaired
Stuttering

1. A student who is ten years old still has difficulty pronouncing the phoneme /r/. He may have a(n) _____.

2. The tendency to repeat or elongate words when speaking is called _____.

3. A student in your class is constantly out of her seat and has difficulty focusing on the lesson. She may be exhibiting signs of _____.

4. A child who cannot benefit from corrective lenses may be classified as _____.

5. A child whose form of mental retardation is caused by a chromosomal abnormality is said to have _____.

6. Children who experience repeated failure often develop a sense of _____.

7. You notice one of your students cannot understand your directions well unless he can see you as you speak. This may be a sign that he is _____.

8. Significantly below-average intellectual and adaptive social behavior may be a sign of _____.

9. A student in the classroom exhibits overly tight muscles and poor coordination; this may indicate a case of _____.

10. More students are categorized as having a(n) _____than any other category .

DEFINITIONS: Cognitive and Learning Styles

Write explanations for the following pairs of terms. Your explanation should clearly distinguish the two from one another. Check the text to see if your explanations are equivalent.

Field dependent/Field independent _____

_____

Impulsive/Reflective _____

_____

Global/Analytic _____

_____

APPLICATION: Students with Learning Challenges

Suppose you have a student in your class who is experiencing one of the physical challenges listed below. Describe how you would accommodate this student in a regular classroom. Include in your answer how you would modify the physical environment of the classroom, as well as changes you would make in the curriculum or your teaching methods.

Vision impaired _____

_____

_____

Hearing impaired_____

_____

_____

APPLICATION: Educating Exceptional Children

Suppose you are a regular education teacher and you believe one of your students may benefit from special education. For each category below, describe briefly what information you are responsible for including in your referral.

Background history _____

_____

Review of school records _____

_____

Other teachers' experience with the student _____

_____

Documentation of students' work in your class _____

_____

Previous strategies you have tried_____

_____

CASE STUDY: Cognitive and Learning Styles

Gina is a student in your second grade classroom. She rushes through her arithmetic problems, making many mistakes and seldom checking for errors. When writing, her words are jumbled together, and she erases so often that she sometimes makes holes in the paper. You suspect that she may be an impulsive learner. What interventions would you recommend that would help her to develop a reflective learning style?

CASE STUDY: Educating Exceptional Children

Your principal had adopted a philosophy of <u>full inclusion</u>, in which all disabled students, no matter how handicapped, should be in the regular classroom, learning alongside their peers. Consequently, a child who has been evaluated to have mild mental retardation has been placed in your fifth grade classroom. What are some of your concerns about this student's social, cognitive, and emotional adjustment to the situation? What are some strategies that you can use to assist this child to adjust to your classroom?

PRACTICE TEST: Multiple Choice

Select the <u>best</u> answer for each of the following items. To check your answers, see Answer Key.

1. Guilford divided cognitive abilities into three categories he called
    a. faces of intellect.
    b. intelligence levels.
    c. intellective types.
    d. categories of intelligence.

2. The original formula for deriving I.Q has been replaced by the concept of
    _____ IQ.
    a. average

    b.   derived

    c.   deviation

    d.   normative

3. Individual intelligence tests are more reliable than group tests for all the following reasons EXCEPT

    a.   they are less susceptible to distractions.

    b.   the examinee is more likely to be motivated by individual attention.

    c.   they require more reading and writing skills.

    d.   the examiner has more control over the testing.

4. What is the typical correlation between IQ and school achievement?

    a.   Weak negative

    b.   About zero

    c.   Weak positive

    d.   Moderate to strong positive

5. Most psychologists today believe that intelligence is influenced

    a.   75% by heredity, 25% by environment.

    b.   25% by heredity, 75% by environment.

    c.   minimally by either heredity or environment.

    d.   about equally by heredity and environment.

6. Almost every definition of mental retardation includes the idea that mentally retarded individuals

    a.   have IQ scores below 75.

    b.   are functionally immature.

    c.   cannot adapt adequately to their environment.

    d.   have limited verbal abilities.

7. The trend today in educating mentally retarded students involves giving greater emphasis to _____ skills.

    a.   psychomotor

    b.   aesthetic appreciation

    c.   sensory

    d.   self-help and domestic

8. Beliefs about teaching the gifted now

    a.   clearly favor acceleration over enrichment.

    b.   clearly favor enrichment over acceleration.

c. view neither acceleration nor enrichment as beneficial.

d. view both acceleration and enrichment as beneficial.

9. What type of intervention appears most successful for learning disabled students?

   a. Direct training of perceptional processes
   b. Teaching study skills and learning methods in specific subjects
   c. Direct training of social skills
   d. Use of behavioral management strategies, such as contingency contracts

10. Which of the following is the least restrictive special education placement?

   a. Special day placement
   b. Homebound instruction
   c. Self-contained special education
   d. Resource class with part-time mainstreaming

PRACTICE TEST: Essay

A. You have a student in your first grade class who has an exceptional ability in mathematics. After individual testing, the school psychologist has concurred that the child's IQ is in the upper 2% of those her age. Describe activities in the classroom that would constitute an enriched mathematics program for this student. In contrast, what would an accelerated program involve for this child?

Answer Key

MATCHING: Measurement of Intelligence

1. e
2. h
3. f
4. k
5. l
6. a
7. i
8. j
9. b
10. c
11. d
12. g

COMPLETION QUESTIONS: Exceptionalities

1. Articulation disorder
2. Stuttering
3. Attention deficit-hyperactive disorder
4. Educationally blind
5. Down syndrome
6. Learned helplessness
7. Hearing impaired
8. Mental retardation
9. Cerebral palsy
10. Specific learning disorder

PRACTICE TEST: Multiple Choice

1. a   Guilford divided cognitive ability into three categories he called <u>faces of intellect</u>. The categories are mental operations, contents, and products.

2. c   The original intelligent quotient formula for determining IQ has been replaced by the concept of <u>deviation IQ</u>. This new conception bases IQ on how individuals perform in relation to others (a norming sample of the same age).

3. c   The factor that would <u>not</u> help to account for the greater reliability of individual IQ tests relative to IQ group tests would be a greater requirement for <u>reading and writing skills</u>. In fact, because individual tests place less emphasis on such skills, they tend to be more reliable than group tests.

4. d   The typical correlation between IQ and school achievement is about .65, indicating a <u>moderate to strong</u> positive relationship.

5. d   Psychologists today believe that intelligence is influenced about <u>equally by heredity and environment</u>. Heredity determines one's potential, while environment shapes the level of intelligence that is actually attained. Both are therefore important determinants.

6. c   Almost every definition of mental retardation includes the idea that mentally retarded individuals <u>cannot adapt adequately to their environment</u>. Specific deficiencies such as immaturity or poor verbal skills are considered less important.

7. d   The trend today in educating mentally retarded students involves greater emphasis to <u>self-help and domestic skills</u>.   This emphasis is called transition programming.

8. d   Beliefs towards teaching the gifted now view <u>both acceleration and</u>

enrichment as beneficial. Acceleration means skipping grades; enrichment means giving student more challenging and sophisticated work in their regular grades.

9. b   In general, learning disabled students appear to benefit most from being taught study skills and learning methods in specific subjects. The Kansas Learning Strategies Curriculum is an example of this approach. Attempts to "train" perceptual processes have been less successful.

10. d   A resource class with part-time mainstreaming would be least restrictive. Compared to other alternatives (day school placement, homebound instruction, and self- contained special education), it would provide a child with significantly greater contact with normal students in regular classrooms.

PRACTICE TEST: Essay

A.   An enriched mathematics program would include sophisticated activities for this student to provide a creative or challenging addition to the regular curriculum. These activities might include computer-based instruction, games, or simulations. The accelerated program would mean skipping a grade, or having the student visit a classroom in a higher grade to receive math instruction.

5

The Impact of Culture and Community

Teaching Outline

I. What Do You Think?

II. Today's multicultural classrooms
   A. Old views: The students must adapt
      1. New immigrants expected to enter cultural melting pot, adopt beliefs and behaviors of the Anglo middle class
      2. Cultural deficit model: Students' home culture inferior
      3. Expectations of schools typically reflect white, Anglo-Saxon, middle-class,
   B. New views: Multicultural education
      1. All students regardless of culture should have a full and equal opportunity to learn
      2. Educational reform to seek breakdown barriers to education regardless of culture, ethnicity, and gender
         a. Some focus on improving human relations
         b. Others press for in-depth studies of various racial and ethnic groups
         c. Others hope to help students learn to be politically effective
   Point/Counterpoint: Should Multicultural Education Emphasize Similarities or Differences?
   C. American cultural diversity
      1. Cultural group membership is defined by the knowledge, rules, traditions, attitudes, and values that guide behavior in a particular group
      2. Cautions in interpreting cultural differences
         a. Differences should not be considered in isolation; children are many overlapping groups
         b. Membership in a particular group does not determine behavior but makes certain types of behaviors more probable

III. Social class differences (socioeconomic status)
   A. Who are the poor?
      1. One in five Americans under age 18 live in poverty
      2. Defined as income less than $13,359 for a family of four
      3. U.S. has highest rate of poverty for children among industrialized nations
   B. SES and achievement
      1. High-SES students of all ethnic groups score higher on achievement tests, get higher grades, and stay in school longer
         a. Relationship between SES and achievement is weaker when SES is measured solely in terms of parents' education, income, or job
         b. Relationship between SES and achievement is stronger when SES measurement includes attitudes and behavior of child's family
      2. Low SES may cause low expectations and low self-esteem
      3. Repeated failure may result in learned helplessness

4. Resistance cultures: The idea that making it in school means selling out
5. Low SES students may be tracked into "general ability" class where focus is on memorization and passive behavior
6. Childrearing styles may differ between low SES and middle class families

IV. Ethnic and racial differences: Differences based on geography, religion, race, or language
    A. Changing demographics: By 2020, almost half of the U.S. population will be from African-American, Asian, Hispanic, or other ethnic groups
    B. Cultural differences: There are visible as well as hidden differences
        1. Cultural conflicts
            a. Differences in conducting interpersonal relationships
            b. Misunderstanding arising from mannerisms, gestures
        2. Cultural compatibility
            a. Some cultural patterns fit into schools well; e.g. Vietnamese children value motivation and education
            b. Parents of Asian children support school philosophy
    C. Ethnic and racial differences in school achievement
        1. Major concern: Some ethnic groups score lower than the average (Table 5.3)
        2. Differences may be due to discrimination or product of cultural mismatches
    D. The legacy of discrimination
        1. Two-thirds of all African-American students attend schools where at least half of students are minority-group members
        2. Integrating students in same building does mean students will respect each other
    E. Continuing prejudice
        1. Certain groups still feel some prejudice from other groups
        2. Education is one of the strongest influences counteracting prejudice
    F. The development of prejudice
        1. Prejudice may be learned in from family and friends
        2. Extreme prejudice may develop as part of an authoritarian personality
    G. Continuing discrimination
        1. African-Americans and Hispanic groups form 20 percent of the total population but only 4 percent of scientists, engineers, and mathematicians and 6.8 percent of the teachers
        2. Minority groups are more often tracked into basic skills classes

V. Women and men: Differences in the classroom
    A. Gender-role identity: Children learn male and female roles very early from parents
        1. Androgynous children rate themselves highly on both masculine and feminine traits
        2. Gender-role stereotyping in the preschool years
            a. Boys are encouraged to be physically active and independent
            b. Girls encouraged to be affectionate and tender
        3. Gender bias in the curriculum: Stereotyped views of gender roles
            a. Books in the 1970s often portrayed males and females in sexually stereotyped roles
            b. Books in the 1990s may still portray females as more helpless

      c. Teacher attitude about sex differences are influential

   4. Sex discrimination in classrooms

      a. Teachers give boys more comments, praise, criticism, and correction, than girls

      b. Teachers can perpetuate stereotypes by asking boys to do physical tasks; be leaders; asking girls to arrange flowers, be secretaries

  B. Sex differences and mental abilities

   1. In early years little difference in mental and motor development

   2. In school years little difference in intelligence tests but tests have been balanced so that neither sex is favored

   3. Sex and mathematics

      a. Prior to 1974, males outperformed females but recently differences seem to be disappearing

      b. In beginning of high school, boys and girls take an equal number of math classes but by end of senior year boys have taken more math courses (Table 5.4)

      c. Teachers treat males and females differently in mathematics classes

   4. Eliminating gender bias

      a. In schools where no significant gender-based mathematic differences occur, teachers are enthusiastic about and have strong backgrounds in mathematics, engineering, or science

      b. Girls tend to do better in math when they work in cooperative groups

      c. Guidelines: Avoiding sexism in teaching

VI. Language differences in the classroom

  A. Dialects: Language variations of language spoken by particular ethnic, social, or regional groups

   1. Dialects and language skills: Differences from standard English pronunciation may cause confusion in spelling and usage

   2. Dialects and teaching

      a. Best approach is to focus on understanding child and accepting dialect as valid but teaching as alternative the standard form of English or dominant language

      b. Teachers may need to repeat instructions using different words

      c. Guidelines: Teaching Dialect-Dominant Students

  B. Bilingualism

   1. What does bilingualism mean?

      a. Mastering the knowledge necessary to communicate in two cultures

      b. Being able to deal with potential discrimination

   2. Becoming bilingual

      a. Higher degrees of bilingualism are associated with increased cognitive abilities

      b. When two languages develop simultaneously, there is some slow down in language acquisition in toddlers; this problem diminishes by age four

      c. In language studies contextualized language skills (face-to-face communication) takes 2 years in a good program to develop

      d. Decontextualized language skills (academic uses of language and grammar): takes five to seven years

3. Bilingual education: Two approaches
   a. Teach all subjects in English as early as possible
   b. Teach students in their primary language and increase English-language instruction over time

VII. Creating culturally compatible classrooms: Eliminating racism, sexism, and prejudice
  A. Social organization: Classrooms need to be organized based on child's culture
  B. Learning styles
    1. Hispanic Americans: Tendency to be field-dependent preferring holistic concrete, social approaches to learning
    2. African Americans: Visual /global style, preferring reasoning by inference rather than formal logic
    3. Native Americans: Global and visual style with a preference to learn privately, through trial-and-error
    4. Asian Americans: Field dependence; tendency to be global in problem solving, passive, and learn best in cooperative settings
    5. Criticisms of learning-styles research
      a. Validity of research questioned
      b. Identifying ethnic-group differences may be misleading
  C. Sociolinguistics: Study of the courtesies and conventions of conversations across cultures
    1. Participation structures: Students need to learn overt as well as subtle, nonverbal cues
    2. Sources of misunderstandings
      a. Different groups of children bring different participation structures
      b. Teachers need to teach clear and explicit rules for communications and activities
  D. Bringing it all together: Teaching every student
    1. Know your students
    2. Respect your students
    3. Teach your students
    4. Guidelines: Creating culturally compatible classrooms

VIII. Summary
IX. Key terms and concepts
X. What Would You Do?
XI. Teachers' casebook

Key Points

See if you understand the main points that are covered in this chapter:

Today's Multicultural Classrooms

- Old views: The students of all cultures must adapt values of dominant culture

   - Children are supposed to become mainstreamed Americans, master

English and adopt beliefs and behaviors of the middle-class, including being on time, getting good grades, and going to college or getting a good job

- Melting pot: A philosophy that values absorbing and assimilating immigrants into the mainstream of society so that ethnic differences vanish

- Cultural deficit model: A model that explains the school achievement problems of ethnic-minority student by assuming that their culture is inadequate and does not prepare them to succeed in school

- Multicultural education helps students and teachers accept one another's cultures and promotes school achievement for students by offering students a full and equal opportunity to learn in school and be respected

- New views: Various approaches to multicultural education

  - The human relations approach focuses on improving students' respect for all people

  - The in-depth study approach calls for a curriculum of study of racial and ethnic groups

  - The infusion approach modifies the curriculum so that all contents have racial and ethnic material included

  - The transformation approach tries to empower minorities to reshape society

- Cultural diversity affects education in all American schools

  - Culture and group membership is defined by the knowledge, rules, traditions, attitudes, and values that guide behavior in a particular group

  - Culture: The knowledge, values, attitudes, and traditions of a group of people that guide their behavior and allow them to solve the problems of living in their environment

  - Cautions in interpreting cultural differences:

    - Children are complex beings; they are individuals as well as members of cultural groups

    - Membership in a particular group does not determine behavior but makes certain types of behaviors more probable

Social class differences and socioeconomic status

- Socioeconomic status (SES): Relative standing in society based on income, power, background, and prestige

- One in five Americans under age 18 live in poverty (income less than $13,359 for a family of four); U.S. has highest rate of poverty for children of industrialized nations

- High-SES students of all ethnic groups score higher on achievement tests, get higher grades, and stay in school longer

- Lack of income may not be as important for school achievement as attitudes and behaviors of child's family

  - Low expectations may cause low self-esteem

  - Children may exhibit learned helplessness after repeated failure

  - Resistance culture: A group that shares values and beliefs about refusing to adopt the behaviors and attitudes of the majority culture

  - Low ability students are often tracked into classes where focus is on passive schooling

    - Academic socialization: The ways that children are taught how to be students, the value of learning, and their own role in schooling

    - Child-rearing styles that emphasize teaching rather than telling prepares children for academic success

Ethnic and racial differences based on geography, religion, race, or language

- Ethnicity: A cultural heritage shared by a group of people

- Race: A group of people who share common biological traits that are seen as self-defining by the people of the group

- Minority group: A group of people who have been socially disadvantaged-- not always a minority in actual numbers

- Changing demographics: By 2020, almost half of the population will be from African-American, Asian, Hispanic, or other ethnic groups

- Cultural differences can be either superficial or hidden from view

- Cultural conflicts can be caused by differences in conducting interpersonal relationships

- Some cultures are more congruent with mainstream values (e.g., Vietnamese children value motivation and education)

- Ethnic and racial groups differ in school achievement; differences may be due to discrimination or product of cultural mismatches

- Discrimination has left a legacy of unequal schooling and integration without positive human relations

- Certain groups still feel some prejudice toward other groups, although education is one of the strongest influences counteracting prejudice

- Prejudice is not innate, but develops as an attitude learned from others

  - Prejudice may develop as a part of an authoritarian personality, and also as a set of cultural values

  - Children develop schemas and stereotypes about other social groups

- Discrimination may be ongoing, as minority groups are more often tracked into basic skills classes

Women and men: Differences in the classroom

- Gender-role identity: Children learn male and female roles very early from parents and schools

  - Gender role stereotyping: Holding rigid beliefs about characteristics and behaviors associated with one sex as opposed to the other

  - Gender bias: Treating males and females differently, often favoring one gender over the other

    - Teachers and textbooks often foster stereotyped views of sex roles

    - Sex discrimination often takes place in classrooms as teachers give boys more interaction, including feedback (praise, criticism, and correction) and more specific comments

    - Boys are asked to do physical tasks and be leaders, while girls are asked to perform more "feminine" tasks

- In early years, little gender difference is shown in mental and motor development

- In school years, little difference in intelligence tests is shown, but by end of senior year boys excel in a number of courses

    - Evidence suggests that teachers treat males and females differently in mathematics classes

    - In schools where no significant mathematic differences occur, teachers have strong backgrounds in science and mathematics, are enthusiastic, and females and males are grouped together for instruction

Language differences in the classroom

- Teaching may be affected by negative stereotypes about language

    - Dialect: Rule-governed variation of a language spoken by a particular group

    - Best approach is to focus on understanding child and accept dialect as valid, teaching as alternative the standard form of English or dominant language

- Bilingual education is one way of dealing with potential discrimination

    - Bilingualism: Speaking two languages fluently

    - English as a Second Language (ESL): Programs and classes to teach English to students who are not native speakes of English

    - Limited English Proficiency (LEP): Students who have limited mastery of English

    - Second language acquisition: The process of learning a second language, very similar to the process of first-language acquisition.

    - Monolingual: Individual who speaks only one language

    - Semilingual: Not proficient in any language, speaking one or more languages inadequately

    - Higher degrees of bilingualism are associated with increased cognitive abilities

    - Contextualized language skills (face-to-face communication) takes two years in a good program to develop

- Decontextualized language skills (academic uses of language and grammar) takes five to seven years in a good program to develop

- One approach to bilingual education is to teach English as early as possible (research does not indicate that this is an effective model)

- A preferred approach involves teaching the student in their primary language and increasing English instruction over time

Creating culturally compatible classrooms: Eliminating racism, sexism, and prejudice

- <u>Culturally compatible classrooms</u>: Classrooms in which procedures, rules, grouping strategies, attitudes, and teaching methods do not cause conflicts with the students' culturally influenced ways of learning and interacting

- Classrooms need to be socially organized based on children's culture

- Research suggests that different cultures have varied learning styles

- Some cultures may be field-dependent, preferring holistic, concrete, social approaches to learning; others favor reasoning by inference rather than formal logic; others favor learning privately, through trial-and-error; some may prefer cooperative settings

  - Teachers need to be cautious about stereotyping ethnic learning styles

- <u>Sociolinguistics</u>: The study of the formal and informal rules for how, when, about what, to whom, and how long to speak in conversations within a given cultural group

  - <u>Participation structures</u>: The formal and informal rules for how to take part in a given activity

  - Different groups of children come to school having learned different participation structures

  - Teachers need to teach clear and explicit rules for communications and activities

Concept Map: CULTURALLY COMPATIBLE CLASSROOMS

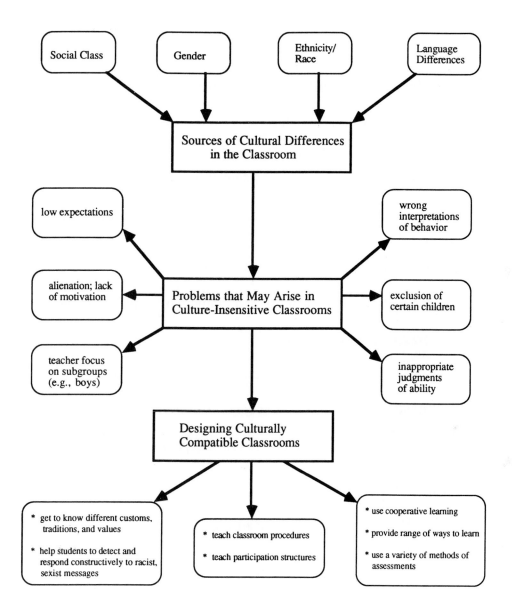

Do You Know This?

Answering these questions will help you to check yourself on your mastery of the chapter objectives.

Today's Multicultural Classrooms

Can you compare the old notion of the melting pot with current views about multicultural education?

Can you define culture and list the various groups that make up <u>your</u> cultural identity?

Social class differences and socioeconomic status

Can you explain why the school achievement of low income students often falls below that of middle- and upper-class students?

Ethnic and racial differences based on geography, religion, race, or language

Can you give examples of conflicts and compatibilities between home and school cultures?

Women and Men: Differences in the Classroom

Can you describe the school's role in the development of gender differences?

Language Differences in the Classroom

Can you summarize the arguments for and against bilingual education?

Creating Culturally Compatible Classrooms

Tell how you would incorporate multicultural concepts in your teaching.

Key Terms and Concepts

MATCHING: Culture and Multicultural Education

Match the letters of the descriptions on the right with the corresponding items on the left. Use each definition only once.

_____	1. Melting pot	a. A group that shares common, self-defining biological traits
_____	2. Cultural deficit model	
_____	3. Multicultural education	b. A group that refuses to adopt values of majority culture
_____	4. Culture	
_____	5. Resistance culture	c. Philosophy of absorption of ethnic differences into mainstream
_____	6. Academic socialization	
_____	7. Ethnicity	d. Relative standing in society based upon income, power, or profession
_____	8. Race	
_____	9. Minority group	

_____   10. Socioeconomic status

e. Explaining minority students' failure
     in school as due to cultural
     shortcomings
f. Cultural heritage shared by a
     group of people
g. A group that has been socially
     disadvantaged
h. Teaching the value of cultural diversity
i. Knowledge, values, traditions
     that guide the behavior of a group
j. The ways that children are taught
     how to be students

DEFINITIONS: Language Differences in the Classroom

Write explanations for the following pairs of terms. Your explanation should clearly distinguish the two from one another. Check the text to see if your explanations are equivalent.

Bilingualism/Semilingual _____

_____

Monolingual/Limited English Proficient _____

_____

Second Language Acquisition/English as a Second Language _____

_____

Sociolinguistics/Participation structures _____

_____

APPLICATION: Old Views versus New Views of Culture in the Classroom

In the space below, contrast the characteristics of the old views of culture in the classroom with the view that is represented by current practices in multicultual education.

Old views _____

_____

_____

Multicultural education _____

_____

_____

APPLICATION: Effect of Socioeconomic Status on Education

Imagine that you are a teacher in a school that is situated in a neighborhood where residents are of low socioeconomic status. At "Back-to-School Night," you have the opportunity to address a group of the parents of students in your class. What suggestions can you give them that will help their children be successful in school? For each of the factors below that are associated with low SES, write a sentence that you would use to explain to parents how they can be of help to their children.

Attitudes about the importance of education _____

_____

Aspirations for school success _____

_____

Family activities which promote intellectual achievement _____

_____

Good health habits and medical care _____

_____

CASE STUDY: Language Differences in the Classroom

You are the chair of the English department of a local high school. You have been given the responsibility of eliminating all tracking practices in the English class in your school. From now on, all students, regardless of ability and language proficiency, will be grouped together. What suggestions will you give the teachers in your department in planning lessons to meet all the individual needs of the students, including the needs of those students with limited English proficiency?

CASE STUDY: Bilingual Education

One of your second grade students with limited English proficiency who has been in a bilingual program since kindergarten want the child redesignated and placed in an all-English program. What defense could you give of the values of bilingual education?

PRACTICE TEST: Multiple Choice

Select the best answer for each of the following items:

1. The traditional philosophy regarding immigrant students is that they

    a. deserve special treatment given the obstacles they have overcome.
    b. are just as prepared for school as other students.
    c. come from an inferior culture that leaves them at a disadvantage.
    d. achieve higher than American students because of their greater motivation.

2. The main impact of the multicultural movement of today is to

    a. promote the concept of the "melting pot."
    b. value variations between different ethnic and racial groups.
    c. suppress the infusion of material in the school curriculum that conveys cultural differences.
    d. promote much heated debate, but no tangible changes.

3. Which of the variables is considered a highly accurate meaure of socioeconomic status?

    a. Political power
    b. A high-status profession
    c. Wealth
    d. None of the above

4. It is predicted that in the next 25 years, the number of poor children will

    a. increase substantially.
    b. increase slightly.
    c. remain fairly consistant.
    d. decrease slightly.

5. Marco decides that he doesn't want to be like the "rich kids who sell themselves out to the system." Accordingly, he prides himself on not learning what the school is trying to teach. Which of the following terms best characterizes his behavior?

    a. Learned helplessness
    b. Tracking
    c. Academic antisocialization
    d. Resistance culture

6. Which of the following is true of minority groups?

    a. According to sociologists' definition, they comprise less than 50% of the population.
    b. Their number is decreasing slightly in most states.
    c. The largest minority group in the United States is African-American.
    d. All of the above.

7. In discussing different cultures, your textbook conveys the view that intelligence

   a. is higher for certain cultural groups than for others.
   b. is the main factor affecting how different cultural groups perform in school.
   c. is defined by the cultural group, based on the types of behaviors it cultivates.
   d. does not differ between cultural groups when measured by standardized tests, such as the WAIS.

8. Which of the following differences between males and females is most clearly documented in the <u>current</u> literature?

   a. Males are significantly superior in spatial abilities.
   b. Males have a strong advantage in verbal skills.
   c. Males have a slight advantage in mathematic skills.
   d. Females are faster at rotating figures in space.

9. In interacting with children who speak in a nonstandard dialect, teachers are encouraged to

   a. accept the dialect but teach Standard English.
   b. verbally correct the child when the dialect yields incorrect grammar.
   c. disallow the use of the dialect for communicating in class.
   d. assign those children to special language classes where they can receive individual help.

10. The current view is that bilingualism is _____ for cognitive development.

   a. extremely harmful
   b. somewhat harmful
   c. somewhat beneficial
   d. neither harmful nor helpful

PRACTICE TEST: Essay

A. Describe a parent's verbal interaction with a young child that demonstrates the providing of intellectual support, or "scaffolding."

B. What evidence indicates that certain minority groups (Hispanic- and African-Americans) are still being discriminated against educationally?

Answer Key

MATCHING: Culture and Multicultural Education

1. c
2. e
3. h
4. i
5. b
6. j
7. f
8. a
9. g
10. d

PRACTICE TEST: Multiple Choice

1. c   The traditional philosophy was that immigrant students <u>come from an inferior culture that leaves them at a disadvantage</u>. This philosophy engendered the cultural deficit model of educating these students.

2. b   The multicultural movement of today directly supports <u>valuing variations between different ethnic and racial groups</u>. The fundamental idea is that all students, regardless of ethnic or cultural background, should have an equal opportunity to learn in school and be respected.

3. d   <u>No single variable</u> appears to be an effective measure of SES. Thus, none of the choices (political power, a high-status profession, or wealth) is correct.

4. a   Based on projections, the number of poor children will <u>increase substantially</u> over the next 25 years. Specifically, it is estimated that by the year 2020 schools will have to teach 5.4 million more poor students than they taught in 1984.

5. d   A <u>resistance culture</u> is represented by lower-class students' rejection of middle-class values. This behavior is exemplified by Marcos purposeful not to learn what the school is trying to teach (to "the rich kids").

6. c   <u>The largest minority group in the United States is African-American</u>. Minority populations are increasing in most states. Although, technically a minority refers to a group that is underrepresented in size in a population, sociologists use the term to label a group of people who receive discriminatory treatment.

7. c   Your textbook conveys the view that intelligence is <u>defined by the culture</u>. What one culture regards as intelligent or adaptive behavior may be viewed less positively by another culture.

8. c   The most clearly documented gender ability difference in the current literature is that males have a slight <u>advantage in mathematics</u>. This advantage appears attributable to external factors, such as males receiving more encouragement

to learn and achieve in mathematics.

9.   a   When interacting with children who speak in a nonstandard dialect, teachers are encouraged to <u>accept the dialect</u>, but teach Standard English. In this way, the teacher shows respect for the child's language while allowing him/her to communicate freely. Learning Standard English also seems fairly easy for most of these children provided that they have good models.

10.   c   It is currently believed that being bilingual is <u>somewhat beneficial</u> for cognitive development. Specifically, higher degrees of bilingualism are associated with increased concept formation, creativity, knowledge of language, and cognitive flexibility. This positive view of bilingualism contrasts with earlier negative interpretations supported by more poorly designed studies.

PRACTICE TEST: Essay

A.   Hess and Shipman's research, among others, have shown that in interacting with their children, middle-class mothers were less likely than lower-class mothers to impose solutions. They talk more; give verbal guidance, and provide encouragement; help their children understand the causes of events, make plans, and anticipate consequences; direct their children's attention to the relevant details of a problem; and encourage children to solve problems themselves.

B.   Even though more than 20% of the total population is Hispanic or African-American, only 4% of the scientists, engineers, and mathematicians and only 6.8% of the teachers in the United States belong to these ethnic groups. They are chosen less often for gifted and acceleration/enrichment programs, and they are more likely to be tracked into "basic skills" classes.

6

Behavioral Views of Learning

Teaching Outline

I. What do you think?

II. Understanding learning
   A. Learning: A definition
      1. Permanent changes in knowledge or behavior brought about by experience, not merely through maturation or temporary conditions
      2. Cognitive view: Learning as internal process that cannot be observed directly; changes in behavior reflection of internal change
      3. Behavioral view: Learning as change in observable behavior
   B. Learning is not always what it seems: Learning processes vary

III. Early explanations of learning: Contiguity and classical conditioning
   A. Repeated pairings of two events (stimulus and response) cause them to be associated
   B. Pavlov's dilemma and discovery: Classical conditioning
      1. Pairing neutral stimulus with an unconditioned stimulus
      2. Classical conditioning: Unconditioned responses becomes conditioned to the formerly neutral stimulus (Figure 6.1)
   C. Generalization, discrimination, and extinction
      1. Generalization: Responding to new stimuli similar to the original stimulus as it were the original stimulus
      2. Discrimination: Responding differently to two similar but not identical stimuli
      3. Extinction: Gradual disappearance of conditioned response when conditioned stimulus is presented repeatedly but not followed by the unconditioned stimulus
      4. Guidelines: Using Principles of Classical Conditioning

IV. Operant conditioning: Trying new responses
   A. The ABCs of operant conditioning: Antecedents--behavior--consequences
      1. Operants: Deliberate actions influenced by the consequences that follow them
      2. Operant conditioning: Effort to influence learning control of the consequences of behavior
   B. The work of Skinner
      1. Behavior can be changed by changes in its antecedents (stimuli that precede it) and /or its consequences and/or consequences
      2. Skinner boxes: Controlled environment where effects of consequences of behavior can be studied
   C. Types of consequences
      1. Reinforcement: Use reinforcers to strengthen behavior
         a. Positive reinforcement: Presentation of a pleasant stimulus

   b. Negative reinforcement: Disappearance or avoidance of an aversive stimulus

  2. Punishment: Use of punishers to decrease or suppress behavior

   a. Presentation punishment: Presentation of a punisher

   b. Removal punishment: Disappearance of removal of a reinforcer

 D. Reinforcement schedules

  1. Continuous reinforcement: Reinforcing behavior every time it occurs to each a new behavior faster

  2. Intermittent reinforcement: Reinforcing behavior periodically (not every time) to maintain an established behavior (Table 6.1)

   a. Interval schedules (based on time interval): Fixed or variable

   b. Ratio schedules: fixed or variable (based on number of responses)

 E. Summarizing the effects of reinforcement schedules

   a. Speed of performance: Ratio schedules produce faster response time than interval schedules

   b. Persistence: Variable schedules produce behaviors more resistant to extinction then those on fixed schedules

  4. Extinction: Removal of reinforcement leads to ceasing of behavior

 F. Antecedents and behavior change

  1. Antecedents (events preceding a behavior): Provide information about which behaviors will lead to positive and negative consequences

  2. Cuing: Providing an antecedent stimulus just before a certain behavior is to occur nonjudgemental cues help prevent negative confrontations

  3. Prompting: Providing students help in responding to cues (See Figure 6.3)

V. Applied behavior analysis: Application of behavioral learning to change behavior

 A. Methods for encouraging behavior

  1. Reinforcing with teacher attention

   a. Behavior improves when teachers give attention to constructive behavior while making rules explicit and ignoring problem behavior

   b. Praise must be contingent on the desired behavior, the behavior must be specified, and praise must be believable

   c. Guidelines: Using Praise Appropriately

  2. Selecting the best reinforcers

   a. Premack principle using preferred activity as reinforcer for a less-preferred activity

   b. Important: The less-preferred activity must precede the preferred activity

  3. Guidelines: Using Reinforcement

  4. Task analysis: identifying the small steps that lead to a final goal

  5. Shaping: Reinforcing progress in successive approximations

   a. Reinforce each subskill

   b. Reinforce improvements in accuracy

   c. Reinforce longer and longer periods of performance

   d. Reinforce longer and longer periods of patricipation

  6. Positive practice: When students make academic errors, having them practice correct responses

 B. Coping with undesirable behavior

  1. Negative reinforcement

2. Satiation: Requiiring students to continue inappropriate behavior until they are tired of it
3. Reprimands: Private, quiet reprimands most effective
4. Response cost: Loss of a reinforcer
5. Some cautions: Teachers should pair punishment with reinforcement
6. Guidelines: Using Punishment Appropriately

VI. Social Learning Theory:
   A. Bandura's social cognitive theory: Importance of both behavioral principles and internal factors (reciprocal determinism)
   B. Learning by observing others (modeling)
      1. Vicarious conditioning: Learning based on seeing others rewarded or punished for their actions
      2. Imitation: Copying behavior of model
      3. Example from Bandura's research: Learning aggressive behavior through modeling
   C. Elements of observational learning
      1. Attention: Teachers must attract student's attention to critical features of lessons
      2. Retention: To imitate behavior one has to remember it
      3. Production: Practice makes behavior smoother and more expert
      4. Motivation and reinforcement: Incentives may encourage performance and maintenance of newly acquired skills
   D. Observational learning in teaching
      1. Teaching new behaviors: Teacher's own behavior may be most prevalent influence on learning
      2. Encouraging already-learned behaviors: Children receive cues by observing others
      3. Strengthening or weakening inhibitions: "Ripple effect" means tendency to imitate or not imitate behavior depending upon the observed consequences of that behavior
      4. Directing attention: Observation can direct attention to new aspects of situation
      5. Arousing emotion: Observation can cause fears or anxieties to develop
      6. Guidelines: Using Observational Learning
VII. Self-regulation and cognitive behavior modification
   A. Focus on helping students take control of their own learning
   B. Self-management
      1. Goal-setting: Setting specific goals and making them public
         a. Higher standards lead to higher performance
         b. Student-set goals have a tendency to decline; need monitoring and reinforcement of high standards by teacher
      2. Recording and evaluating performance
      3. Self-reinforcement: Rewards for a job well done
      4. Guidelines: Instituting Self-Management Programs
   C. Cognitive behavior modification: Adds emphasis on thinking and self-talk to behavior change program
      1. Direct teaching of how to use self-instruction through "private speech"

2. Other methods: Dialogue, modeling, guided discovery, motivational strategies, feedback, etc.
VIII. Problems and issues
   Point/Counterpoint: Should students be rewarded for learning?
   A. Behavioral strategies may be used responsibly or irresponsibly
   B. Ethical issues surround choices of goals and strategies
      1. Goals should go beyond mere classroom decorum
      2. Strategies can have negative side effects such as modeling aggression
   C. Criticisms of behavioral methods
      1. Decreased interest in learning
      2. Impact on other students
   D. Guidelines: Making Ethical Use of Behavioral Methods
IX.   Summary
X.   Key terms and concepts
XI.   What would you do?
XII. Teachers' casebook

Key Points

Understanding Learning

- <u>Learning</u>: Process that causes permanent change in knowledge or behavior

- <u>Behavioral learning theory</u>: Explanation of learning that focuses on external events as the cause of changes in observable behaviors

- <u>Cognitive learning theory</u>: Explanation of learning that focuses on internal processes that cannot be observed directly; behavior change is a reflection of internal change

- <u>Contiguity</u>: Association of two events because of repeated pairings

- <u>Stimulus</u>: Event that activates behavior

- <u>Response</u>: Observable reaction to a stimulus

Classical conditioning: Pairing automatic responses with new stimuli

- <u>Unconditioned stimulus</u> (US): Stimulus that automatically produces an emotional or physiological response

- <u>Unconditioned response</u> (UR): Naturally occurring emotional or physiological response

- <u>Conditioned stimulus</u> (CS): Stimulus that evokes an emotional or physiological response after conditioning

- Conditioned response (CR): Learned response to a previously neutral stimulus

- Generalization: Responding to similar stimuli in the same way

- Discrimination: Responding differently to similar stimuli

- Extinction: Gradual disappearance of a learned response

- Classical conditioning may be a cause of emotional reactions to various situations; students may need to be taught more adaptive emotional responses

Operant Conditioning: Trying new responses

- Antecedents: Events that precede an action

- Behavior: Observable action influenced by its antecedents (stimuliwhich precede it)

- Consequences: Events that follow an action

- Respondent: A (generally automatic or involuntary) response elicited by a specific stimulus

- Operant: A voluntary (and generally goal-directed) behavior emitted by a person or an animal

- Operant conditioning: Learning in which voluntary behavior is strengthened or weakened by consequences or antecedents

- Thorndike's Law of Effect: Any act producing a satisfying effect in a given situation will tend to be repeated in that situation

- Skinner box: A controlled environment where effects of antecedents and consequences of behavior can be studied

- Reinforcer: Any event that follows a behavior and increases the chances that the behavior will occur again

- Reinforcement: Consequence that strengthens behavior

- Positive reinforcement: Strengthening behavior by presenting a desired stimulus after the behavior

- Negative reinforcement: Strengthening behavior by removing an aversive stimulus

- Punishment: Anything that weakens or suppresses behavior

    - Presentation punishment: Decreasing the chances that a behavior will occur again by presenting an aversive stimulus following the behavior; also called Type I punishment

    - Removal punishment: Decreasing the chances that a behavior will occur again by removing a pleasant stimulus following the behavior; also called Type II punishment

- Reinforcement schedules: Reinforcement should occur in a structured format

    - Continuous reinforcement schedule: Presenting a reinforcer at every appropriate response

    - Intermittent reinforcement schedule: Presenting a reinforcer after some, but not all responses

    - Fixed interval reinforcement schedule: Reinforcing a behavior after set intervals

    - Variable interval reinforcement schedule: Reinforcing a behavior after varying amounts of time

    - Fixed ratio reinforcement schedule: Reinforcement is given after a fixed number of responses

    - Variable ratio reinforcement schedule: Reinforcement is given after varying numbers of responses

- Antecedents : Providing information about which behaviors will lead to positive and negative consequences

- Cuing: Providing a stimulus that "sets up" a desired behavior

- Prompt: A reminder that follows a cue to make sure that the student reacts to the cue

Applied behavior analysis

- This is sometimes called behavioral modification, and is the application of behavioral learning to understand and change behavior

- Praise-and-ignore: Teachers give attention to constructive behavior while making rules explicit and ignoring problem behavior

- Premack principle: A more preferred activity can serve as a reinforcer for a less preferred activity

- Shaping: Reinforcing each small step of progress towards a desired goal or behavior

- Positive practice: Practicing correct response immediately after errors

- Negative reinforcement: Increasing behavior by removal of an aversive stimulus

- Satiation: Repeating a positive behavior past the point of interest or motivation

- Reprimands: Criticisms for misbehavior; rebukes

- Response cost: Punishment through loss of reinforcers

- Social isolation (timeout): Removal of a disruptive student for 5 or 10 minutes

Social Learning Theory

- Theory that emphasizes learning through observing others (modeling)

- Reciprocal determinism: An explanation of behavior that emphasize the mutual effects of the individual and the environment on each other

- Observational learning: Learning by observing and imitating others

- Self-efficacy: A person's sense of being able to deal effectively with a particular situation

- Vicarious reinforcement: Increasing the chances that you will repeat a behavior by observing another person being reinforced for that behavior

- Self-reinforcement: Providing positive consequences to yourself, contingent on accomplishing a particular behavior

- Social cognitive theory asserts that cognitive factors underlie behavior; operant learning does not adequately explain mediated learning

  - The teacher influences learning by modeling appropriate behaviors

- Ripple effect: "Contagious" spreading of behaviors through imitation

Cognitive behavior modification and self-regulation

- Helps students get in control of their own learning, regulating and managing own lives, setting own goals and providing own reinforcement as a preparation for adult life

- Self-management: Using behavioral learning principles to manage one's own behavior

- Cognitive behavior modification: Procedures based on both behavioral and cognitive learning principles for changing your own behavior by using self-talk and self-instruction

DO YOU KNOW THIS?

Answering these questions will help you to check yourself on your mastery of the chapter objectives.

Understanding Learning

Can you give a definition of learning, contrasting it with maturation?

Early Explanations of Learning: Contiguity and Classical Conditioning

Can you give examples of contiguity learning, classical conditioning, and operant conditioning?

How can a teacher understand children's emotional responses by utilizing principles of classical conditioning?

Operant Conditioning: Trying New Responses

Can you give examples of four different kinds of consequences that may follow any behavior and the effect each is likely to have on future behavior?

Applied Behavior Analysis

Can you choose a common academic or behavior problem and design an intervention based on applied behavior analysis?

Social Learning Theory

Can you describe a situation in which a teacher may decide to use modeling?

Self-Regulation and Cognitive Behavior Modification

Can you compare self-management and cognitive behavior modification?

Problems and Issues

Can you discuss potential dangers and ethical issues involved in the use of any behavioral change technique?

Concept Map: APPLYING BEHAVIOR ANALYSIS

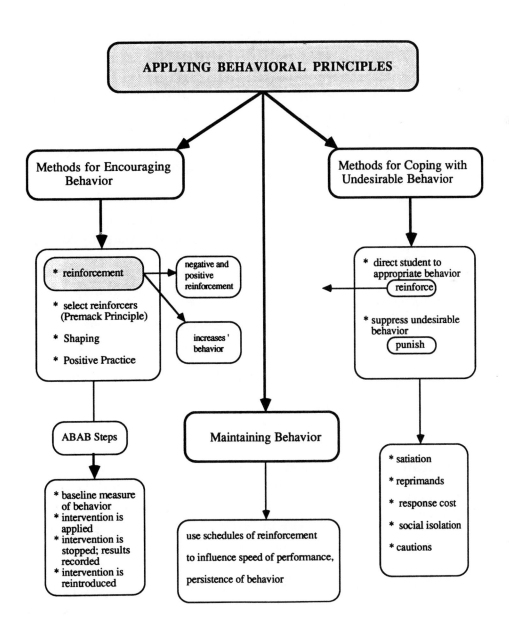

Key Terms and Concepts

MATCHING: Learning Through Classical Conditioning

Match the letters of the descriptions on the right with the corresponding items on the left. Use each definition only once. To check answers, see Answer Key.

1. _____ Contiguity
2. _____ Stimulus
3. _____ Response
4. _____ Unconditioned stimulus
5. _____ Unconditioned response

6. _____ Conditioned stimulus
7. _____ Conditioned response
8. _____ Generalization
9. _____ Discrimination
10. _____ Extinction

a. **Responding to similar stimuli in the same way**
b. **Gradual disappearance of a learned response**
c. **Observable reaction to a stimulus**
d. **Produces an emotional or physiological reaction**
e. **Responding differently to similar stimuli**
f. **Naturally occurring emotional or physiological reaction**
g. **Event that activates behavior**
h. **Evokes an emotional or physiological reaction after conditioning**
i. **Association of two events because of repeated pairings**
j. **Learned reaction to a previously neutral stimulus**

DEFINITIONS: Concepts in Operant Conditioning

Write explanations for the following pairs of terms. Your explanations should clearly distinguish one from the other. Check the text to see if your explanations are equivalent.

Presentation Punishment/Removal Punishment _____

_____

Punishment/Negative Reinforcement _____

_____

Continuous/Intermittent Reinforcement Schedules _____

_____

Fixed Interval/Variable Interval Reinforcement Schedule _____

_____

Fixed Ratio /Variable Ratio Reinforcement Schedule_____

_____

COMPLETION QUESTIONS: Operant Learning

Fill in the blanks with the following concepts. Each term is used only once. For answers, see Answer Key.

Extinction   **Negative reinforcement**
Operants   **Punishment**   **Praise**
Operant conditioning   **Reinforcer**   **Discriminate**
Antecedents   **Cuing**   **Shaping**
Consequences   **Prompting**

1.   A teacher needs to establish consistent _____ for positive and negative behaviors.

2.   Deliberate actions are called _____.

3.   Instructing students to recognize which _____ can be associated with positive consequences will help them manage their own behavior.

4.   Mr. Patterson used to scold Jason for speaking out of turn; Mr. Patterson now ignores Jason's comments and praises other students for their cooperation. Mr. Patterson is using _____ by withholding his former attention to Jason's misbehavior.

5.   Students need to _____ among various antecendent conditions so they will learn which behaviors will gain rewards.

6.   To decrease students' pushing each other on the playground, the playground supervisor pulls misbehaving students off the playground immediately and assigns detention. This is an example of _____.

7.   Miss Chu wants to teach Joshua to raise his hand when he wants to answer a question. Therefore, she praises him each time he raises his hand appropriately. Eventually, she wants him to answer questions without being reinforced. She is attempting to use small successive steps or _____ to modify his behavior.

8.   The teacher frowns at off-task students until they resume working. This is an example of _____.

9. _____ involves voluntary behaviors strengthened or weakened by reinforcement or punishment.

10. _____ is the act of providing an antecedent stimulus just before a particular behavior is to take place.

11. By watching what children choose to do with their free time, the teacher can identify what an appropriate _____ might be for those children.

CHARTING: Task Analysis

In the chart below, create a task analysis for the steps necessary to solve a long division problem of this type: 50 divided by 5. The first step has been completed for you. You will need to add more boxes.

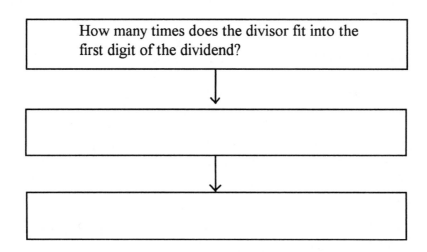

How many times does the divisor fit into the first digit of the dividend?

APPLICATION: Social Learning Theory

Lunchtime at Curtis Middle School is pandemonium. Teachers who are asked to be lunch monitors find it difficult to keep the noise level under control. Students who are assigned to after-school detention too often return to the next day's lunch without the detention experience improving their behavior. The principal has decided to implement a social learning program. She calls students to her office whom she regards as role models for other students (although some of these have not provided models of positive behavior in the past). How can the principal use social learning principles to persuade these students to affect the lunchroom behaviors of the other students?

APPLICATION: Self-Regulation and Cognitive Behavior Modification

Trisha is a sixth grade student who finds it difficult to complete seatwork assignments without a continuous monitoring by the classroom teacher. She is distractible, talkative, and does not organize her materials such as paper and pencils so that they are available when she needs them. Mrs. Rigby wants to increase Trisha's self-management skills. For each category below, suggest ideas that would help Trisha improve her ability to complete her social studies seatwork assignments without continual reminders from Mrs. Rigby.

Set goals _____

_____

Observe own work _____

_____

Keep records _____

_____

Evaluate own performance _____

_____

Self reinforcement _____

_____

CASE STUDY: Appropriate Use of Operant Conditioning

Brock's behavior has troubled Miss Yokomura since the first day of school. Several parents have complained during parent conferences that their children come home with bruises that Brock has inflicted on the playground. The positive reinforcement that Miss Yokomura is using has proven ineffective in stopping Brock from bullying classmates. While discussing the situation with the principal, Miss Yokomura has identified two aspects of behavior that must be targeted: stopping the bullying and shaping Brock's positive leadership qualities on the playground. Propose specific reinforcement techniques that will accomplish these two objectives.

CASE STUDY: Applied Behavior Analysis

It was taking all Mr. Reber's self-control to remain calm with his third grade class. Between activities, students often wander around the room, sharpening pencils, poking their fingers in the rabbit cage, and fiddling with the science exhibits. How can Mr. Reber use prompts and cues to help students make more appropriate transitions between class activities? Give examples.

IDENTIFICATION: Reinforcement Schedules

For each blank, choose one of the four reinforcement schedules given below. When you finish, check your answer with the Answer Key at the end of this chapter.

Fixed Interval (FI)
Variable Interval (VI)
Fixed Ratio (FR)
Variable Ratio (VR)

1. _____ The teacher is walking slowly around the classroom to monitor students' seatwork. Students directly in front of the teacher are working hard to produce answers. Students behind the teacher slow down briefly because they have already received teacher attention.

2. _____ Students who receive a sticker after every ten problems they complete will temporarily slow down after each sticker.

3. _____ Students who raise their hands to volunteer to answer during recitation teaching are never sure how many times they will be called upon to answer. This keeps the hand-raising at a high rate.

4. _____ The computer program for a math drill shows students a comic character after every fifth correct problem. This results in a steady performance.

5. _____ In the language laboratory, the instructor tunes in to listen to students one after the other. Students are never sure when they will be monitored. This results in a uniform level of students listening and responding to the tapes.

6. _____ When a midterm and final examination are the only two tests scheduled, studying increases in magnitude and frequency just before the tests and drops dramatically just after the test is given.

PRACTICE TEST: Multiple Choice

1. In an experiment, an electric can opener is used to open a can, and no salivation by the subject is detected. After a number of pairings between the can opener's operation and food, any time the can opener is used the subject salivates. The conditioned response in this study is the

   a. salivation to the can opener.
   b. saliavation to the food.

   c. can opener.

   d. food.

2. During physical education class, Julia enthusiastically swings at each pitch and strikes out. One of the other students comments, "You are the strike out queen!" Julia turns beet red. The next week she feels ill when it is time to go to physical education class. Her reaction illustrates

   a. social learning.

   b. classical conditioning.

   c. cognitive learning.

   d. unconditioned stimulus.

3. The study by Madsen, Becker, and Thomas (1968) confirmed that one effective and available reinforcer for young students is

   a. free time.

   b. tokens or extrinsic rewards.

   c. teacher attention.

   d. points toward their final grade.

4. Elimination of all negative consequences in classrooms tends to lead to

   a. fewer disruptive behaviors when praise is increased.

   b. fewer disruptive behaviors when teachers ignore misbehaviors.

   c. a continuation of disruptive behaviors and less work involvement.

   d. no noticeable increase or decrease in disruptive behaviors.

5. The Premack principle states that

   a. a preferred activity is withheld until rewards are earned.

   b. a less-preferred activity is postponed until after a preferred one.

   c. less-preferred activities are effective as punishment.

   d. a preferred activity is a reinforcer for a less-preferred activity.

6. Which of the folllowing is an example of the use of "negative reinforcement?"

   a. The noisy class loses 30 minutes of recess.

   b. John disrupts the class and is sent out of the room.

   c. The class becomes quiet and is allowed to leave for recess.

   d. Louise makes a rude noise and is forced to continue until bored.

7. Which of the following is NOT true of the use of "social isolation"?

   a. Time-out longer than 20 minutes is most effective.

   b. A student is placed in an uninteresting room.

   c. The teacher must ensure student stay in the "time-out" situation.

   d. It is more frequently used in special education classes.

8. The "ripple effect" uses

   a. peer tutoring to help others learn.

   b. teacher modeling to demonstrate good behavior.
   c. imitation to spread new behaviors.
   d. emotional reactions of children to established attitudes toward new materials.

9. A common criticism of behavioral methods is that they

   a. are ineffective.
   b. result in decreased interest in learning when rewards are unavailable.
   c. are not based on accepted principles of learning.
   d. are highly time-consuming to implement compared to other methods.

10. Following classical conditioning, an extinction procedure would be intiated by presenting

   a. the conditioned stimulus alone.
   b. negative reinforcement.
   c. the unconditioned stimulus alone.
   d. a new neutral stimulus with the unconditioned stimulus.

PRACTICE TEST: Essay

A. As Marcia's mother drops her off at kindergarten, Marcia cries as if her heart would break. Marcia's mother is becoming more and upset and does not want to leave her daughter. Mr. Robles, the kindergarten teacher, suspects that Marcia's mother's reluctance to leave may be reinforcing Marcia's crying. How can he help to extinguish Marcia's crying behavior?

B. As part of the discipline policy at Redwood Elementary, the principal of the school regularly stands misbehaving children in small red circles on the playground at recess time. Several parents of students in your clasroom have complained to you about this practice. How would you support or not support this policy? First, given reasons why this may be an appropriate technique. Then, propose an alternative practice.

Answer Key

MATCHING: Learning Through Classical Conditioning

1. i
2. g
3. c
4. d
5. f
6. h
7. j
8. a
9. e
10. b

COMPLETION QUESTIONS: Operant Learning

1. **Consequences**
2. **Operants**
3. **Antecedents**
4. **Extinction**
5. **Discriminate**
6. **Punishment**
7. **Shaping**
8. **Negative reinforcement**
9. **Operant conditioning**
10. **Cuing**
11. **Reinforcer**

IDENTIFICATION: Reinforcement Schedules

1.	**FI**	4.	**FR**
2.	**FR**	5.	**VI**
3.	**VR**	6.	**FI**

PRACTICE TEST: Multiple Choice

1. a   The conditioned response in this experiment would be <u>salivation to the can opener</u>. Prior to the pairing to the neutral stimulus, can opener, with the unconditioned stimulus, food, this response did not occur. It needed to be learned or "conditioned."

2. b   For Julia, feeling ill at the prospect of going to physical education class illustrates <u>classical conditioning</u>. This conditioing was produced by the other student's inadvertent pairing of the previously neutral stimulus, physical education class, with feelings of embarassment.

3. c   Madsen, Becker, and Thomas' (1968) study demonstrated that teachers can improve student behavior by praising students who are following rules and ignoring rule-breakers. The implication is that <u>attention</u> is an effective and available reinforcer for young adults.

4. c   Research has suggested that when teachers eliminate all negative consequences and try only positive consequences to manage the class, the <u>disruptive behaviors will continue and work involvement will decrease</u>. The suggestion is that the praise- and-ignore approach should be considered for dealing with minor misbehavior or used as supplement with other strategies.

5. d   The Premack Principle uses a preferred activity as a reinforcer for a less preferred activity. An example is, "<u>Clean your room and then you can watch

<u>T.V.</u>"

6.   c   Negative reinforcement is the removal of an aversive condition to reinforce a response. An example would be <u>allowing a quiet class to leave early for recess</u>. (The "aversive" condition is staying in the regular class.)

7.   a   Social isolation or time out involves placing a misbehaving student in an uninteresting room, usually for less than 15 minutes. It is more frequently used in special education classes than in regular classes. <u>Time out as long or longer than 20 minutes is not recommended</u>.

8.   c   The "ripple effect" uses <u>imitation to spread good behaviors</u>. A positive example is when the teacher disciplines a high status individual and every one else immediately behaves properly. The good behavior "ripples" through the class.

9.   b   A common criticism of behavioral methods is that result in <u>decreased interest in learning when rewards are unavailable</u>. In other words, when students are rewarded they may become conditioned in a sense to expect rewards. Extrinsic rewards may thus reduce intrinsic (natural) motivation for learning.

10.   a   To extinguish a conditioned response, present the <u>conditioned stimulus alone</u> (without the unconditioned stimulus). In Pavlov's experiment, one would sound the tone (conditioned stimulus) day after day without presenting food. Eventually, the dog will stop salivating to the tone.

PRACTICE TEST: Essay

A.   Extinction is accomplished by reducing or removing the reinforcers which have been a consequence of inappropriate behavior. Mr. Robles may wish to suggest to Marcia's mother that despite Marcia's crying, the mother should bring Marcia to kindergarten and promptly leave. Over time, Marcia's crying behavior will cease. At the same time, Mr. Robles should shape Marcia's adjustment by making a reinforcing activity available to interest Marcia when she arrives at class.

B.   To defend the punishment policy, it is important to remember that inappropriate playground behaviors may be dangerous to other students and must be stopped immediately. Making the children stand in circles may be an appropriate consequence because it is adapted to their infraction. It deals with their behavior rather than their personal qualities. It uses negative reinforcement in that when they have stood for a while, they are ready to behave properly to avoid further standing. An alternative would be for them to pick up litter on the playground or to be placed in a detention room instead of the playground.

7

Cognitive Views of Learning

Teaching Outline

I. What Do You Think?

II. Elements of the cognitive perspective
   A. Comparing cognitive and behavioral views
      1. Cognitive view: Changes in knowledge make changes in behavior possible
         a. Cognitive methods: learning is studied in a wide range of situations
         b. Focus is on individual and developmental differences in cognition
      2. Behavioral view: New behaviors themselves are learned
         a. Behavioral methods: Goal is to identify a few general laws of learning that apply to all higher organisms
         b. Research studies animals in controlled laboratory settings
   B. The importance of knowledge and learning
      1. Knowledge is the outcome of learning
      2. Prior knowledge is important in determining what information can be learned

III. The information processing model of memory
   A. Kinds of knowledge
      1. General vs. domain-specific
      2. Declarative, procedural, or conditional
   B. Information processing: Three memory stores
      1. Sensory memory
         a. Capacity, duration, and contents
         b. Perception
         c. The role of attention
         d. Attention and teaching: See Table 7.2
      2. Short-term memory
         a. Capacity, duration, and contents
         b. Retaining information in short-term memory
         c. Forgetting
      3. Long-term memory
         a. Capacity and duration
         b. Contents of long-term memory
         c. Propositions and propositional networks
         d. Images
         e. Schema
         f. Episodic memory
         g. Procedural memory
         h. Storing information in long-term memory
         i. Retrieving information from long-term memory
         j. Forgetting and long-term memory
      4. Another view of information processing: Levels of processing

   a. Memory is determined not by where it is stored but by the process of analysis and connection as it is processed during input

   b. Strategies or level of processing moves information from one stage to the next

  5. Connectionism: Another alternative to the three-store model

   a. Parallel distributed processing: PDP

   b. Accounts for more than recall and explains incremental human learning

IV. Metacognition, self-regulation, and individual differences

 A. Executive control processes select and guide information processing

  1. Metacognition: Involves declarative & procedural as well as conditional knowledge

  2. Cognitive monitoring: The use of metacognitive abilities

 B. Individual differences in working memory

  1. Developmental and individual differences in short-term memory

  2. Children develop strategies as they mature such as rehearsal, organization

  3. Some strategies (e.g. oversimplification, skipping steps) are incorrect

 C. Individual differences in long-term memory

  1. Children are different in their ability to utilize prior knowledge

  2. Children gradually develop more useful previous knowledge

   a. Domain-specific declarative and procedural knowledge provides organizing background

   b. Conditional knowledge is useful in knowing when to apply previous information

V. Becoming knowledgeable: Some basic principles

 A. Development of declarative knowledge

  1. Rote memorization: applied to information with no inherent meaning

   a. Part learning: concentrating on limited number of items

   b. Serial position effect: better memory for items at beginning and end of list

   c. Distributed practice: use of brief study periods with rest times

   d. Massed practice may cause fatigue and loss of motivation

  2. Mnemonics

   a. Loci: connecting information to imagined familiar places

   b. Peg-type: associating new information with familiar

   c. Acronyms: using the first letter of each word in a list

   d. Chain mnemonics: connecting each item to the previous and following items

   e. Keyword method: associating new word with similar sounding cue word and using imagery to connect the meaning of each

  3. Making it meaningful

   a. Organizing new information so it relates to previous knowledge

   b. Clarifying with more familiar words

   c. Giving examples of analogies

 B. Becoming an expert: Development of procedural knowledge

  1. Stages in the development of automated basic skills

   a. Cognitive: Relying on declarative knowledge and general problem-solving strategies

   b. Associative: Individual steps of a procedure are chunked into larger units

c. Autonomous: Whole procedure can be accomplished without much attention
2. Domain-specific strategies: Conscious organization of thoughts, actions needed to reach a goal
C. Becoming an expert student: Learning strategies and study skills
1. Learning strategies and tactics
a. Strategies: plans for accomplishing learning goals
b. Tactics: specific learning techniques
2. Study skills
3. PQ4R (a variation of SQ3R, a study aid to improve reading comprehension)
a. Preview: introduce yourself to chapter; survey major topics and sections
b. Question: for each major section generate questions related to reading purposes
c. Read: answer questions; adjust speed to difficulty and purpose
d. Reflect: elaborate and connect new ideas to previous knowledge while reading
e. Recite: think about initial purposes and answer questions without looking back at text; reread if necessary
f. Review: Frequent cumulative review helps commit new material to long-term memory
VI. Constructivism: Challenging symbolic processing models
A. Knowledge: Accuracy versus usefulness
B. Learning: Individual versus social
VIII. Summary
IX. Key terms and concepts
X. What Would You Do?
XI. Teachers' casebook

Key Points

Elements of the cognitive perspective

- Cognitivist view of learning: A general approach that explains learning as an active mental process of acquiring, remembering, and using knowledge

  - Cognition involves the study of concept learning and problem solving; it is a reflection of mental processes and organization

  - Cognition involves studying structures of knowledge and the processes that create them

  - Topics studied by cognitivists include memory, perception, attention, problem- solving, comprehension, and concept learning

The information processing model of memory

- Cognitive psychologists distinguish several kinds of knowledge

  - <u>General knowledge</u>: Information that is useful in many different kinds of tasks; information that applies to many situations

  - <u>Domain-specific knowledge</u>: Information that is useful in a particular situation or that applies only to one specific topic

  - <u>Declarative knowledge</u>: Verbal knowledge; facts; knowing "what"

  - <u>Procedural knowledge</u>: Knowledge that is demonstrated when we perform a task; knowing "how"

  - <u>Conditional knowledge</u>: Knowing "when" and "why" to use declarative and procedural knowledge

- The information processing model of learning relies on the computer as a metaphor

  - Like a computer, the human brain is involved with encoding (input devices), temporary storage for workspace, permanent storage (internal or off-line) and retrieval

    - <u>Encoding</u>: Gathering and representing information in sensory registers

    - <u>Temporary storage</u>: Holding information in short-term or working memory

    - <u>Retrieval</u>: Getting information when needed from long-term memory

    - <u>Executive control processes</u>: Processes such as selective attention, rehearsal, elaboration, and organization that influence encoding, storage, and retrieval of information in memory

Information processing: three memory stages

- <u>Sensory register</u>: System of receptors holding sensory information very briefly

  - <u>Receptors</u>: Parts of the human body that receive sensory information

  - Contents of the sensory register are coded in patterns resembling original stimulus

- Perception: Interpretation of sensory information

- Feature analysis (bottom-up processing): Perceiving based on noticing separate defining features and assembling them into a recognizable pattern

- Perception based on knowledge and context (top-down processing): Perceiving based on the context and the patterns you expect to occur in that situation

- Paying attention to certain stimuli and ignoring others determines what information will be processed

- New processes initially requiring attention and concentration gradually become automatic (automaticity: The ability to perform thoroughly learned tasks without much effort)

- Short-term memory: Working memory holding a limited amount of information briefly

- Working memory: Information that you are focusing on at a given moment

  - Maintenance rehearsal: Keeping information in working memory by repeating to yourself

  - Elaborative rehearsal: Keeping information in working memory by associating it with something else you already know

  - Chunking: Grouping individual bits of data into meaningful larger units

  - Forgetting: Loss of information from short-term memory

- Long-term memory: Permanent store of knowledge with unlimited capacity

  - Stimuli coded both visually and verbally are easier to remember

  - Semantic, or meaning, memory is a type of long-term coding

    - Propositional network: An interconnected set of concepts and relationships in which long-term knowledge is held

    - Images: Representations based on perceptions

    - Schemas: Basic structures for organizing information or concepts

- Story grammars: Typical structures or organizations for stories

- Scripts: Schemata or expected plan for the sequence of steps in a common event or behavior

- Episodic memory: Long-term memory for information tied to a particular place and time, especially memory of the events in a person's life

- Procedural memory: Long-term memory for how to do things

- Storing information in long-term memory can be facilitated

- Elaboration: Adding and extending meaning by connecting new information to existing knowledge

- Organization: Ordered and logical network of relations

- Context : Factors associated with an event

- Retrieving information from long-term memory is a problem-solving process

- Retrieval: Searching for and finding information in long-term memory

- Reconstruction: Recreating information by using memories, expectations, logic, and existing knowledge

- Spread of activation: area of memory activated at one time

- Forgetting and long-term memory: Using cues for retrieval

- Interference: Newer or older memories confuse encoding

- Decay: Information lost from memory through time

- Levels of processing theory: Recall of information is determined not by where it is stored but by the process of analysis and connection as it is processed during input

- Connectionism: Brain assembles storage of information in a network of processing units that are more basic than symbolic codes

- Subsymbolic units work together to activate memories, thoughts

Metacognition, self-regulation, and individual difference

- Components of metacognition are executive control processes, declarative and procedural knowledge about strategies

    - Metacognition: Knowledge about our own thinking processes

    - Cognitive monitoring: Monitoring of thinking and learning strategies ability to use self-regulatory mechanisms to complete a task

- Individuals differ in use of sensory memory, working memory, and long-term memory

    - Learning abilities, preferences, cognitive style, and culture affect perception

    - Memory span improves with age in children, either from capacity increase or improved strategy use, or from neurological changes which bring improved memory efficiency

    - Children develop organizational and elaboration strategies, and more useful prior knowledge

Becoming knowledgeable: Some basic principles

- Rote memorization: Remembering information by repetition without necessarily understanding the meaning of the information

    - Part Learning: Breaking a list of rote items into shorter lists

    - Serial position effect: Remembering the beginning and end, but not the middle of the list

    - Distributed practice: Use of brief study periods with rest intervals

    - Massed practice: Practice for a single, extended period

- Mnemonics: Art of memory; also, techniques for remembering

    - Pegword method: Associating items with a previously memorized word list

    - Loci: Connecting information to imagined familiar places

    - Acronyms: Technique for remembering names, phrases, or steps by using the first letter of each word to form a new, memorable word

    - Chain mnemonics: Memory strategies that associate one element in a series with the next element

- Keyword method: Associating new words or concepts with similar-sounding cue words

- Making information meaningful enhances long-term storage

- Developing procedural knowledge entails having automated skills

    - Experts go through cognitive, associative, and autonomous stages

    [a] Domain-specific strategies assist in problem-solving

- Learning strategies: General plans for approaching a learning task

    - Learning tactics: Specific techniques for learning, such as using mnemonics or outlining a passage

    - PQ4R: A method for studying text that involves preview, question, read, reflect, recite, and review

Constructivism: Challenging symbolic processing models

- Knowledge is constructed in social settings by individuals with unique perspectives

    - Particular ideas are useful within a community of practice

- Gestalt Theory: Holds that people organize their perception into coherent wholes

    - Gestalt: German for "pattern" or "whole"

Do You Know This?

See if you understand the main points that are covered in this chapter:

Elements of the Cognitive Perspective

Can you discuss the role of knowledge in learning?

Can you describe three different models of learning based on information processing?

The Information Processing Model of Memory

Can you compare the roles of perception and attention in learning?

Can you contrast general and domain-specific knowledge? Declarative, procedural, and conditional?

How do schemas and scripts influence learning and memory?

Can you explain why we remember some things and forget others?

Can you describe how knowledge is represented as patterns of activation?

Metacognition, Self-regulation, and Individual Differences

Can you describe the stages in the development of cognitive skills?

Can you explain how individuals differ in short-term and long-term memory?

Becoming Knowledgeable: Some Basic Principles

Could you use a variety of memory strategies and study skills derived from cognitive theory to prepare for the test you may have to take on this chapter?

Can you develop a plan for teaching learning strategies and tactics to your students?

Constructivism: Challenging Symbolic Processing Models

Can you contrast information processing and social constructivist perspectives on learning?

Concept Map: MEMORY

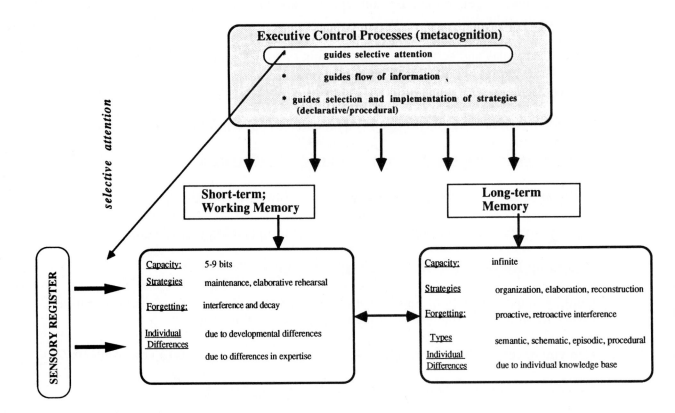

Key Terms And Concepts

DEFINITIONS: Concepts of Cognition

Write definitions for the following terms. Then check the Glossary of your textbook to see if your definition is appropriate.

Cognitive view of learning _____

_____

General knowledge _____

_____

Domain-specific knowledge _____

_____

Declarative knowledge _____

_____

Procedural knowledge _____

_____

Conditional knowledge _____

_____

DEFINITIONS: Concepts of Memory

Write explanations for the following pairs of terms. Your explanation should clearly distinguish the two from one another. Check the text to see if your explanations are equivalent.

Top-down/Bottom-up processing _____

_____

Elaborative/Maintenance rehearsal _____

_____

Images/Schemata _____

_____

Episodic/Semantic memory_____

_____

MATCHING: Concepts of Memory

Match the letters of the descriptions on the right to the corresponding items on the left. Use each definition only once. To check answers, see Answer Key.

_____	1.	Schema	a. Knowledge about our own thinking processes
_____	2.	Story grammar	
_____	3.	Script	b. Searching for, and finding,

_____ 4. Elaboration
_____ 5. Context
_____ 6. Reconstruction
_____ 7. Retrieval
_____ 8. Spread of activation
_____ 9. Levels of processing
_____ 10. Executive control processes
_____ 11. Metacognition
_____ 12. Rote memorization
_____ 13. Connectionist models
_____ 14. Chunking

information in long-term memory

c. Expected plan for the sequence of steps in a common event

d. Adding meaning by connecting new information to existing knowledge.

e. Remembering information by repetition

f. Basic structure for organizing information

g. Typical structure for organizing narratives

h. Memory depends on how well it is connected to existing information

i. Organize encoding, storage, and retrieval of information in memory

j. Factors associated with an event

k. Information currently in working memory

l. Recreating information by using memories, expectations, and existing knowledge

m. Memory is built through sub-symbolic networks

n. Grouping individual bits of data into meaningful larger units

APPLICATION: Mnemonic Devices

Below is a list of mnemonic devices that some students have found useful in remembering items which must be memorized. In the applications below, choose which mnemonic device is being described. Write the correct mnemonic device on the blank beside the description.

Chaining   Keyword method   Method of loci   Acronym   Pegword

_____ 1. Imagine the stores in a sequence along the main street of your hometown. Now place in the window of each store an image which represents the seven largest cities of the United States: New York, Los Angeles, Chicago, etc.

_____ 2. Use the letters PLACK to remember these five mnemonic devices: Pegword, Loci, Acronym, Chaining, Keyword.

_____   3.   You remember Mr. Patterson's name by imagining it sounds like "PAT HER SON" and you make an image of him patting a woman's child.

_____   4.   You memorize items in a list by imaging the items holding hands in a row.

_____   5.   You "hang" new vocabulary words on the names of members of your family.

CHARTING: Information Processing

Below is a list of cognitive activities. Enter each item in the box where it best fits.

1. Catching the name of a new acquaintance during an introduction.
2. Saying a telephone number over and over until dialing is complete.
3. Tracking an incoming plane on the screen in an air traffic control booth.
4. Using college Spanish when traveling in South America.
5. Learning a part in a play.
6. Hearing your name across the room in a crowded party.
7. Remembering a definition from last week's vocabulary list.
8. The child follows along in a reading book and knows when it's her turn.
9. Children are able to focus on the teacher's verbal instructions.
10. Recognizing whose voice is on the telephone when you answer.

Sensory Register	Working (short-term) memory	Long-term memory

APPLICATION: Semantic Map

Convert parts of Table 7.4 of your text to a semantic map by writing a concept on each numbered blank of the map below. The answer to #1 is "Procedural information." To check your answers, see Answer Key.

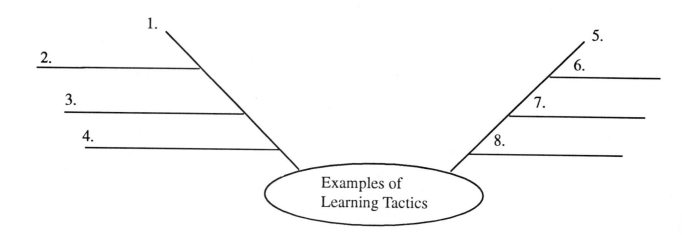

CASE STUDY: Working Memory

Your twelfth grade American Government class is studying the Bill of Rights. You have noticed that students tend to oversimplify the task of learning what each Article contains. For example, the Fifth Amendment to the Constitution is often remembered as, "A person cannot be required to incriminate himself in a court of law." However, the Fifth Amendment also states the rights of due process (what legal procedural rights citizens have) and protection from double jeopardy (one cannot be tried twice for the same crime). You think it is important for your students to know each of the rights in each Amendment. Using Case's (1985b) research explain how you could implement a better strategy for students to enhance their working memory capacity.

CASE STUDY: Procedural Memory

Your fifth grade students are struggling to master double digit multiplication (ex. 32 x 48). You need to teach this as procedural memory, so that the students will retain what they learn. Describe how this task can be divided into a chain of small steps (condition-action rules, or productions) which become automatic rules. For example, the first step in solving 32 x 48 is the following: Multiply 8 x 2; enter 6 in the one's column, and carry 1.

PRACTICE TEST: Multiple Choice

1. Which of the following interpretations is most consistent with a cognitive viewpoint?

   a. "Reinforcement has little influence over learning."
   b. "Reinforcement is a source of motivation."
   c. "Reinforcement serves a cueing function."
   d. "Reinforcement is source of feedback."

2. The more you think about something, the more likely you are to remember it. This idea is most strongly emphasized the _____ theory.

   a. levels of processing
   b. dual memory
   c. artificial intelligence
   d. Gestalt

3. "In one ear and out the other" best describes which component of memory?

   a. sensory
   b. short-term
   c. episodic
   d. long-term

4. Top-down processing is distinguished by its reliance on a(n)

   a. assembly of elements into a meaningful pattern.
   b. downward scanning of the eyes.
   c. search for familiar features or elements.
   d. understanding the context of a situation

5. Research has shown that the capacity of the short-term memory is limited to about _____ chunks.

   a. 2-4
   b. 5-9
   c. 11-12
   d. 13-15

6. You are shown a math problem to solve. As you try to remember the formula, which memory system is being searched?

   a. Sensory register
   b. Long-term
   c. Short-term
   d. Schematic

7. A student provides an explanation of why water evaporates. But his description

leaves out some of the details the teacher provided, while including some new information. Cognitive theorists would attribute this to

a. elaboration.
b. time decay.
c. reconstruction.
d. rote learning.

8. Which if the following most clearly illustrates elaboration?

a. John relates the calculation of percentages that he is learning in math to his batting average in Little League.
b. Mary follows procedural steps for computing percentages.
c. Alicia defines percentages exactly the way it is presented in the text.
d. Bart checks his calculations as he does his homework problems.

9. Which of the following is not a component of metacognition?

a. Awareness of resources
b. Awareness of strategies
c. Knowledge of facts concerning a subject
d. Knowledge of how to perform a strategy.

10. To help students become better learners it is recommended that

a. they be taught strategies, but not specific tactics.
b. they master one strategy only.
c. strategies training focus on procedures rather than motivation.
d. exposure to a variety of strategies be provided.

PRACTICE TEST: Essay

A. Describe how a first grade child and a sixth grade child use strategies to remember information. Be sure to include differences in working memory, long-term memory, and metacognition.

B. Describe how learning is constructed by means of an apprenticeship model.

Answer Key

MATCHING: Concepts of Memory

1. f
2. g
3. c

4. d
5. j
6. l
7. b
8. k
9. h
10. i
11. a
12. e
13. m
14. n

APPLICATION: Mnemonic Devices

1. Loci
2. Acronym
3. Keyword
4. Chaining
5. Pegword

CHARTING: Information Processing

1. Sensory register
2. Short-term memory
3. Sensory register
4. Long-term memory
5. Long-term memory
6. Sensory register
7. Long-term memory
8. Short-term memory
9. Sensory register
10. Sensory register, long-term memory

APPLICATION: Semantic Map

1. Tactics for learning procedural information
2. Pattern learning
3. Self-instruction
4. Practice
5. Tactics for learning verbal information
6. Attention focusing
7. Schema building
8. Idea elaboration

PRACTICE TEST: Multiple Choice

1. d   Cognitive psychologists regard reinforcement as a source of <u>feedback</u> because it provides information about what is likely to happen if the behaviors (that were reinforced or punished) were repeated. (Behaviorists view reinforcement as an incentive or motivator for behavior.)

2. a   <u>Levels of processing</u> theory assumes that what determines how well information is remembered is the degree to which it was actively processed during acquisition. More extensive processing produces stronger connections to existing knowledge.

3. a   <u>Sensory memory</u> is very brief in duration-- between one and three seconds. Unless the information is processed, it will be lost (thus, the saying "in one ear and out the other").

4. d   Top-down processing involves using the <u>context of the situation</u> as a basis for recognizing (or perceiving) something. In contrast, bottom-up processing bases perception on analyzing specific features of the stimulus and "mentally assembling" the whole from the parts.

5. b   The capacity of short-term memory is from <u>5-9</u> separate "bits" or pieces of information. By comparison, long-term memory is theorized to have an unlimited capacity.

6. b   The <u>long-term</u> semantic memory is our memory for meaning. This information represents our knowledge of the world (formulas, facts, scripts, words, etc.).

7. c   <u>Reconstruction</u> involves recalling information based on what we (a) actually remember and (b) fill in based on related experiences or what seems logical. Because of these variables, different people will often remember very different things after experiencing the same event.

8. a   <u>John is relating his study of percentages</u> to his existing knowledge about baseball. As a result of this elaboration, the material on percentages will be better connected with other information in long-term memory, and thus be more easily remembered.

9. c   Metacognition means knowledge about cognition-- the processes of learning. This domain would encompass awareness of context (or resources), strategies, and how to perform strategies. It would <u>not</u> include <u>knowledge of facts concerning a subject</u>.

10. d   Research has suggested that students should be exposed to a number of <u>different strategies</u>. Also, specific tactics, such as mnemonic techniques,

should be learned.

PRACTICE TEST: Essay

A. Older children are better at memory rehearsal and do not simplify inappropriately. They can form associations and images, organize new material to make it easier to remember, and apply test-taking techniques, outlining, and note taking. They can decide how to apportion time and effort, switching strategies to overcome difficulties.

B. In an apprenticeship system of learning, those who are new to a task (novices) are supported as they learn with the help of an expert guide or model. They gradually take on more and more responsibility until they are able to function independently. Learning takes place in a social situation and is embedded in a particular social and cultural context, affected by the community of practice that prevails at the workplace.

8

Concept Learning, Problem Solving, Creativity, and Thinking

Teaching Outline

I. What Do You Think?

II. The importance of thinking and understanding

  A. Garner: The capacity to take knowledge, skills, and concepts and apply them appropriately in new situations

  B. Baron: Good thinking is thinking that achieves its goal

III. Learning and teaching about concepts

  A. Views of concept learning

    1. Defining attributes: Distinctive features which have traditionally defined a concept

      a. Feature analysis (bottom-up processing) is involved in perception

      b. Most concepts lack a defining attribute

    2. Prototype: (best representative of a category); defines members, not concepts

      a. Categories have graded membership: some are more representative than others

      b. Exemplars are actual members

    3. Concepts and schemas

      a. Schematic knowledge provides a background of expectations and context

      b. Prototypes may be an average of all previous exemplars

  B. Strategies for teaching concepts (traditional: rely on analysis of defining attributes)

    1. Lesson components

      a. Name of the concept (label)

      b. Define the concept: give the general category and the defining attribute

      c. Relevant and irrelevant attributes

      d. Examples and nonexamples (positive and negative instances)

      e. Use of visual aids such as models, graphs, diagrams, or maps improve learning

    6. Lesson structure: Start with prototypical examples. Watch for undergeneralizing (exclusion of valid instances) or overgeneralizing (inclusion of wrongful examples)

IV. Problem solving: Creating new solutions when routine or automatic responses do not fit

  A. Problem-solving general or domain-specific?

    1. General: some strategies are useful in many domains

    2. Specific: strategies that are useful in particular disciplines

    3. People may move between general and specific approaches

    4. Steps in problem solving (Bransford and Stein: IDEAL)

      a. Identify that a problem exists
      b. Define and represent the problem
      c. Explore possible strategies
      d. Act on the strategies
      e. Look back and evaluate the effects of your activities

B. Defining and representing the problem
   1. Identify relevant information
   2. Understanding the words: Linguistic comprehension helps to develop an accurate representation of the situation
      b. Relational propositions describe relations between elements
      c. Assignment propositions assign a value to an element
      d. Part-whole relations govern which elements are subsumed under others
   3. Understanding the whole problem
      a. Assemble all the sentences into an accurate understanding
      b. An incorrect representation may rely solely on surface features
   4. Translation and schema training
      a. Recognize and categorize problem types
      b. Represent problems graphically or in words
      c. Select relevant and irrelevant information from problems
   5. Results of problem representation
      a. An immediate solution is a result of an available schema
      b. It may take a while to match problem to existing schema
      c. Schema-driven problem solving uses "schema activated routes"

C. Exploring possible solution strategies
   1. Algorithmic procedure
      a. Step-by-step prescription for reaching goal
      b. Highly domain-specific
   2. Heuristic strategy: A strategy with a reasonable chance of resulting in a solution
      a. Guesses or general procedures of trial and error
      b. Means-end analysis: problem divided into a number of subproblems and each is tackled one by one
      c. Work backwards: Starting at the goal (if known) and working backward to the initial problem
      d. Analogic thinking: Limiting search for solutions to situations that resemble problem
      e. Verbalization: trying to put into words what you are doing and why

D. Acting on the strategies and looking back
   1. Execute the plan
   2. Look for characteristic "bugs" or erroneous algorithms
   3. Evaluate the results
      a. Check for evidence that confirms or contradicts the solution
      b. Apply a checking routine

E. Factors that hinder problem solving
   1. Functional fixedness
      a. Seeing materials in their characteristic function
      b. Failure to consider unconventional uses of materials may inhibit problem

solving

  c. Response set: The tendency to respond in most familiar way

 2. The importance of flexibility

  a. Insight: Sudden realization of a solution or reconceptualization of problem

  b. Recognition of new problem as a disguised version of an old problem

V. Effective problem-solving: What do the experts do?

 A. Expert pattern recognition

  1. Experts have a supply of knowledge, facts, concepts, and procedures

  2. Knowledge is elaborated and organized and easy to retrieve, well-practiced

  3. Experts have declarative, procedural, and conditional knowledge

 B. Becoming an expert problem solver: ACT* theory

  1. Interpretive state: Problem solver recalls specific examples (declarative knowledge)

  2. With practice, problem solver shifts to use of procedural knowledge using condition-action rules

  3. With expertise, problem solving becomes automatic

 C. Expert knowledge

  1. Experts solve problems using pattern recognition

  2. Short cuts are available using schema-activated paths

  3. Experts perceive large, meaningful patterns; are quick; deal with problems at a deeper level, have superior short and long-term memories, and take time to analyze

 D. Novice knowledge

  1. Novices have misconceptions or intuitive notions that may be difficult to modify by merely collecting more information on a subject

  2. Curriculum designed to confront common misconceptions appears to be beneficial

 E. Helping novices become experts

  1. Present needed facts as well as several examples of using the facts in problem solving

  2. Allow for practice with new tools in actual problem solving

  3. Provide a way that students can monitor their strategy use as they work

  4. Guidelines: Problem Solving

VI. Creativity and creative problem-solving

 A. Creativity: trait or process?

 B. Creativity and cognition

  1. Sternberg: use of knowledge-acquisition components in an insightful way

  2. Ability to restructure a problem, to arrange extensive knowledge in a flexible way

 C. Assessing creativity

  1. Can creativity be equated with divergent thinking?

   a. Divergent thinking is marginally related to real-life creative activity

   b. Divergent thinking is a marginally stable trait

  2. Paper-and pencil tests of creativity

   a. Torrance - Verbal and graphic tests

   b. Scored for originality, fluency, and flexibility

  3. Teachers' judgments of creativity

         a. According to Torrance's research, teachers' judgments have no relation to creativity of students in later life

         b. Sattler's Checklist for Identifying Creative Children (see Table 8.2)

  D. Creativity in the classroom

     1. Teachers must learn to set up an encouraging and accepting atmosphere

     2. Brainstorming strategy

         a. Separate the generation of ideas from the judgment of their worth

         b. Generate many ideas as a group, then evaluate at a separate time

     3. Allow students time for play in order for ideas to be created, nurtured, and restructured

VII. Teaching and learning about thinking: analyzing, evaluating, generating new ideas

  A. Stand-alone programs for developing thinking

     1. Students do not need extensive subject-matter knowledge to master thinking skills

     2. General skills may not be applied by children outside stand-alone program

  B. Developing thinking skills in every class

     1. Create a culture of thinking in the classroom

     2. Model thinking; provide direct instruction in thinking; encourage practice

     3. The language of thinking: analyze, hypothesize, guess, doubt

     4. Critical thinking: defining and clarifying problems; judging information related to a problem; drawing conclusions

     5. Thinking as a "state of mind"

         a. Being "mindful" is an open, creative state

         b. Students can become able to take intellectual risks, seek challenges, invest effort

VIII. Teaching for transfer: Previous learning effects current learning

  A. Defining transfer

     1. Positive transfer: Previously learned material applied appropriately in new situation

     2. Negative transfer: Applying familiar but inappropriate strategies in new situation

     3. Specific transfer: Rule, fact, or skill learned in one situation is applied in second similar situation

     4. General transfer: Dealing with new problems based on principles and attitudes learned in other situations

     5. Contemporary views on transfer

         a. Low-road transfer: Spontaneous, automatic transfer of highly practiced skills

         b. High-road transfer: Conscious applying abstract knowledge from one situation to another using "mindful abstraction"

         c. Forward-reaching transfer: Looking forward to applying knowledge gained

         d. Backward-reaching transfer: Looking back on previous problems for clues

  B. Teaching for positive transfer

     1. Transfer is difficult because most learning is situated in a particular situation

     2. What is worth learning?

        a. Stress general as well as basic skills

        b. Present information necessary for future success

    3. How can teachers help?

        a. Incorporate new information into existing schemata

        b. Teach for deep processing, permanent storage, and easy retrieval

        c. Involve students in the learning process

        d. Help students to form abstractions that can be applied later

        e. Teach for forward- and backward-reaching transfer

        f. Practice should take place under authentic contexts

        g. Practice new skills in simulated conditions

        h. Encourage overlearning to combat forgetting

IX. Cognitive models of teaching

  A. Discovery learning: Bruner

    1. Structure of the subject matter: Teachers provide problem situations; stimulate students to discover fundamental ideas, relationships, or patterns

    2. Concepts and coding systems (hierarchy of related concepts): allow people to go beyond information given which is the most characteristic aspect of mental life

    3. Inductive reasoning: also called eg-rule method (abstracting from examples)

    4. Discovery in action

        a. Teachers should nurture intuitive thinking: make imaginative leaps to workable solutions

        b. Distinction between discovery learning: where students work on their own to a great extent; and guided discovery: teachers provide more direction and feedback

        c. Guidelines: Applying Bruner's Ideas in the Classroom

  B. Reception learning: Ausubel

    1. Meaningful learning should occur through reception, not discovery; as teachers present material in a carefully organized form

    2. Expository teaching: Model designed to encourage verbal interaction between students and teacher

        a. Use of examples, drawings, diagrams, pictures

        c. Deductive reasoning: general concepts presented before more specific concepts (rule-eg method)

        d. Sequential and carefully organized exposition from subsumer (the concept at the top of the hierarchy) on down

    3. Characteristics of the expository teaching model

        a. Advance organizers: Introductory statement that fits new material into a student's present schemata, proving scaffolding for new information or conceptual bridge between new material and current knowledge

        b. Categories of advance organizers: comparative (activate already existing schemata) or expository (provide new knowledge on which upcoming information is based)

    4. Steps of an expository lesson

        c. Use advance organizers; show relationships using examples (both similarities and differences), revisit advance organizer and goals of lesson, making modifications as necessary

5. Making the most of expository teaching
   a. Most appropriate when teaching relationships among concepts, not concepts themselves
   b. Requires mental manipulation of ideas: generally more appropriate at or above junior-high level
   c. Research indicates that advance organizers do help students learn; in order to be effective, organizer must be processed and understood by students and must encompass and show relationship among basic concepts
6. Guidelines: Applying Ausubel's Ideas in the Classroom

X.   Summary
XI. Key terms and concepts
XII. What would you do?
XIII. Teachers' casebook

Key Points

The importance of thinking and understanding

- Understanding: The capacity to apply knowledge, skills, and concepts in new situations

- Concepts: A category used to group ideas, objects, people, or events whose members share certain properties

- Defining attributes: Distinctive features shared by members of a category

  - Prototype: Best representative of a category

  - Graded membership: The extent to which something belongs to a category

  - Exemplar: A specific example of a given category that is used to classify an item

  - Schemata also organize knowledge

- Strategies for teaching concepts beyond simply giving definitions

  - Label the concept, giving the general category and the defining attribute

  - Provide relevant and irrelevant attributes

  - Give examples and nonexamples (positive and negative instances) to clarify concept boundaries; start with prototypical examples.

- <u>Undergeneralizing</u>: Exclusion of some true members from a category

- <u>Overgeneralizing</u>: Inclusion of non-members in a category; wrongful examples

- <u>Concept mapping</u>: Students diagram their understanding of a concept

Problem solving

- <u>Problem solving</u>: Creating new solutions when routine or automatic responses do not fit

  - General problem-solving features strategies that are useful in many domains

  - Domain-specific problem-solving features strategies that are useful in particular situations

- IDEAL Steps in problem solving (Bransford and Stein)

  - <u>I</u>dentify that a problem exists

  - <u>D</u>efine and represent the problem

  - <u>E</u>xplore possible strategies

  - <u>A</u>ct on the strategies

  - <u>L</u>ook back and evaluate the effects of your activities

- Translation and schema training helps students to solve problems by presenting a variety of problem types, practicing a variety of representations, and selecting relevant information

- <u>Schema-driven problem solving</u>: Recognizing a problem as a disguised version of an old problem for which you already have a solution

- <u>Algorithmic solution strategy</u>: Step-by-step procedure for reaching goal

- <u>Heuristic solution strategy</u>: General strategy used in attempting to solve problems

  - <u>Means-end analysis</u>: Heuristic in which problem is divided into a number of subproblems and each is tackled one by one

  - <u>Working backwards</u>: Starting at the goal (if known) and working backward to solving the initial problem

- Analogic thinking: Heuristic in which search is limited to solutions to situations that resemble problem at hand

- Verbalization: Putting your problem solving plan and its logic into words

- Debugging: Looking for "bugs" or erroneous algorithms

- Some factors can hinder understanding or interfere with representation of a problem

  - Functional fixedness: Inability to use objects or tools in a new way

  - Response set: Rigidity, tendency to respond in the most familiar way

  - Insight: Sudden realization of a solution or reconceptualization of problem

Effective problem-solving: What do the experts do?

- Experts have a fund of declarative, procedural, and conditional knowledge

  - Experts use pattern recognition to represent a problem quickly

  - Experts have a large store of condition-action schemata or productions to aid in understanding and solving problems

  - Novices have misconceptions or intuitive notions that may be resistant to merely "collecting" more information on a subject

- Becoming an expert: The ACT* theory

  - To become expert problem solvers people must move from the interpretive stage where they try to use declarative knowledge (specific examples and analogies) to solve new problems to the procedural stage where solving problems is more automatic -- a particular set of conditions automatically triggers certain actions.

Creativity and creative problem-solving

- Creativity: Imaginative, original thinking for problem-solving

  - Problem restructuring: Conceiving a problem in a new or different way

- • <u>Incubation</u>: An unconscious solution while away from a problem

- • Can creativity be equated with divergent thinking?

  - • <u>Divergent thinking</u>: Coming up with many possible solutions

  - • <u>Convergent thinking</u>: Narrowing possibilities to one simple answer

  - • Tests of creativity are scored for originality, fluency, and flexibility

  - • <u>Brainstorming</u>: Generating many ideas as a group, then evaluating at a separate time

  - • Allow students time for play, for ideas to be created, nurtured, and restructured

Teaching and learning about thinking

- • <u>Stand-alone thinking skill programs</u>: Programs that teach thinking skills directly without need for extensive subject matter

- • <u>Developing thinking in every class:</u> Teachers can develop a culture of thinking in the class by <u>direct instruction</u>, <u>modeling</u>, <u>practice</u>, and <u>interaction</u>.

- • The classroom should be filled with a rich <u>language of thinking</u> -- many and varied ways of describing thoughtful learning.

- • <u>Critical thinking</u>: Evaluating conclusions by logically and systematically examining the problem, the evidence, and the solution.

Teaching for transfer

- • <u>Transfer</u>: Influence of previous learned material on new material

  - • <u>Positive transfer</u>: Previously learned material applied appropriately in new situation

  - • <u>Negative transfer</u>: Previously learned material hinders new learning

  - • <u>Specific transfer</u>: Rule, fact, or skill learned in one situation is applied in second similar situation

  - • <u>General transfer</u>: Dealing with new problems based on principles and attitudes learned in other situations

- • Contemporary views on transfer

- Low-road transfer: Spontaneous, automatic transfer of highly practiced skills

- High-road transfer: Consciously applying abstract knowledge from one situation to another using "mindful abstraction"

- Forward-reaching transfer: Looking forward to applying knowledge gained

- Backward-reaching transfer: Looking back on previous problems for clues

- Overlearning: Practicing a skill past the point of mastery

Cognitive models of teaching

- Discovery learning (Bruner): Teachers provide problem situations; stimulate students to discover for themselves the structure of the subject matter

  - Structure of a subject matter: Fundamental framework of ideas

  - Inductive learning (eg-rule method): Formulating general principles based on knowledge of examples and details

  - Coding system: Hierarchy of related concepts

  - Guided discovery: Teachers provide more direction and feedback

- Reception learning (Ausubel): Meaningful verbal learning; focused and organized relationships among ideas and verbal information

  - Expository teaching: Teachers present material in complete, organized form, moving from broadest to more specific concepts

  - Deductive reasoning (rule-eg method): Drawing conclusions by applying rules or principles; logically moving from a general rule or principle to a specific solution

  - Advance organizer: Statement of inclusive concepts to introduce and sum up material that follows

Concept Map: PROBLEM-SOLVING

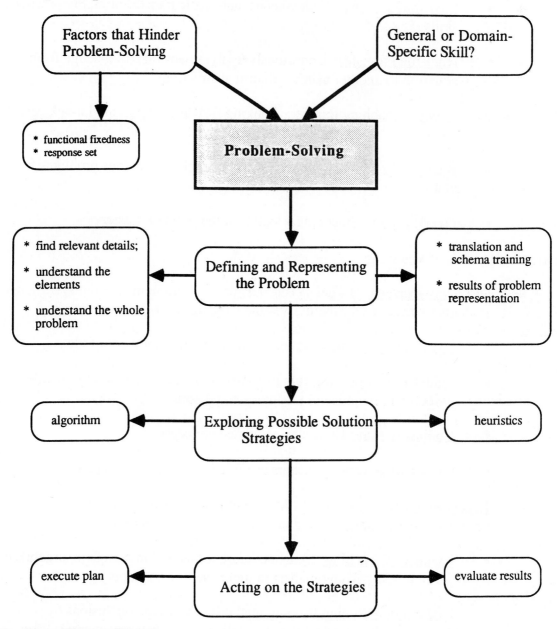

Do You Know This?

See if you understand the main points that are covered in this chapter:

The Importance of Thinking and Understanding

Can you recall an instance when you thought you understood a concept but found it difficult to apply in a new context?

Learning and Teaching about Concepts

Can you design a lesson for teaching a key concept in your subject area?

Problem-Solving

List the steps in solving complex problems and explain the role of problem representation .

Expert Problem Solving

Can you compare how novices and experts solve problems?

Creativity and Creative Problem-Solving

Can you identify three ways that you might encourage creativity in your students?

Teaching and Learning about Thinking

What are implications of cognitive theories for teaching critical thinking?

Teaching for Transfer

Can you list three ways that a classroom teacher might promote positive transfer of learning?

Cognitive Models of Teaching

Develop a lesson using Bruner or Ausubel's approach.

Key Terms and Concepts

CHARTING: Concepts and Categories

Many categories have <u>graded membership</u>; that is, some members of the category are much more characteristic of the category than others. These function as <u>prototypes</u> of the category. For the categories and members below, place each member on the continuum of each category depending on whether it is prototypical, average, or atypical.   To check your answers, see Answer Key.

<u>Category</u>	<u>Members</u>
FURNITURE	DESK, TELEPHONE, LAMP
VEHICLE	SPACE SHUTTLE, ROLLER SKATE, CAR
CAKE	PANCAKE, FRUITCAKE, CHOCOLATE LAYER
BIRD	FINCH, ROBIN, DODO

	Prototypical	Average Member	Atypical Member
FURNITURE	<-->		
VEHICLE	<-->		
CAKE	<-->		
BIRD	<-->		

DEFINITIONS: Concepts of Thinking and Problem Solving

Write explanations for the following pairs of terms. Your explanation should clearly distinguish the two from one another. Check the text to see if your explanations are equivalent.

Means-ends analysis/Working backwards strategy _____

_____

Algorithm/Heuristic _____

_____

Analogical thinking/Critical thinking _____

_____

Undergeneralization/Overgeneralization _____

_____

APPLICATION: Problem Solving

Using the IDEAL problem solving format, observe the way two teachers come to a different solution concerning the problem below.   Then fill out the IDEAL steps as indicated.

Problem: A young boy in the second grade comes to school with a hygiene problem. His hair is uncombed, his clothes are often soiled, and his smell is offensive. The other students ostracize him, make fun of him, and in general are cruel and do not include him in their play groups.

IDEAL problem solving steps	Teacher A	Teacher B

1. _____   The boy has a hygiene .   The group is cruel to
                            problem   him.

2. _____   Parents are not concerned Group social skills are
                            about boy's hygiene.   inadequate.

3. _____   Teacher contacts parents; has Teacher reads a story
                            them meet with counselor to   to children which
                            reprimand parents   portrays consequences
                                                           of group cruelty to
                                                           misunderstood person

4. _____   Teacher sends boy home to   Class role-plays scenes
                            change soiled clothes and   from story to simulate
                            bathe   group acceptance of
                                                        misunderstood person

5. _____   Child feels ashamed; grades Classmates give boy
                            drop, absences increase   acceptance despite
                                                         hygiene problem; boy
                                                         makes own efforts to
                                                         improve hygiene.

APPLICATION: Using Critical Thinking

The paragraph below is a Letter to the Editor of a local newspaper. Each sentence has
been put on a separate numbered line. Using the list of critical thinking skills to the right,
enter the number of the line whose text illustrates the principle involved. To check your
answers, see Answer Key.

1. Dear Editor,   _____ Irrelevant information
2. I am sick and tired of the Japanese saying   _____ Unsubstantiated opinion
3. that Americans don't work hard enough.   _____ Illogical conclusion
4. Just yesterday I worked 12 hours. Then I   _____ Sidetrack from main point
5. picked up my dog at the vet. Everyone   _____ Unstated assumptions
6. knows that Americans are smarter than   _____ Bias, propaganda
7. the Japanese: We beat them in World War II,   _____ Stereotype or cliché
8. didn't we? America is the greatest country   _____ Inadequacy of data
9. in the world, and they can't accept that. They've
10. bought out three banks in my hometown. It's
11. obvious that they are taking over all our
12. financial assets. Then they will control all our
13. destinies. Everyone, especially bankers and other
14. loafers, needs to work harder.

MATCHING: Concepts of Transfer

Match the numbers of the descriptions on the right to the corresponding items on the left. Use each definition only once. To check your answers, see Answer Key.

_____   1.   Transfer

            a.   Looking ahead to applying knowledge

_____   2.   Positive transfer

            b.   Solving problems based on previously learned principles and attitudes

_____   3.   Negative transfer

            c.   Previous solution applied appropriately to new situation

_____   4.   Specific transfer

_____   5.   General transfer

            d.   Spontaneous, automatic transfer of highly practiced skills

_____   6.   High-road transfer

_____   7.   Low-road transfer

            e.   Influence of previous learned material on new material

_____   8.   Forward-reaching transfer

            f.   Looking back on previous problems for transfer clues

_____   9.   Backward-reaching transfer

            g.   Rule, fact, or skill learned in one situation is applied in second, similar situation

            h.   Applying of abstract knowledge learned in one situation to a different situation

            i.   Previously learned material hinders

CASE STUDY: Teaching for Creativity

You are an art teacher in a primary school. A number of classroom teachers have used trite seasonal activities in their classrooms; for example, one teacher draws holiday art ideas from a book entitled, *1000 Uses for Paper Plates*. As an art teacher, describe an art activity on a winter theme which would genuinely promote your students' creativity.

CASE STUDY: Expert Versus Novice Learning

You are a band teacher in a middle school. Some students have had several years of instrumental training before entering the band while some are just beginning. Using the categories below, how would you promote the novice learners' rapid transition to expertise in reading music?

Pattern recognition _____

Declarative knowledge _____

Procedural knowledge _____

Conditional knowledge _____

PRACTICE TEST: Multiple Choice

1.   A prototype for a particular concept is an instance that

    a. is most representative of its category.
    b. has only one defining attribute.
    c. is a member of two or more concept categories.
    d. is rarely associated with the concept.

2.   Traditional views of concept learning suggest that we recognize examples of a concept by

    a. imaging prototypes.
    b. deductive reasoning.
    c. top-down processing.
    d. identifying defining features.

3.   Which of the following is the sequence of procedures recommended by your textbook for teaching concepts?

    a. Less obvious examples, nonexamples, then prototype
    b   Nonexamples, less obvious examples, then prototype
    c. Prototype, less obvious examples, then nonexamples
    d. Less obvious examples, prototype, then nonexamples

4.   Two mathematic statements are the following: (A) John is three inches shorter than Helga, and (B) Helga is 48 inches tall. Based on studies of linguistic comprehension, which of the following is true?

    a. B is a relational proposition.
    b. A is an assignment proposition.
    c. Problems based on B will be more difficult to understand.
    d. Problems based on A will be more difficult to understand.

5.   Maurice has forgotten his combination and cannot open his lock. Which of the following is an example of an algorithm?

    a. He takes a hammer and breaks the lock.
    b. He remembers that this type of lock tends to use even 2-digit numbers, such as 24, 30,36, so he tries some combinations using those.
    c. He starts at 0-0-0 and overtime, systematically tries every combination of three numbers.
    d. He asks of each of his 10 friends to provide 10 combinations and tries all 100

suggestions.

6. Which of the following best illustrates the state of functional fixedness?

   a. A student who is used to making "d's" look like "b's" continues to make this error.
   b. A third grade teacher sees the second grade achievement scores for her new class and begins to form expectancies about individuals' abilities.
   c. A student who is trying to solve a math problem explores many different strategies until she gets a reasonable answer.
   d. A student who is using a ruler for drawing lines fails to realize that he can use its metal edge as a scraper to remove paint from his desk.

7. Overlearning is the process of practicing a skill

   a. for too long such that reactive inhibition develops.
   b. for too long such that proactive inhibition develops.
   c. past the point of mastery such that retention is improved.
   d. that is similar to a skill previously learned such that positive transfer is realized.

8. A comparative organizer would typically be used to

   a. introduce new information.
   b. review what has been taught following a lesson.
   c. activate existing knowledge.
   d. provide an experiential basis for inductive processing.

9. Ms. McDonald's class learns to list the names of all the U. S. vice-presidents in order. Ausubel would probably consider this to be rote learning because it

   a. involves non-essential information.
   b. is not expository.
   c. is not connected to existing knowledge.
   d. meets no behavioral objective.

PRACTICE TEST: Essay

A. How can you use the concept of "debugging" to help students take a different attitude toward error correction?

B. One way to teach fifth grade students about the Westward Expansion of America is for the teacher to use expository teaching to help students master concepts such as resource management, pioneer life, and trail exploration. Explain how the use of the computer simulation *Oregon Trail* teaches these same concepts through discovery learning.

Answer Key

CHARTING: Concepts and Categories

Category	Prototype	Average Member	Atypical Member
FURNITURE	DESK	LAMP	TELEPHONE
VEHICLE	CAR	SPACE SHUTTLE	ROLLER SKATE
CAKE	CHOCOLATE LAYER	FRUITCAKE	PANCAKE
BIRD	ROBIN	FINCH	DODO

APPLICATION: Using Critical Thinking

1-3	Stereotype or cliché
4	Sidetrack from main point (What does one individual working 12 hours have to do with the issue?)
4-5	Irrelevant information (Taking the dog to the vet is irrelevant)
5-7	Unsubstantiated opinion (Everyone knows...)
8	Illogical conclusion (Being smarter has to do with winning the war)
8-9	Propaganda ("America is the greatest...")
9-11	Inadequacy of data (Hard to generalize from three hometown banks to finance in general)
12-13	Unstated assumptions (Controlling banks = controlling destinies)
13-14	Stereotyping (Bankers do not work hard)

MATCHING: Concepts of Transfer

1.	e	6.	h
2.	c	7.	d
3.	i	8.	a
4.	g	9.	f
5.	b		

PRACTICE TEST: Multiple Choice

1. a   A prototype for a particular concept is defined as the example that <u>is most representative of the category concerned</u>. Thus, if Morris thinks of an apple

when he hears the word "fruit," apple would be a prototype of the concept "fruit."

2. d   For many years, it was thought that examples of concepts were recognized by identifying their distinctive attributes or <u>defining features</u>. This traditional view emphasizes bottom-up processing over top-down processing.

3. c   To help establish the concept category, start with a <u>prototype</u> or best example. Then present <u>less obvious examples</u> to reduce tendencies for undergeneralization. Finally present <u>nonexamples</u> to reduce tendencies for overgeneralization.

4. d   <u>Problems based on "A" will be more difficult to understand</u> because A ("John is 3 inches shorter than Helga") is a relational proposition that compares two measures. In contrast, B is an assignment proposition that simply defines the value of something.

5. c   It may take Maurice a long time, but his only recourse (aside from calling the lock manufacturer) <u>is to try every combination systematically (e.g. starting with 0-0-0 etc.)</u> This algorithm will guarantee a solution (eventually).

6. d   <u>The ruler can be used as a scraper as well as a tool for drawing lines</u>. Due to functional fixedness, however, the student recognized the latter, more common function only.

7. c   <u>Overlearning involves practicing a skill past the point of mastery so that performance is more rapid and enduring</u>. An example is learning the alphabet in elementary school.

8. c   By relating new information to what is already known, comparative organizers function to <u>activate existing knowledge</u>. In contrast, expository organizers provide new knowledge to serve as scaffolding for the information to be learned.

9. c   Learning to list the vice-presidents in order is a rote memorization task that will <u>not involve connecting the material to existing knowledge</u>. That is, students generally approach such tasks without having relevant knowledge that would help them to know, without being told, who the vice presidents are. Ausubel would not regard this as meaningful learning.

PRACTICE TEST: Essay

A.   When students use algorithms in a particular subject area to solve problems, they may develop systematic errors. For example, when children subtract, they may consistently subtract the smaller number from the larger number, regardless of which one is on top. Once teachers discover a bug, they can give specific tips about reworking problems. This corrective feedback is much more helpful than merely pointing out errors. In a sense, we only learn through wrong answers.

B. The *Oregon Trail* computer simulation is a program that allows students to equip a wagon train with a given amount of supplies, and as they face a random set of hardships and opportunities on the way to Oregon, they discover or recreate the conditions faced by pioneers during the Westward Expansion. This helps them to understand the structure of the subject, to use inductive reasoning to solve problems, and to identify key principles for themselves rather than simply accepting teachers' explanations.

9

Motivation: Issues and Explanations

Teaching Outline

I. What Do You Think?
II. What is motivation? (an internal state that arouses, directs, and maintains behavior)
  A. Intrinsic and extrinsic motivation
    1. Is motivation stable or temporary?
      a. Motivation can be seen as traits, or stable characteristics of individual
      b. Motivation can also be seen as a temporary state
    2. Intrinsic
      a. Intrinsic motivation is associated with activities that are their own reward
      b. Enjoyment of task or sense of accomplishment that it brings
    3. Extrinsic
      a. Motivation created by external factors like rewards and punishments
      b. Not interested in activity for its own sake, but instead for possible gains
    4. Locus of causality explains the students' reason for performing tasks
      a. Internal/intrinsic locus: Students freely choose to perform an activity
      b. External/extrinsic locus: Students are influenced by someone or something outside them
    5. Teachers must nurture intrinsic interest in learning while providing extrinsic motivators
  B. Four general approaches to motivation
    1. Behavioral approaches to motivation
      a. Reward is an attractive object or event supplied as a consequence of a particular behavior
      b. Incentive is an object or event that encourages or discourages behavior
    2. Humanistic approaches to motivation
      a. Reaction against behaviorism and Freudian psychoanalysis
      b. Emphasis on personal freedom, choice, self-determination, and personal growth
      c. Role of needs is central; people are motivated to fulfill their potential
    3. Cognitive approaches to motivation
      a. Behavior is determined by thinking, not simply by reward or punishment for past behavior
      b. People is initiated and regulated by plans, goals, schemas, expectations, and attributions
      c. A central assumption is that people respond not to external or physical conditions or events, but to interpretations
      d. People are seen as active and curious, searching for information to solve personally relevant problems
    4. Social learning approaches to motivation
      a. Integration of behavioral and cognitive approaches
      b. Expectancy X value theories: motivation is the product of two forces,

expectation of success combined with the value of the goal (example, Bandura's Social Cognitive Theory).

   C. Motivation to learn in school
      1. "Student tendency to find academic activities meaningful and worthwhile"
      2. Includes planning, concentration on a goal, metacognitive awareness, what is intended and how; accurate search for information, clearly perceiving feedback, pride in achievement; no anxiety for fear of failure

III. Goals and motivation
   A. Goal: What an individual is striving to accomplish
   B. Types of goals
      1. Most effective: Specific, moderately difficult, within reach
         a. Provide clear standards for judging performance
         b. Realistic challenge (moderate difficulty)
         c. Not likely abandoned
      2. Performance goal
         a. Focus: Seeming competent in the eyes of others
         b. Anxious to avoid risks; give up when difficult
      3. Learning goal
         a. Focus is on improving abilities regardless of performance
         b. Seek challenges; persist under difficulty
   C. Feedback and goal acceptance
      1. Feedback: An accurate sense of where one is and how far one has to go
      2. Goal acceptance: Students accept goals set by teachers or establish own goals
   D. Goals: Lessons for teachers
      1. Learning goals: clear, specific, moderately challenging, attainable in short time
      2. Emphasis should be on learning and improving, not just performing well

IV. Needs and motivation
   A. Needs: What a deficiency person requires or thinks he/she requires for overall well-being; needs activate motivation
   B. Maslow's hierarchy
      1. Needs function as hierarchy
      2. Deficiency needs (four)
         a. Survival, safety, belonging, self-esteem
         b. Must be satisfied first
      3. Being needs (three)
         a. Intellectual achievement, aesthetic appreciation, and self-actualization
         b. Never completely fulfilled, endlessly renewed
      4. Enables look at full person: physical, emotional, and intellectual needs interrelated
      5. Educational implications
         a. Students with deficiency needs will not seek knowledge and understanding
         b. Student needs and teacher's goals may conflict
   C. Achievement motivation: desire to excel for the sake of achieving
      1. Origins in the family and cultural group of the child
      2. Resultant motivation
         a. When the achievement motivation is greater than the need to avoid failure, a moderate amount of failure can often enhance desire to pursue problem
         b. When the achievement motivation is less than the need to avoid failure,

student will usually be discouraged by failure and encouraged by success

    D. The need for self-determination
        1. The desire to have our own wishes rather than external rewards
        2. People strive to become the causal agent for their own behavior
        3. DeCharms model: Origins versus pawns
    E. Need for relatedness: The need to develop bonds with others in order to be connected to important people in our lives
        1. Involvement: The degree to which teachers are interested in and involved with children's interests and experiences
        2. Autonomy support: The degree to which teachers and parents encourage children to make their own choices
    F. Needs and motivation: Lessons for teachers
        1. Meet lower level needs first, providing a secure learning environment
        2. Make sure that tasks offer a sense of achievement
        3. Students need to form positive relationships with others
        4. Teachers need to make students feel secure, competent, and cared-for
        5. Students need to feel like origins rather than pawns
V. Attributions, beliefs, and motivation
    A. Attribution theory describes how an individual's justifications and excuses influence motivation (B. Weiner)
        1. Locus: internal/external dimension
            a. Internal locus related to confidence and self-esteem, or loss of self-esteem
            b. Students with internal locus feel responsible for success through skill and effort
            c. Students with external locus prefer to work in situations governed by luck
        2. Stability: stable or unstable dimension; related to expectations about future
            a. If success attributed to stable factors, similar expectation of past to future
            b. If success attributed to unstable factors, expectation is future will differ from past
        3. Responsibility: Whether a student can control the causes of success; it is related to emotional reactions
            a. If attribution is that success or failure is due to controllable factors, the outcome is feeling of pride or shame
            b. If attribution is to uncontrollable factors, outcome will be gratitude for good luck
        4. Locus of control (Rotter) is closely related to Weiner"s "locus"
            a. Distinguishes self-determination and control by others
            b. Learned helplessness (extreme of external locus): a feeling that nothing and no one can help
            c. Helplessness causes cognitive, motivational, and affective deficits
        5. Attributions and student motivation
            a. Positive, adaptive mastery-oriented response: failure attributed to lack of effort (internal and controllable); focus on strategies for succeeding next time
            b. Negative, unmotivated: failure attributed to internal, stable, and uncontrollable causes (resigned to failure and apathetic)
        6. Cues about causes
            a. Graham (1981): teachers' responses can give cues about attribution
            b. If teacher is critical or angry, suggests that student is responsible (i.e.

powerful)

    c. If teacher responds with pity, suggests that student is of low-ability (lacks power)

    d. Certain ethnic groups may be receiving low-ability cues which are demoralizing

C. Beliefs about ability

  1. Entity view: Intelligence fixed, stable, uncontrollable

    a. Young children hold this view

    b. Tend to set performance goals

    c. Blame poor performance on not studying or test anxiety

    d. May protect self-esteem by not trying at all

  2. Incremental view: Intelligence is a set of skills that can be changed; it is unstable, yet controllable

    a. Children over 11 years tend to share this view

    b. Tend to set learning goals

    c. Failure is not as threatening

    d. Tend to set moderately difficult goals which are the most motivating

D. Beliefs about efficacy

  1. (Bandura): Self-efficacy refers to our beliefs about competency in a certain area

  2. Sense of self-efficacy affects motivation through goal-setting

  3. Self-efficacy related to self-attributions

E. Attributions, achievement motivation, and self-worth

  1. Mastery-oriented students set learning goals, assume responsibility for success and failure; competitive

  2. Failure-avoiding students set performance goals, seek to protect image, take few risks; may decide they are incompetent

  3. Failure-accepting students: Where failure-avoiding leads

  4 Help failure-avoiding students to set realistic goals, to avoid their becoming failure-accepting

  5. Avoid self-defeating sexual or ethnic achievement stereotypes

F. Attributions and beliefs: Lessons for teachers

  1. Students' perceptions are responsible for their success

  2. Guidelines: Encouraging Students' Self-Worth

VI. Anxiety in the classroom

A. Definition: General uneasiness or feeling of tension

  1. Improves performance on simple tasks; interferes on complex tasks

  2. Anxiety is negatively related to almost all school achievement

B. What causes anxiety in school?

  1. Pressures to perform, severe consequences for failure, and competitive comparisons among students

  2. Anxious students divide their attention between information to be learned and their feelings of nervousness, are more easily distracted by irrelevant aspects of the learning task, cannot focus on significant details, and have poor study habits

  3. Test-taking skills poor; "freeze and forget"

C. Helping anxious students

  1. Set realistic goals

  2. Work at moderate pace; for example, on tests; eliminate time pressures

3   Provide structure such as repetitive lessons
    D. Lessons for teachers: See Guidelines for Dealing with Anxiety
VII.   Summary
VIII.   Key terms and concepts
IX.   What would you do?
X.   Teachers' casebook

Key Points

What is motivation?

- <u>Motivation</u>: A general process by which behavior is initiated and directed toward a goal

    - <u>Traits</u>: Stable, individual human characteristics

    - <u>States</u>: Temporary situations which can impact motivation

    - <u>Intrinsic motivation</u>: Motivation associated with activities that are their own reward

    - <u>Extrinsic motivation</u>: Motivation created by external factors like rewards and punishments

    - Teachers must balance the effort to stimulate intrinsic interest in learning with some provision for extrinsic motivators

- Behavioral approaches to motivation emphasize extrinsic reinforcement

    - Rewards (attractive consequences) and incentives (encouragements and discouragements) influence behavior.

    - Motivation is explained by such principles as contiguity, reinforcement, punishment, and modeling

- Humanistic approaches to motivation emphasize personal freedom, choice, and self-determination

    - Focus is on intrinsic needs of students for self-esteem and personal control over self-directed learning

- Cognitive approaches to motivation builds on people's intrinsic need to understand and cope with environment

    - Motivation is directed by our thinking, beliefs, and interpretation of events

- Social learning approaches to motivation integrate behavioral and cognitive approaches

- Expectancy X value theories: Explanations of motivation that emphasize the individual's expectations for success combined with their valuing of the goal

    - Self-efficacy: Beliefs about personal competence in a particular situation

    - Teacher efficacy: A teacher's belief that she or he can reach even difficult students to help them learn

Motivation to learn in school

- Students need to find learning meaningful and worthwhile

    - Includes planning, focus on goal, understanding of intention to learn, active involvement, pride in achievement.

    - Teachers must create a state of motivation without undermining the trait of life-long learning

Goals and motivation

- Goals that are most effective are specific, moderately difficult, and within reach

    - Performance goal: An intention to seem competent or perform well in the eyes of others

    - Learning goal: An intention to improve your abilities and understand regardless of how performance may suffer

Needs and motivation

- Need: A biological or psychological requirement; a state of deprivation that motivates a person to take action towards a goal

- Maslow's Hierarchy interrelates physical, emotional, and intellectual needs

    - Deficiency needs: Survival, safety, belonging, self-esteem must be satisfied first

    - Being needs: Intellectual achievement, aesthetic appreciation, and self-actualization

    - Self-actualization: Fulfilling your potential

- Students with deficiency needs will not seek knowledge and understanding

- Students' needs and teacher's goals may conflict

- <u>Achievement motivation</u>: Desire to excel; striving for excellence and success

  - <u>Resultant motivation</u>: Whichever is the strongest tendency-- the need to achieve or the need to avoid failure

Attributions, beliefs, and motivation

- Attribution theory describes how an individual's justifications and excuses influence motivation

  - Internal locus of control related to confidence and self-esteem, or loss of self-esteem

    - Students with internal locus feel responsible for success through skill and effort

    - Students with external locus prefer to work in situations governed by luck

  - If attribution is <u>stable</u>, future is thought to resemble past; if <u>unstable</u>, future represents a discontinuity from past

  - If attribution is that success or failure is due to <u>controllable</u> factors, the outcome is feeling of pride or shame; if attribution is to <u>uncontrollable</u> factors, outcome will be gratitude for good luck or blame for failure

  - If student has a positive, adaptive mastery-oriented response, failure is attributed to lack of effort (internal and controllable)

  - If student has a negative response, student is resigned to failure and apathetic (stable, and uncontrollable)

    - <u>Learned helplessness</u>: A feeling that nothing and no one can help

- Teachers' responses can give cues about attribution

  - Critical or angry response suggests that student is responsible; pity suggests that student is of low ability

  - Certain ethnic groups may be receiving low-ability cues that are demoralizing

- <u>Entity view about ability</u>: The belief that intelligence is fixed, stable, uncontrollable

- Students with entity view tend to set performance goals

- Incremental view about ability: The belief that intelligence is a set of skills that can be changed

  - Students with incremental belief tend to set learning goals

- Attributions, achievement motivation, and self-worth affect goal attainment

  - Mastery-oriented students: Students who focus on learning goals to increase their skills because they value achievement and see ability as improvable

  - Failure-avoiding students: Students who avoid failure by sticking to what they know, by not taking risks, or by claiming not to care about their performance

  - Failure-accepting students: Students who believe their failures are due to their low ability and there is little they can do about it

- Teachers can help students to set realistic goals and emphasize student progress; keep portfolio of good work and periodically review progress

  - Avoid self-defeating sexual or ethnic achievement stereotypes

  - Make specific suggestions for improvement, then reward when improvement is made; have evidence that "trying harder" pays off

Anxiety in the classroom

- Anxiety in the classroom improves performance on simple tasks; interferes on complex tasks

  - General uneasiness or feeling of tension is negatively related to almost all school achievement

  - Anxious students are more easily distracted by irrelevant aspects of learning task and cannot focus on significant details

  - To help anxious students, set realistic goals; work at moderate pace; and provide structure such as repetitive lessons

151

Concept Map: ATTRIBUTION AND MOTIVATION

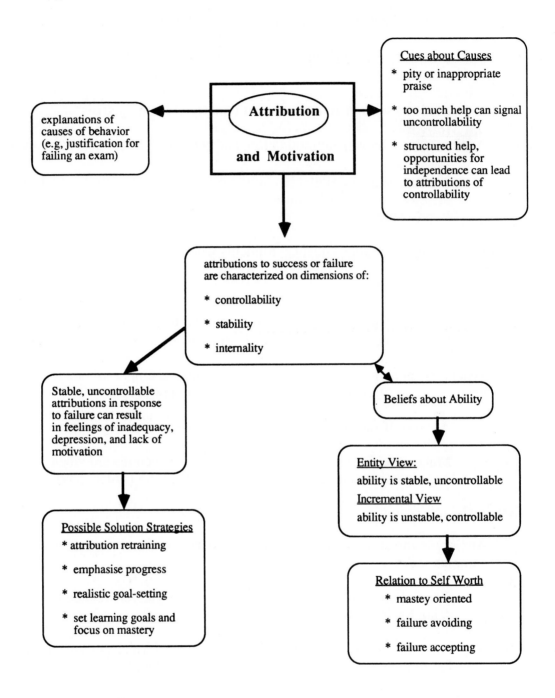

Do You Know This?

See if you understand the main points that are covered in this chapter.

What is Motivation?

Can you give classroom examples of intrinsic and extrinsic motivation?

Compare and contrast perspectives on motivation from the behavioral, humanistic, cognitive, and social learning points of view

Motivation to Learn in School

Can you explain the concept of student motivation to learn?

Goals and Motivation

Can you set goals that motivate you and your students?

Needs and Motivation

Can you list Maslow's seven levels of needs and give a classroom example of each?

Attributions, Beliefs, and Motivation

Can you explain how to encourage the need for achievement in your classroom?

What are the possible motivational effects of success and failure, and how do these effects relate to beliefs about ability?

What are characteristics of mastery-oriented, failure-avoiding, and failure-accepting students?

Anxiety on the Classroom

Can you develop a plan for helping an anxious student to improve?

Key Terms and Concepts

DEFINITIONS: Concepts in Motivation

Write explanations for the following pairs of terms.   Your explanation should clearly distinguish the two from one another. Check the text to be sure that your explanations are equivalent.

Arousal/Anxiety _____

_____

Performance goals/Learning goals _____

_____

External/Internal locus of control _____

_____

Intrinsic/Extrinsic motivation _____

_____

Entity/Incremental view of ability _____

_____

IDENTIFICATION: Maslow's Hierarchy of Needs

Read each description below of how to motivate certain students. In the preceding blank, write which level of Maslow's Hierarchy best fits the description. The levels have been provided for you. To check your answers, see Answer Key.

Self-actualization
Aesthetic appreciation
Intellectual achievement
Self-esteem
Belonging
Safety
Survival

1. _____ "Finish your work so you can go outside with the others."

2. _____ "I could tell you <u>my</u> opinion of your writing, but it's most important that you write to please <u>yourself</u>."

3. _____ "Eat all the lunch in your bag before you go play. You'll need that energy for your work this afternoon."

4. _____ "These essays show real improvement and excellent knowledge of the subject."

5. _____ "When you hear the fire siren, line up quickly so we can all leave the classroom as fast as possible."

6. _____ "Draw the diagram for each science experiment carefully. When you look back on what you've studied, you can enjoy each picture that you have drawn so neatly."

7. _____ "Let's all give Alison a hand for being elected Student of the Month."

8. _____ "In the Summer Book Club, it's not how many books you read that is important, but that you read what you want to read and learn to select and treasure some favorite authors."

9. _____ "Because this is the first day of school, we will need some rules to help us get along with one another. Who can give me a rule that help us all feel like valued members of the group?"

COMPLETION QUESTIONS: Beliefs, Attributions, and Motivation

Fill in the blanks with the following concepts. Each concept is used only once. To check your answers, see Answer Key.

Attribution	**Stable attribution**
Locus of control	**Unstable attribution**
Internal locus of control	**Entity view**
External locus of control	**Incremental view**
Failure-accepting student	**Cues about attribution**

1. Japanese parents believe that mathematics ability is not so much innate but is a result of hard daily effort. This would be regarded as a(n) _____ of ability.

2. Students feel pride in completing their assignments because they believe that success or failure is due to their own efforts. This is an example of a(n)_____

3. After trying to perform a somersault about a dozen times during physical education class, Timothy quit trying, saying, "I'll never get this right. I'm just a klutz." He is becoming a(n) _____.

4. Where people place responsibility for successes or failures -- inside or outside of their domain of responsibility -- determines their _____.

5. Thong Toc told his mother, "My teacher feels sorry for me. That means she doesn't think I can really learn English." The teacher is giving this student _____ that make him believe he is not capable.

6. "My spelling test scores have always been low. I'll never be good in spelling." This characterizes a student with a _____ about spelling performance.

7. Believing that musical ability is inborn is a(n)_____ of ability.

8. "The principal picks on me. I never know when she will call me in off the playground for something I'm doing. I'm just unlucky." This student exhibits a (an)_____.

9. When we succeed or fail at a task, we naturally think about who or what was responsible. We have a(n) _____that governs our subsequent behavior.

10. "Whether or not I do well on my history tests seems to depend on the mood I'm in at the time." This student has a(n) _____ about ability in history.

APPLICATION: Attribution of Motivation

For each description below, indicate whether it is a Controllable (C) or Uncontrollable (U) attribution. To check your answers, see Answer Key.

1. _____ "I don't feel I'm a born teacher."

2. _____ "Sometimes when I study, I'm lucky enough to remember until the test."

3. _____ "I was too tired from working late last night to do well on the math final."

4. _____ "Too many of my friends came over, so I couldn't study for the test."

5. _____ "The teacher always gives F's in this class. She's too tough on grading."

6. _____ "I'm too lazy to put much effort into this assignment."

7. _____ "I must have been unlucky in my choice of answers-- I've never done this poorly."

8. _____ "I really put a lot of work into this report."

9. _____ "I can't play volleyball. I'm not very athletic."

10. _____ "If I practice piano every night, I can aspire to become a concert pianist."

CASE STUDY: Intrinsic and Extrinsic Motivation

Ms. Judson was hired in January to substitute for a teacher on sick leave. The previous teacher used many extrinsic rewards to encourage students to achieve and behave. For example, when students completed their seatwork assignment, they could come to the teacher's desk for a piece of candy. Arriving to class on time in the morning would earn each student a small sticker; ten stickers could be traded for a privilege such as free time to play games. Ms. Judson is concerned that students seem to have little intrinsic desire to learn. Describe how Ms. Judson could gradually transform the students from extrinsic learners to intrinsic learners.

CASE STUDY: Teacher's Cues of Attribution

Maria Inez is a recent immigrant from Mexico. Although she previously studied English in a private girl's school in Mexico City, when she raises her hand in science class, Maria Inez's teacher does not call upon her for an oral response. The teacher has explained to her that she does not want to embarrass her in class. In contrast, Stefan, a recent immigrant from Albania, makes as many mistakes in English, but is called upon frequently and sometimes even corrected verbally by the teacher. Even though initially

Maria Inez showed an interest in science, she is gradually losing her desire to perform well in this class. Explain what may be happening to Maria Inez in terms of attribution cues from the teacher.

PRACTICE TEST: Multiple Choice

1. Maria spent many hours trying to complete her geometry proofs. Which of the following would be a <u>cognitive</u> interpretation of her motivation?

    a. She is trying to acquire understanding of how the different theorems work.
    b. She is trying to feel accomplished to raise her self-esteem.
    c. She wants her friends to be more likely to accept her.
    d. She knows that a good grade will bring a reward from her parents.

2. An "expectancy x value" theory would predict that motivation will necessarily be

    a. low if self-efficacy and the perceived value of the goal are low.
    b. zero if self-efficacy and the perceived value of a goal are low.
    c. zero only if expectation to succeed and the perceived value of a goal are zero.
    d. zero if either expectation to succeed or the perceived value of a goal is zero.

3. When highly anxious students set educational goals for themselves, they tend to

    a. set fairly realistic goal.
    b. set too-difficult or too-easy goals.
    c. lack organization to accomplish the goals.
    d. work too slowly to accomplish the goals.

4. Students with performance goals are largely concerned with

    a. achievement motivation.
    b. looking good in front of others.
    c. bettering themselves in terms of skill competencies.
    d. finishing tasks so that they can seek new challenges.

5. Which of the following is a correct implication of Maslow's hierarchy for education?

    a. A student with low self-esteem will probably have little motivation to belong to and be liked by a group.
    b. A student who is feeling or unsafe may show little interest in academic performance.
    c. Failure to satisfy aesthetic needs will prevent a student from having high self-esteem.
    d. A student who is frustrated in her search for knowledge may show little interest in her physiological well-being.

6. As need for achievement increases relative to fear of failure, _____ will increase.

    a. apathy
    b. self-esteem
    c. deficiency needs
    d. achievement motivation

157

7. Which of the following is consistent with the idea that "practice makes perfect?"
   a. Incremental view of ability
   b. External locus of control
   c. Performance goals
   d. Entity view of ability

8. Which of the following orientations are associated with higher academic motivation and performance?
   a. Performance goals and an entity view
   b. External locus of control and entity view
   c. Failure avoidance and external-uncontrollable attributes
   d. None of the above

9. Pedrita sets very unrealistic goals for herself. Since she is so unsure of herself, we could say that she is
   a. failure-avoiding.
   b. mastery-oriented.
   c. failure-accepting
   d. failure-oriented.

PRACTICE TEST: Essay

A. Explain how a behaviorist, humanistic, or cognitivist theory of motivation would influence a teacher's choice of activities for students. Give several examples of activities consonant with each philosophy.

Answer Key

IDENTIFICATION: Maslow's Hierarchy of Needs

1. Belonging
2. Self-actualization
3. Survival
4. Intellectual achievement
5. Safety
6. Aesthetic appreciation
7. Self-esteem
8. Self-actualization
9. Belonging

COMPLETION QUESTIONS: Beliefs, Attributions, and Motivation

1. Incremental view
2. Internal locus of control
3. Failure-accepting student
4. Locus of control
5. Cues about attribution
6. Stable attribution
7. Entity view
8. External locus of control
9. Attribution
10. Unstable attribution

APPLICATION: Attribution of Motivation

1. U (ability)
2. U (luck)
3. C (action)
4. C (action)
5. U (difficult task)
6. C (effort)
7. U (luck)
8. C (effort)
9. U (ability)
10. C (effort)

PRACTICE TEST: Multiple Choice

1. a Cognitive theories of motivation are concerned with the quest to learn and understand things. In this case, Maria's behavior in geometry would be explained as interest in understanding her theorems, not in obtaining recognition (social theory or behavioral), rewards (behavioral), or self-esteem (humanistic).

2. d Motivation will be zero if either expectation to succeed or the perceived value of a goal is zero. This is because social cognitive theory views these variables as multiplicatively related: Motivation = Expectancy x Perceived value.

3. b Highly anxious students tend to set goals that are too difficult or too easy. Both types of goals remove pressure. (That is there is not a stigma associated with failure on a difficult task while success on easy tasks is guaranteed, but allows for little satisfaction.)

4. b Students who have performance goals want to look good in front of others. Thus, they are less concerned with what they learn than with how they appear.

5. b Maslow's hierarchy is based on the assumption that we first try to satisfy lower-level needs before we attend to higher-level needs. Accordingly, someone who

is <u>feeling ill or unsafe, (survival needs) may show little interest in academic achievement</u>. The other multiple-choice alternatives all depict reverse orderings (higher-level before lower-level).

6.   d   Resultant motivation is the difference between the need to achieve and the need to avoid failure. Whichever tendency is greater will determine which behavior pattern (<u>achievement motivation</u> or failure-avoidance) will have more influence on behavior.

7.   a   <u>An incremental view of ability</u> assumes that ability is unstable and controllable Thus, if you are willing to try hard, you can improve your abilities and your achievement. This philosophy is consistent with the idea that "practice makes perfect."

8.   d   <u>None of the choices is correct</u>. Higher academic performance is associated with: learning goals (not performance goals), an internal (not external) locus of control, a mastery orientation (not failure avoidance), and internal-controllable (not external-uncontrollable) attributions.

9.   a   <u>Failure avoiding</u> students do not want to fail, so they select goals that are <u>unrealistic</u>. An example might be "D" students setting a goal of scoring 95%, an overly high goal on the physics exam. When they do not obtain it, no one can blame them. In contrast, failure-accepting students are resigned to failure and do not have a need to protect themselves from it.

PRACTICE TEST: Essay

A. **Behaviorist motivation**: Skills tasks that feature immediate feedback; teaching by modeling; use of primary and secondary reinforcers. Examples: Weekly spelling tests, with number of right answers posted by stars on a wall chart; praising students aloud who are behaving well; using tokens, stickers, and snacks to shape motivation.

Humanistic motivation: Activities that promote self-esteem, personal goal-setting, and self-directed learning. Examples: Daily journal writing, oral language development in sharing circles, students evaluate their own progress in reading and are encouraged to establish lifelong learning habits.

Cognitivist motivation: Activities are directed by student's intrinsic curiosity, with the need to understand and construct learning inductively. Examples: Science experiments involve discovery learning, with conclusions formulated by cooperative experimental teams; students are encouraged to bring observations and questions about nature to share with the class; students are encouraged to think critically about current events.

10

Motivation, Teaching, and Learning

Teaching Outline

I.   What Do You Think?
II. The ultimate goal of teaching: Life-long learning
  A. Self-regulated learning
    1. Combination of academic skills and self-control that makes learning easier
    2. Integrates effective learning research and motivation
    3. Learner's knowledge: To be self-regulated, learners need knowledge about themselves, the subject, the task, strategies for learning, and context in which to apply learning
    4. Motivation: Self-regulated learners are motivated to learn
    5. Volition: Self-regulated learners know how to protect themselves from distractions
    6. Creating environments for self-regulated learning
  B. On TARGETT: for self-regulated learning (See Table 10.1)
III. Tasks for learning
  A. Academic tasks can be interesting or boring; have a subject content; involve facts, concepts, opinions or principles
  B. Tapping interests and arousing curiosity
    1. Student interests are a key part of lesson planning
    2. Interests can be determined by discussion, questionnaire, observation
    3. Curiosity can be aroused by displays or activities
  C. Task operations (Doyle): Four categories of academic tasks
    1. Memory tasks: recognize or reproduce information
    2. Routine or procedural tasks: use algorithm to solve a problem
    3. Comprehension tasks: transform, combine, or choose best information
    4. Opinion tasks: state a preference
  D. Risk and ambiguity
    1. Risk: Some tasks involve more likelihood of failure
      a. Few risks: memory or procedural tasks
      b. High risks: longer and more complex memory or procedural tasks
    2. Ambiguity: How straightforward the expected answer is
      a. Ambiguous: opinion and understanding tasks
      b Unambiguous: memory and procedural tasks
    3. Relationship with motivation
      a. Students motivated to lower risks and decrease the ambiguity in schoolwork
      b. When risk and ambiguity are reduced, a state of motivation may seem to increase
      c. This "task negotiation" may increase motivation to perform, but not to learn
      d. Caution: fostering trait of motivation requires higher risk and more

ambiguity
- E. Task value
    1. Expectations related to the strength of motivation
    2. Attainment value: importance of doing well on the task
    3. Intrinsic or interest value: enjoyment obtained from a task
    4. Utility value: contribution of a task to meeting goals
    5. Authentic task is one that has some connection to real-life challenges
    6. Problem-based learning: students meet an ill-structured problem before they receive any instruction
- IV. Supporting autonomy and recognizing accomplishment in the classroom
    - A. Advantages of autonomy in the classroom
        1. Classroom environments that support student autonomy are associated with greater student interest, sense of competence, self-esteem, creativity, conceptual learning, and preference for challenge
        2. Discomforting: Students and parents seem to prefer more controlling teachers, even though students learn more when teachers support autonomy
    - B. Information and control
        1. Cognitive evaluation theory explains that various events (reminders, grading,) can be controlling and informational
        2. If information is provided that increases a sense of competence, students' intrinsic motivation will be enhanced
        3. If events are controlling, intrinsic motivation is decreased
    - C. Autonomy supporting class climates
        1. Teacher takes the perspective of the student
        2. Opportunities for student choice and initiative about activities, approaches, and materials
        3. Teacher explains why limits are necessary
        4. Teacher forewarns students that they might have negative emotional reactions to the limits imposed or the work assigned
        5. Limit controlling messages to students and make sure information adds to sense of competence
    - D. Recognizing accomplishments
- V. Grouping: Cooperation and competition
    - A. Goal structures: how students strive toward a goal in relation to others
        1. Cooperative
        2. Competitive
        3. Individualistic
    - B. Cooperative learning
        1. Setting up cooperative groups
            a. Balance number of boys and girls
            b. For the shy and introverted, individualistic learning may be better
            c. Only those who take responsibility and participate will learn
        2. Student Teams-Achievement Divisions system (STAD)
            a. Students previous work used as base score to rate improvement
            b. Improvement, regardless of ability level, contributes to group score
        3. Teams-Games-Tournament (TGT)
            a. Heterogeneous groups help students to prepare for weekly tournaments

          b. Students compete across groups with students of similar ability

          c. Caution: research shows that students on unsuccessful teams were unhappier

    4. Cooperative Integrated Reading and Composition (CIRC)

          a. Traditional reading ability-level groups are used

          b. Pairs from each reading group work in teams to study

          c. Teams are rewarded on average performance of all their members

    5. Reciprocal questioning

          a. Students work in pairs to develop questions of the material they are studying

          b. This encourages deeper thinking about the material

VI. Evaluation and time

  A. Evaluation

    1. Emphasis on competitive grading results in performance goals rather than learning goals, and ego-involvement rather than task-involvement

    2. Deemphasize grades and emphasize learning

  B. Time

    1. Individuals need time to learn, rather than be pressured for group's pace

    2. Students need time to process knowledge rather than "cover" it

    3. Students develop persistence and efficacy if they are allowed to stick with an activity

VII. Teacher expectations

  A. Origins of the construct

    1. "Pygmalion in the classroom" effect in elementary classrooms

    2. Dispute of Rosenthal and Jacobson's research findings remains

  B. Two kinds of expectation effects

    1. Self-fulfilling prophecy: incorrect expectation confirmed because it has been expected

    2. Sustaining expectation effect: teacher's, initially accurate, but unchanging expectation sustains student's achievement at the expected level

          a. Students given more time and encouragement to answer questions will perform better academically

          b. Teachers with low expectations for certain students will assign them less work, move at slower pace, accept lower quality answers, and make fewer demands

    Point/Counterpoint: Can Teacher Expectations Affect Student Learning?

    3. Expectations, motivation, aspiration level, and self-concept

          a. Teachers' behavior provides mirror for students to see themselves

          b. Teachers' views affect self-esteem of young, dependent, or conforming students

  C. Sources of expectations (See Figure 10-3)

  D. Teacher behavior and student reaction

    1. Instructional strategies

          a. Ability grouping: have effect on students and teachers; preference for higher ability groups

          b. Pace and quantity of instruction: increase as soon as students ready

          c. Problem: teachers sometimes select inappropriate teaching methods

     2. Teacher-student interactions that communicate expectations
        a. High achieving students get asked harder questions, are given more chances, and longer time to respond, with more clues, prompts, and encouragement
        b. Lower achieving students are asked easier questions, given less time for answering, and are less likely to get prompts and praise
        c. See Table 10-3 for self-test
     3. In summary: the effects on students
        a. Decreased motivation follows lowered expectations
        b. Lowered performance because of lower motivation "confirms" teacher's expectation
        c. Misbehavior and disruption may follow; discourages teacher's attention for academic work
  D. Guidelines: Avoiding the Negative Effects of Teacher Expectations
VIII. Strategies to encourage motivation and thoughtful learning
  A. Necessary conditions in the classroom
     1. Classroom organized and free from constant interruptions
     2. Teacher patient and supportive of mistakes
     3. Challenging but reasonable work
     4. Worthwhile learning tasks
  B. Can I do it? Building confidence and positive expectations
     1. Begin work at the students' levels, moving in small steps to assure students' understanding
     2. Emphasize clear, specific, attainable learning goals
     3. Stress self-comparison, not comparison with others
     4. Communicate that academic ability is improvable
     5. Model good problem-solving
  C. Do I want to do it? Seeing the value of learning
     1. Intrinsic and attainment value
        a. Class activities tied to student needs and interests
        b. Arouse curiosity
        c. Make the learning task fun
        d. Use novelty and familiarity
     2. Instrumental value (See Chapters 5 and 6)
        a. Explain to students the connections between school and life outside of school
        b. Provide incentives for learning when needed
        c. Use ill-structured problems and authentic tasks
     3. What do I need to do to succeed? Staying focused on the task
        a. Frequent opportunities to demonstrate skills, permitting more corrective feedback
        b. Have students create a finished product
        c. Avoid competitive evaluation
        d. Model the motivation to learn
        e. Teach particular learning tactics
  D. How do beginning teachers motivate students?

    1. Research: Over half of the motivational strategies used by new teachers were reward/punishment
    2. Teachers also tried to focus student attention
    3. Minor strategies were commenting on the importance of the material and building students' confidence
        a. Commenting on relevance was positively correlated with on-task behavior
        b. The use of rewards and punishments was negatively correlated

IX.   Summary
X.   Key terms and concepts
XI.   What would you do?
XII.   Teachers' casebook

Key Points

Life-long learning

- <u>Self-regulated learning</u>: Academic skills plus self-control

  - Learners need knowledge about themselves, the subject, the task, strategies for learning, and the contexts in which to apply learning

Tasks for learning

- <u>Academic tasks</u>: The work the student must accomplish, including the content covered and the mental operations required

- Student interests are a key part of lesson planning

- <u>Task operations</u>: Categories of academic tasks are memory, procedural, comprehension, and opinion tasks

- Risk and ambiguity vary with the type of task operation

  - Memory or procedural tasks are low risk

  - Longer and more complex memory or procedural tasks are high risk

  - Opinion and understanding tasks are ambiguous

  - Memory and procedural tasks are unambiguous

  - When students convince teachers to reduce risk and ambiguity, a state of motivation may seem to increase, but this "task negotiation" may increase motivation to perform, not to learn

  - Fostering trait of motivation requires higher risk and more ambiguity

- <u>Task value</u> : Expectations related to the strength of motivation

  - <u>Attainment value</u>: Importance of doing well on the task

  - <u>Intrinsic or interest value</u>: Enjoyment obtained from a task

  - <u>Utility value</u>: Contribution of a task to meeting goals

  - Age, needs, beliefs, and goals influence value

- Teachers can support autonomy and recognize accomplishment in the classroom

  - Classrooms that support autonomy are associated with greater student interest, sense of competence, self-esteem, creativity, challenge

  - Cognitive evaluation theory explains why autonomous classrooms are intrinsically motivating

  - Teachers can limit controlling messages to enhance self of competence

Grouping: Cooperation and competition

- <u>Goal structures</u>: The way students strive towards a goal in relation to others

  - Cooperative goals are effective with complex tasks; they encourage taking others' perspectives, enhance ethnic relations; increase self-esteem, and lead to greater acceptance of handicapped and low-achieving students

  - Competitive goals foster belief that students will only reach their goals if other students do not reach theirs

  - Individualistic goals are based on belief that reaching a goal is not related to other students' attempts to reach goals

- In cooperative learning, those who take responsibility and participate will learn

  - Student Teams-Achievement Divisions system (STAD)

    - Uses students' previous work as base score to rate improvement, which contributes to group score

  - Teams-Games-Tournament (TGT)

167

- Uses heterogeneous groups to help students to prepare for weekly tournaments in which students compete across groups with students of similar ability

- Cooperative Integrated Reading and Composition (CIRC)

  - Traditional reading ability-level groups are used and teams are rewarded on average performance of all their members

- Reciprocal questioning

  - Students work in pairs to develop questions about the material they are studying, which encourages deeper thinking about the material

Evaluation and time

- Emphasis on grades tends to result in performance goals rather than learning goals

- Students need time to learn, to process knowledge in depth and develop persistence and efficacy

Teacher expectations

- <u>Self-fulfilling prophecy (Pygmalion effect)</u>: An incorrect expectation that is confirmed because it has been expected

- <u>Sustaining expectation effect</u>: Student performance maintained at a certain level because teachers do not recognize improvements

- Ability grouping has an effect on students and teachers, with both preferring higher ability group members

- High expectation students are given more time and encouragement to answer questions, which leads to better performance

- High achieving student get asked harder questions, are given more chances and longer time to respond, with more clues, prompts, and encouragement

- Low expectation students are assigned less work, move at a slower pace, and receive fewer demands

- Lower achieving students are asked easier questions, given less time for answering, and are less likely to get prompts and praise

- Teachers' behavior is a mirror for students to see themselves and can affect the self-esteem of young, dependent, or conforming students

- Decreased motivation follows lowered expectations, which "confirms" teacher's expectation

Strategies to encourage motivation and thoughtful learning

- Necessary classroom conditions for motivation: Classroom organized and free from constant interruptions, teacher patient and supportive of mistakes, work is challenging but reasonable, and learning tasks are worthwhile

- To build confidence and positive expectations, teachers need to begin work at the students' levels, moving in small steps to assure students' understanding; emphasize clear, specific, attainable learning goals; stress self-comparison; communicate that academic ability is improvable; and model good problem-solving

- To increase intrinsic and attainment value of learning, class activities should be tied to student needs and interests; use novelty and familiarity to make learning fun

- To increase instrumental value, explain to students the connections between school and life outside of school

- For students to succeed, they must stay focused on the task, with frequent opportunities to demonstrate skills, receive corrective feedback, avoiding competitive evaluation

Concept Map: **MOTIVATIONAL STRATEGIES: ESTABLISHING THE NECESSARY PRECONDITIONS**

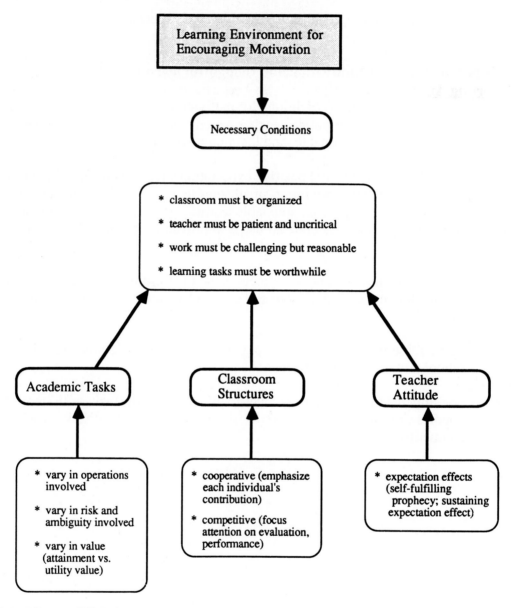

Learning Environment for Encouraging Motivation

↓

Necessary Conditions

↓

* classroom must be organized

* teacher must be patient and uncritical

* work must be challenging but reasonable

* learning tasks must be worthwhile

Academic Tasks

* vary in operations involved

* vary in risk and ambiguity involved

* vary in value (attainment vs. utility value)

Classroom Structures

* cooperative (emphasize each individual's contribution)

* competitive (focus attention on evaluation, performance)

Teacher Attitude

* expectation effects (self-fulfilling prophecy; sustaining expectation effect)

Do You Know This?

See if you understand the main points that are covered in this chapter.

The Ultimate Goal of Teaching: Life-Long-Learning

Can you list some characteristics of a self-regulated learner, and describe how teachers can promote self-regulated learning in the classroom?

Tasks for Learning

Can you describe how the ambiguity and risk of the learning task affect motivation, and explain what can happen when students try to reduce risk and ambiguity?

How does the value of a task affect motivation to learn?

Supporting Autonomy and Recognizing Accomplishment in the Classroom

Can you describe the characteristics of classrooms that support students' autonomy?

Grouping: Cooperation and Competition

Can you explain how grouping arrangements can influence motivation?

Can you design a unit featuring cooperative learning?

Evaluation and Time

Can you explain how evaluation procedures can influence motivation?

Teacher Expectations

Can you describe potential effects on students of teachers' positive and negative expectations?

Strategies to Encourage Motivation and Thoughtful Learning

Can you devise a strategy for teaching your subject to an uninterested student?

Key Terms and Concepts

DEFINITIONS: Tasks for Learning

Write definitions for the following terms. Then check the Glossary of your textbook to see if your definition is appropriate.

Task ambiguity _____

_____

Attainment value _____

_____

Intrinsic (interest) value _____

_____

Utility value _____

_____

IDENTIFICATION: High-Risk vs. Low-Risk Tasks

For each statement below, choose **High-Risk** or **Low-Risk** to describe the task. To check your answers, see Answer Key.

_____ 1. Copying a page of handwriting practice.

_____ 2. Completing a Word Search puzzle looking for spelling words.

_____ 3. Solving a page of story problems involving long-division.

_____ 4. Memorizing the capitals of 50 states.

_____ 5. Making a diorama featuring a State of the Union.

_____ 6. Creating a collage from magazine ads about nutritious foods.

_____ 7. Reciting the Pledge of Allegiance to the flag.

CASE STUDY: Grouping for Cooperation and Competition

Mr. Knoerr has grouped his fourth-grade language arts students into three ability groups: high, medium, and low. The high-ability students often brag about their group rank to the other students and the members of the medium and low ability groups complain that the high group is assigned more interesting activities. Socially, students in the high ability group seem to be chosen most often as playground leaders. Parents of students in the medium and low ability groups have told Mr. Knoerr of their dislike for the practice of ability grouping, claiming that their children's self-esteem is being damaged. What can Mr. Knoerr do to alleviate this situation?

CASE STUDY: Cooperative Learning

Ms. Whitefoot's Advanced Placement European History class takes weekly tests over each unit to prepare for the Advanced Placement test in May. Each student is graded competitively on test performance. Although the students have individualistic academic goals, Ms. Whitefoot would like to organize the class so that they could work together on the units to learn the required information. Choose an appropriate cooperative learning strategy and describe how Ms. Lightfoot could implement this strategy in the classroom.

PRACTICE TEST: Multiple Choice

1. A desirable effect of teachers' deemphasizing grades and emphasizing learning would be to increase students' _____ involvement with what is taught.

    a. attainment
    b. performance
    c. task
    d. state

2. With regard to degree of risk and ambiguity, comprehension tasks can be defined as

    a. low in both.
    b. high in risk, low in ambiguity.
    c. low in risk, high in ambiguity.
    d. high in both.

3. Ms. Owen becomes frustrated by children's failure to comprehend the logic for addition- with-regrouping problems, so she converts the task to one of simply memorizing the correct problem-solving steps. According to your text, a possible danger to this type of approach is

    a. students will not learn how to solve problems.
    b. although state motivation may be increased, trait motivation may be undermined.
    c. although long-term motivation may increase, immediate motivation may be undermined.
    d. attainment value of the learning task will be substantially lowered.

4. After receiving a 97 on his algebra test, Carlos proudly walks around the room "feeling smart." Based on this behavior, the accomplishment most clearly has _____ value for him.

    a. attainment
    b. intrinsic
    c. utility
    d. interest

5. Studies of achievement under different goal structures indicate that

    a. cooperation is generally more effective than competition.
    b. competition is especially effective for low-ability students.
    c. cooperation helps high-ability students but hinders low-ability students.
    d. none of the above.

6. Research on cooperative learning suggests that it is best to

    a. group students of similar abilities together.
    b. balance the number of boys and girls in each group.
    c. make shy or introverted students group leaders.
    d. all of the above.

7. Mrs. Brown was told by another teacher that Johnny was a "slow student and very disruptive in class." By the third day of school, Johnny had been placed in the lowest reading and math groups and had been sent to the principal's office four times. Johnny may indeed be appropriately placed but he may also be a victim of

    a. a low level of aspiration.
    b. the self-fulfilling prophecy.
    c. the fear of failure.
    d. a poor self image.

8. Which of the following is true about the sustaining expectation effect?

    a. Real improvement is not recognized, resulting in the continuation of low expectancies.
    b. The students' true abilities are initially misdiagnosed resulting in inappropriate expectancies being conveyed.
    c. Expectancies about a student are communicated from one teacher to another within a school.
    d. Students are taught to believe in themselves and their ability to succeed.

9. Ms. Gibbons does not expect much of Sally. She thinks Sally is just not very bright. In classroom interactions, she is likely to give Sally

    a. easier questions and less time to answer.
    b. more praise for correct answers.
    c. greater encouragement to succeed.
    d. verbal prompts and cues to the correct answer.

PRACTICE TEST: Essay

A. In Mrs. Lane's eleventh grade analytical geometry class, students often complain that they see little value in learning to graph equations using two variables. What can Mrs. Lane do to help students see the value of this learning task?

B. In classes where exceptional students are mainstreamed, there are sometimes social conflicts in which students do not gracefully accept classmates with disabilities. What advantages in students' interpersonal relations have been shown as a result of cooperative goal structures?

Answer Key

IDENTIFICATION: High-Risk vs. Low-Risk Tasks

1. **Low-risk**
2. **Low-risk**
3. **High-risk**
4. **High-risk**
5. **Low-risk**
6. **Low-risk**
7. **Low-risk**

PRACTICE TEST: Multiple Choice

1. c. <u>Task-involved</u> students are concerned with learning goals rather than performance goals. When teachers deemphasize grades, the message is that learning is important for its own sake (i. e. for personal improvement and increased knowledge) not simply for obtaining extrinsic rewards such as points and grades.

2. d Comprehension tasks are <u>high in both ambiguity and risk</u>. Ambiguity is high because such tasks do not have clear-cut answers. Risk is high because the chances for failure are greater than with simple memory or procedural tasks.

3. b When Ms. Owen converts the task to one of simply memorizing the correct problem-solving steps, she is reducing the risk and ambiguity of the task. The students will be immediately satisfied with the decision and thus develop <u>short-term motivation to perform</u>. Unfortunately, involvement in the simpler tasks will not serve to develop <u>long-term interest in learning</u>.

4. a. The algebra test has primarily <u>attainment value</u> for Carlos. He wants to do well in order to be recognized as being "smart." (If he were naturally interested in algebra, it would have intrinsic value for him.)

5. a Studies have shown that when a task involves complex learning and problem-solving skills, <u>cooperation leads to higher achievement than competition</u>, especially for low-ability students.

6. b Research suggests that <u>it is best to balance the number of boys and girls in each cooperative group</u>. Otherwise, when there are just a few girls in a group, they tend to be left out of group discussions; when there are just a few boys, they tend to dominate.

7. b A <u>self-fulfilling prophesy</u> is a false assumption that comes true because it has been expected. When Mrs. Brown is told by another teacher to expect that

Johnny was "slow...and disruptive," she may have unwittingly promoted this behavior from Johnny.

8.   a   The sustaining expectation effect occurs when teachers are initially accurate in their perception of student abilities, <u>but improvement (or changes) in those abilities are not recognized</u>. As a result, the teacher's perceptions remain unchanged, even though the student's performance has improved.

9.   a   Research on student-teacher interactions indicates that <u>lower-ability students are usually given less time to answer questions than are higher-ability students</u>. Also, they are asked easier questions and are given fewer prompts and cues.

PRACTICE TEST: Essay

A.   As Mrs. Lane's eleventh grade analytical geometry class contains older students, increasing the <u>utility value</u> of the task may help students to see the value of the task. For example, those students planning a career in science, engineering or aerospace will need to learn to graph equations using two variables as a foundation for success in calculus. It is also sometimes used in market analysis in business. To increase the <u>interest value </u> of the task, Mrs. Lane may wish to devise games and simulations in which students need to use two variables.

B.   As a result of cooperative goal structures, students can learn to see the world from another person's point of view, which often increases self-esteem and acceptance for exceptional and low-achieving students who are mainstreamed. This may reduce social conflicts.

11

Creating Learning Environments

Teaching Outline

I. What Do You Think?
II. The need for organization
    A. The ecology of classrooms
        1. Classroom environment and inhabitants are constantly interacting
        2. Characteristics of classrooms
            a. Multidimensional: individuals with differing goals, performing various tasks within particular time pressures
            b. Simultaneity: many things happening at once
            c. Immediacy: very fast pace
            d. Unpredictability: even with best plans, disruptions are likely
            e. Public: students evaluating interactions between teacher and surroundings
            f. Histories: current events frequently depend on past
        3. The basic task: Gain their cooperation
            a. Main management tasks: achieve order by gaining and maintaining student cooperation in class activities
            b. Gaining cooperation: product of many managerial skills, not merely controlling misbehavior
        4. Age-related needs: Four levels of classroom management
            a. Early elementary grades: direct teaching of rules and procedures important
            b. Middle elementary grades: time spent monitoring and maintaining management system more time consuming than direct teaching of rules
            c. Late elementary-early high school grades: motivating students concerned with peers, channeling challenges to authority productively
            d. Late high school grades: managing the curriculum, fitting curriculum to student interest and abilities, helping students become more self-managing in learning
    B. The goals of classroom management
        1. More time for learning:
            a. 25% available time lost to interruptions and rough transitions
            b. Significant relationship between content covered and student learning; increase allocated time
            c. Learning highly correlated with amount of engaged time ("time on task"; time spent attending actively to specific learning tasks)
            d. Academic learning time means students are working with high rate of success
        2. Access to learning
            a. Explicit participation structures: rules defining participation in various activities
            b. Implicit participation structures: students ability to participate influenced by structure in home

    c. Inconsistent rules: cause confusion and increased disruptions

    d. Key: awareness and communication of rules, good fit with students' cultural backgrounds and home experiences

  3. Management for self-management: Help students manage themselves

III. Creating a positive learning environment

  A. Good instructional planning prevents many management problems

    1. Assign work at students' ability level

    2. Make an effort to motivate students

  B. Some research results

    1. How effective teachers were studied as they "got started" in the first weeks of class; connections were made to management problems, and management principles were identified

    2. Teachers who applied these principles had fewer problems, higher achievement

  C. Rules and procedures required

    1. Procedures: describe how to accomplish activities in the classroom (see Guidelines: Establishing Class Procedures)

      a. Administrative routines: taking attendance, etc.

      b. Student movement: entering and leaving room

      c. Housekeeping: taking care of classroom and personal items

      d. Routines for accomplishing lessons: collecting and distributing papers

      e. Interactions between teacher and student

      f. Talk among students

    2. Rules: Specify expected and forbidden actions in the class; have a few general rules

    3. Rules for elementary school

      a. Be polite and helpful

      b. Respect other people's property

      c. Listen quietly while others are speaking

      d. Do not hit, shove, or hurt others

      e. Obey all school rules

    4. Rules for secondary school

      a. Bring all needed materials to class

      b. Be in your seat and ready to work when the bell rings

      c. Respect and be polite to everyone

      d. Respect other people's property

      e. Listen and stay seated while someone else is talking

      f. Obey all school rules

    5. Consequences

      a. Determine beforehand the consequences for following or breaking rules

      b. Logical consequences: have the student go back and do it right

      c. Consequences should be clear and enforceable

  D. Getting started: The first weeks of class

    1. Effective managers for elementary students

      a. Effective teachers organized from the first day, giving children interesting tasks, monitoring behavior as a whole group, teaching rules, and consequating misbehavior immediately

      b. Ineffective teachers gave vague or complicated rules with consistent consequences; procedures were not taught or practiced, and teachers frequently left the room

    2. Effective managers for secondary students

        a. Focus on establishing rules

        b. Standards for academic work and class behavior clearly communicated

        c. Infractions of rules dealt with quickly

        d. In low-ability classes, students given variety of tasks in one period

        e. Overall, student behavior is closely monitored so students cannot avoid work with consequences

IV. Maintaining a good environment for learning

  A. Encouraging engagement

    1. Lesson format

        a. Increasing teacher supervision increases student engaged time

        b. Providing cues on next steps and materials for completion of task

        c. If students are interested, they will be motivated to stay on task

    2. Involvement without supervision

        a. Well-planned systems

        b. Guidelines: Encouraging Student Responsibility

  B. Prevention is the best medicine: Kounin's study of effective classroom managers

    1. Effective managers better at preventing problems

    2. "Withitness"

        a. Being aware of what is happening in the classroom

        b. Stopping minor disruptions before they become major

        c. Avoid target errors: blaming the wrong student for misbehavior

        d. Avoid timing errors: waiting too long before intervening in misbehavior

        e. If two problems occur simultaneously, deal with the most serious one first

    3. Overlapping and group focus

        a. Overlapping: keeping track of and supervising several activities at the same time

        b. Group focus: keeping as many students as possible involved in appropriate class activities

    4. Movement management

        a. Making smooth transitions, maintaining an appropriate pace, and using variety when changes are necessary

        b. Avoid slowdown: taking too much time to start new activities

  C. Dealing with discipline problems

    1. Making sure students get back to work: eye contact, move closer, and use non-verbal signals

    2. Reminding students of procedures

    3. Calmly asking student to state correct procedure

    4. Assertively, telling student to stop misbehavior

  D. Special problems with secondary students

    1. Enforcing established consequences for incomplete work

    2. Students who continually break the same rules:

        a. Seat difficult students away from others who can be influenced

        b. Be consistent about consequences

        c. Encourage self-management techniques

        d. Remain friendly
    3. The defiant, hostile student:
        a. Get out of situation, allow cool down time
        b. Follow through with consequences
        c. Talk privately about outburst
    4. Violence or destruction of property: send for help, get names of participants and witnesses

V. Special programs for classroom management
    A. Group consequences: Positive group consequences can build cooperation among students
        1. Good Behavior Game
            a. Divide class into teams and give a discipline mark if a team member transgresses a "good behavior" rule
            b. Team with the fewest marks receives a special reward or privilege
        2. Reward based on the good behavior of the whole group (e.g. listening to a radio)
        3. Reward to group if a single problem student behaves
        4. Caution in applying group behavioral consequences:
            a. A group can reject a poorly behaving student because whole group suffers
            b. Difficult students may need individual arrangements
    B. Token reinforcement programs
        1. Tokens are symbolic rewards which can later be exchanged for prizes or privileges
        2. Schedules of giving tokens
            a. When system begins, tokens are given continuously, exchanged often for reward
            b. Once system works, intermittent tokens are given and time between exchange is longer
        3. Home-based consequences: parents provide reward based on school report of tokens earned (caution: do not use if parents may punish severely for poor reports)
        4. When to use token reinforcement systems
            a. To motivate students who are completely disinterested and unresponsive
            b. To encourage students who have failed to make academic progress
            c. To deal with a class that is out of control
            d. Mentally retarded students respond to concrete, direct token reinforcement
        5. Before using token system, make sure curriculum and management fit students
    C. Contingency contract programs
        1. Individual contract with a student describing what behavior will earn which reward
            a. Students may participate in deciding on behaviors and rewards
            b. Students learn to set reasonable goals and abide by terms of contract
        2. In this, as in other reward systems, remember extrinsic rewards may undermine intrinsic motivation

VI. The need for communication
    A. Message sent - message received

1. Responding to what one thinks was said or meant, not necessarily to the message sent or intended
   a. Body language, tone of voice, and choice of words convey messages
   b. Students may hear unintended message and react to it
2. Paraphrase rule
   a. Participants must summarize in their own words what the previous speaker said before responding
   b. Speaker explains again if misunderstood
   c. Cycle continues until the speaker agrees that the listener has heard the correct message
B. Diagnosis: Whose problem is it?
   1. If problem is student's: respond with active or empathetic listening
   2. If problem is teacher's: solution is found through problem-solving with student
   3. Deciding problem ownership: does the student's action concretely and tangibly affect me or prevent me from fulfilling my role as a teacher?
C. Counseling: The student's problem
   1. Empathetic listening: hearing student's intent and emotions; reflecting them back through paraphrasing
   2. Four components of empathetic listening:
      a. Blocking out external stimuli
      b. Attending to verbal and nonverbal message
      c. Differentiating between intellectual and emotional content
      d. Making inferences about speaker's feelings
D. Confrontation and assertive discipline
   1. "I" messages
      a. Teacher owns the problem and must intervene to change the student's behavior
      b. Description of student's behavior, how it affects you as a teacher, and how you feel about it
   2. Assertive discipline
      a. Clear, firm, non hostile response style
      b. Teachers make expectations clear and follow through with established consequence
      c. Students have clear choice: follow rules or accept consequences
      d. Mistakes of the passive or non assertive response style
      e. Mistakes of the hostile response style
      f. Assertive response style: communicates teacher's care for student and learning in calm, firm, and confident manner, with expectations clearly stated; rules are not debated
      g. Table 11-2: Passive, Hostile, and Assertive Teacher Responses
   3. Conflict and negotiations
      a. If I-message or assertive response fails to change behavior, a conflict situation arises
      b. Three methods of resolving conflict: teacher imposes solution, teacher gives in to student demands, or "no-lose method" used (define the problem, generate many possible solutions, evaluate each solution, make a decision, determine how to implement the solution, evaluate the success of

the solution)
Point/Counterpoint: Does Assertive Discipline Work?
VII. Spaces for learning
  A. Interest-area arrangements
    1. Note the fixed features that you must deal with
    2. Have easy access to materials in a well-organized place to store them
    3. Provide students with clean, convenient surfaces on which to use equipment
    4. Make sure work areas are private and quiet
    5. Arrange that you can see the students and they can see instruction
    6. Avoid dead spaces and racetracks
    7. Provide choices
    8. Provide flexibility
    9. Give students a place to keep their personal belongings
  B. Personal territories
    1. Action zones: Where participation is the greatest (not necessarily the front)
    2. Home-base formations work well for whole-class instruction and allow for cooperative work
VIII. Summary
IX. Key terms and concepts
X. What would you do?
XI. Teachers' casebook

Key Points

The need for organization

- Classrooms are ecologies -- the environment and inhabitants are constantly interacting

  - Classrooms are multidimensional, with differing individuals who have various goals, and perform various tasks within particular time pressures

  - Classrooms are also characterized by simultaneity, with many things happening at once, and immediacy (very fast pace)

  - Classrooms are unpredictable: Even with best plans, disruptions are likely

  - Classrooms are public: Students are constantly evaluating interactions between teacher and other students and judging teacher's fairness

  - Classrooms have histories

- The main management task is to achieve order by gaining and maintaining student cooperation in class activities

  - Management in early elementary grades emphasizes direct teaching of rules and procedures

  - Management in middle elementary grades involves less time spent teaching new rules than time spent monitoring and maintaining management system

  - Late elementary-early high school grades need teachers to motivate students who are concerned with peer relations; teacher must channel challenges to authority productively

  - In the late high school grades, teachers must fit curriculum to student interest and abilities and help students become more self-managing in learning

The goals of classroom management

- A major goal of classroom management is to provide more time for learning, and reduce time lost to interruptions and rough transitions

  - Allocated time: Time set aside for learning

  - Engaged time: "Time on task"; time spent attending actively to specific learning tasks

  - Academic learning time: Time in which students are actually succeeding at learning task

- Another major goal of learning is to provide access to learning

  - Explicit participation structures are rules that clearly define participation in various activities

  - Implicit participation structures determine students' ability to participate; this is influenced by the participation structures of the home

- Another goal of learning is to encourage student self-management

Creating a positive learning environment

- Procedures: Prescribed steps for an activity in the classroom

  - Administrative routines: Taking attendance, etc.

- Student movement: Entering and leaving room

- Housekeeping: Taking care of classroom and personal items

- Routines for accomplishing lessons: Collecting and distributing papers

- Interactions between teacher and student

- Talk among students

- <u>Rules</u>: Statements specifying expected and forbidden actions in the class

- Consequences should be clear, enforceable, logical, and consistent

- Getting started: Effective teachers are organized from the first day, giving children interesting tasks, monitoring behavior as a whole group, teaching rules, and consequating misbehavior immediately

- Effective managers for secondary students focus on establishing rules; standards for academic work and class behavior are clearly communicated; infractions of rules are dealt with quickly; and student behavior is closely monitored so students cannot avoid work without consequences

Maintaining a good environment for learning

- Student engaged time is increased via lesson formats that provide cues on next steps and materials for completion of task

- Kounin's study of effective classroom managers shows that effective managers are better at preventing problems

    - <u>"Withitness"</u>: Awareness of everything happening in the classroom

        - Avoid <u>target errors</u>: Blaming the wrong student for misbehavior

        - Avoid <u>timing errors</u>: Waiting too long before intervening in misbehavior

    - <u>Overlapping</u>: Supervising several activities at the same time

    - <u>Group focus</u>: Keeping as many students as possible involved in class activities

    - <u>Movement management</u>: Making smooth transitions, maintaining an appropriate pace, and using variety

- Discipline problems can be handled by making sure students get back to work, using eye contact, moving closer, and using non-verbal signals to remind students of procedures

- Special problems with secondary students may involve students who continually break the same rules

  - Be consistent about consequences

  - Encourage self-management techniques

  - Remain friendly

  - For the defiant, hostile student, allow cool down time and talk privately about outburst, but maintain consequences for misbehavior

  - In cases of violence or destruction of property, send for help, get names of participants and witnesses

Special programs for classroom management

- Group consequences: Class as a whole is rewarded or punished for adhering to, or violating, the rules of conduct

- Good Behavior Game: The class is divided into teams and given a discipline mark if a team member transgresses a "good behavior" rule

- Token reinforcement programs: Students earn tokens for academic work and for positive classroom behavior that are periodically exchanged for some desired reward

  - Tokens: Symbolic rewards that can later be exchanged for prizes or privileges

  - When system begins, tokens are given continuously, exchanged often for reward; then an intermittent token schedule is implemented

  - In a home-based consequence system, parents provide reward based on school report of tokens earned

  - Token reinforcement systems can be used to motivate students who are completely uninterested and unresponsive, to encourage students who have failed to make academic progress, and to deal with a class that is out of control

- Contingency contract: A contract between teacher and individual student specifying what the student must do to earn a particular privilege or reward

- Students may participate in deciding on behaviors and rewards

- Students learn to set reasonable goals and abide by terms of contract

The need for communication

- Students sometimes respond to what they think a teacher said or meant, not necessarily to the message intended

- Teachers must decide <u>problem ownership</u>: Does the student's action concretely and tangibly affect me or prevent me from fulfilling my role as a teacher?

  - If problem is student's: Respond with active or empathetic listening

  - If problem is teacher's: Solution is found through problem-solving and empathetic listening with student

  - <u>Empathetic listening</u>: Hearing student's intent and emotions; reflecting them back through paraphrasing

- Using confrontation and assertive discipline may be necessary if problem is "teacher-owned"

  - <u>"I" messages</u>: Give a clear, non-accusatory statement of how something is affecting you

    - Teacher owns the problem and must intervene to change the student's behavior

    - Give a description of student's behavior, how it affects you as a teacher, and how you feel about it

  - <u>Assertive discipline</u>: Clear, firm, non-hostile response style

- Conflict and negotiations: Three methods of resolving conflict include teacher's imposing solution, teacher's giving in to student demands, or using "no-lose method" (defining the problem, generating many possible solutions, evaluating each solution, making a decision, determining how to implement the solution, and evaluating the success of the solution)

Spaces for learning

- Space can be organized by territory (permanent seating) or by function (work centers to which everyone has access)

- Use the setting to attain teaching objectives by first deciding what activities you want the classroom to accommodate and then draw floor plans to match

- Verbal interaction is concentrated in the <u>action zone</u>: The center front and in a line up the center of the classroom

  - Teachers should move around room, making eye contact and involving those at back of room

  - <u>Home-base formation</u>: Arrangement for students' desks suitable for a wide number of teaching-learning situations

Concept Map: PREPARING FOR THE FIRST DAY OF CLASS

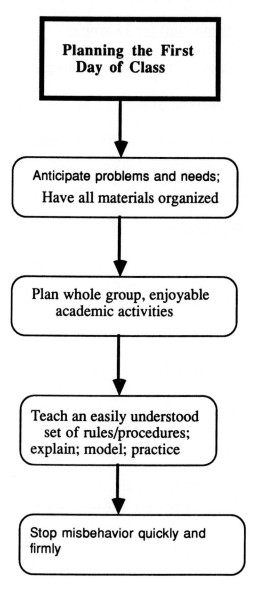

Do You Know This?

Answering these questions will help you to check yourself on your mastery of the chapter objectives.

The Need for Organization

Can you describe the special managerial demands of classrooms and relate these demands to students of different ages?

Creating a Positive Learning Environment

Give a list of rules and procedures for an elementary and a secondary class.

How would you plan for organizing your first week of teaching?

Maintaining a Good Environment for Learning

Can you describe Kounin's suggestions for preventing management problems?

Special Programs for Classroom Management

How might you respond to a student who seldom completes work?

Can you compare the use of various types of group consequences, token reinforcement systems, and contingency contracts to enhance classroom management?

The Need for Communication

What are two different approaches for dealing with a conflict between teacher and student or between two students?

Spaces for Learning

Describe how you would arrange the physical environment of your classroom to fit your learning goals and teaching methods.

Key Terms and Concepts

DEFINITIONS: Concepts in Classroom Management

Write explanations for the following pairs of terms. Your explanation should clearly distinguish the two from one another. Check the text to see if your explanations are equivalent.

Allocated/Engaged time _____

_____

Procedures/Rules _____

_____

Time on task/Academic learning time _____

_____

APPLICATION: Kounin's Management Strategies

Mrs. Graham is considered an effective classroom manager. While she takes roll in the morning, students are writing in their journals. When the children begin their reading lesson, Mrs. Graham makes sure all students are attending to the information. She is aware of each student's behavior, sometimes reminding students at their seats of the need for task focus even when she is occupied with a small group at the rear of the classroom. Describe in Kounin's terms what Mrs. Graham is doing that demonstrate effective management strategies:

Overlapping _____

_____

Group focus _____

_____

"Withitness" _____

_____

APPLICATION: Token Reinforcement Programs

Mr. Fernández has been called in as a long-term substitute to replace a teacher whose classroom management style was overly permissive. The class is disrespectful and disorderly. He decides to use a token reinforcement system. Suggest ways that this might be implemented in the following aspects:

Choice of prizes and privileges _____

_____

Schedule of administering tokens _____

_____

Organizing home-based consequences

IDENTIFICATION: Who Owns the Problem?

For each of the situations below, choose "Teacher" or "Student" to indicate "who owns the problem." For answers, see Answer Key.

_____ 1. A student tears out a page in a literature book.

_____ 2. A child has difficulty concentrating because his parents are getting a divorce.

_____ 3. Marvin is upset because Julio does not want to be his friend.

_____ 4. Kathryn comes in from the playground in tears because the other children not let her play with them.

_____ 5. Terry is not paying attention while another child gives an oral report.

_____ 6. Olivia continually arrives at school tardy.

_____ 7. Ching-Yuan has lost her lunch money twice this week.

_____ 8. Leticia seems depressed and does not want to participate in the spelling bee.

_____ 9. When Mr. Foster was absent, the class showed disrespect to the substitute.

_____ 10. James reports that someone has taken his new pencil eraser from his desk.

APPLICATION: Empathetic Listening

Paraphrase each of the following student statements to demonstrate empathetic listening. The first one has been done for you.

1. "Do we have to have music again today? I hate singing!"

   Paraphrase: _"You don't want to sing today, is that it?"_

2. "I scraped my knee on the playground. It hurts!"

Paraphrase: _____

3.   "My dog got really sick yesterday. We had to take her to the vet."

Paraphrase: _____

4.   "I can't seem to get this portrait sketch right. The chin still looks off-center."

Paraphrase: _____

IDENTIFICATION: Assertive, Hostile or Passive Discipline

In each situation below, several contrasting responses are given. Label each response with one of the following response styles: Assertive, Hostile, or Passive. For correct answers, see Answer Key.

1. Students are leaving the lunch table messy.

    _____   a.   "I'm sick and tired of your acting like pigs. Now pick up everything!"

    _____   b.   "You boys and girls will have to try harder to be clean."

2. You overhear a student making a rude and disparaging remark about another student's appearance.

    _____   a.   "I don't like what I just heard. I want you to come in immediately after school to discuss this."

    _____   b.   "You shouldn't make fun of other people. How would that make you feel?"

3. A kindergarten boy has consistently bullied other students on the playground. You notice that he has just pushed Yoshiko, a tiny girl, and made her cry.

    _____   a.   "You're just a big bully. You should be ashamed of yourself!"

    _____   b.   "We don't push other children. You will have to go inside now."

CASE STUDY: Contingency Contracting

Jeremy entered Washington Elementary School in the middle of the school year. He has not mastered the multiplication tables; this is necessary for learning double-digit multiplication. To encourage Jeremy to master these facts independently, Mrs. Shimatsu arranges for a contingency contract for Jeremy. Describe the details of such a contract.

CASE STUDY: The First Week of Teaching

Mrs. Klein is preparing for her first week of teaching. She wants to start the year off well. What should be her classroom management priorities?

CASE STUDY: Action Zone

Dr. Fitzpatrick is visiting a student teacher's classroom to observe the instruction. She notices that Mr. Llewellyn, the student teacher, uses a recitation technique to solicit and then respond to student's answers. He calls on students seated only in the front row in the middle aisle. After the lesson, she discusses her observation with him. He is surprised that he has been involving only a select group of students. What kinds of suggestions could Dr. Fitzpatrick offer which would help Mr. Llewellyn to expand the number of students in the "action zone"?

PRACTICE TEST: Multiple Choice

1. Which of the following best exemplifies what Doyle means by "multidimensional" classrooms?

   a. Everything happens at once.
   b. Events are unpredictable.
   c. Events rapidly occur.
   d. Students differ in attitudes and abilities.

2. At which age level is the direct teaching of the classroom rules and procedures most critical to effective classroom management?

   a. Early elementary
   b. Middle elementary
   c. Late elementary to middle school
   d. High school

3. One of the most important goals of classroom management is to expand the number of minutes available for learning. The time available for learning is known as _____ time.

   a. allocated
   b. classroom
   c. engaged
   d. academic learning

4. Class rules specify
    a. how to accomplish classroom activities.
    b. appropriate and forbidden actions.
    c. desired behaviors and consequences.
    d. routines for handling materials and completing assignments.

5. Which of the following is a rule that, based on your textbook's recommendations, seems more appropriate for secondary school classes than for elementary school classes?
    a. Bring all needed materials to class.
    b. Respect other people's property.
    c. Listen while others are speaking.
    d. Obey all school rules.

6. At the beginning of the school year, effective managers will
    a. practice school routines such as fire drills.
    b. explain and review rules.
    c. use vague rather than specific criticisms.
    d. all of the above.

7. Greg was trying to pass Bill a note, but Bill kept his eyes on his own work and thought, "Why does Greg do this to me? Mrs. Peeper will spot him for sure. She never misses anything. You would think she could read minds." Mrs. Peeper could be described as
    a. exhibiting overlapping.
    b. being wary.
    c. showing withitness.
    d. a good movement manager.

8. Mrs. Jones always seems to be talking to Jodie and Ruth. The rest of the class is often left to do independent work while she attends to these two students. Mrs. Jones is failing to maintain
    a. group focus.
    b. movement management flow.
    c. participation structuring.
    d. assertive disciplinary action.

9. Your textbook suggests that as a first step in dealing with a discipline problem, teachers should
    a. give a student a soft reprimand.
    b. ask the student to state the correct rule or procedure.
    c. give the student a nonverbal signal to stop.
    d. tell the student in a clear, assertive way to stop the misbehavior.

10. All of the following are components of empathetic listening <u>except</u>

    a. attending to both verbal and nonverbal messages.
    b. taking account of all the stimuli surrounding the speaker.
    c. differentiating between emotional and intellectual content.
    d. making inferences regarding speaker's feelings.

PRACTICE TEST: Essay

A. How are the classroom management demands different between the upper elementary grades and high school?

B. What can you predict might be the results when a teacher punishes the whole class for one student's misbehavior?

Answer Key

IDENTIFICATION: Whose Problem Is It?

1. **Teacher**
2. **Student**
3. **Student**
4. **Teacher**
5. **Teacher**
6. **Debatable: The teacher is inconvenienced, but how much responsibility has the parent assumed for getting the child to school on time? This may depend on the age of the child.**
7. **Student**
8. **Student**
9. **Teacher**
10. **Teacher**

IDENTIFICATION: Assertive, Hostile or Passive Discipline

1.   a. **Hostile**
     b. **Passive**
2.   a. **Assertive**
     b. **Passive**
3.   a. **Hostile**
     b. **Assertive**

PRACTICE TEST: Multiple Choice

1. d   According to Doyle, classrooms are multidimensional because <u>many individuals, all with differing goals, preferences, attitudes and abilities</u>, must share resources, accomplish a number of tasks, and so on.

2. a   <u>Early elementary</u> students are <u>unfamiliar</u> with their roles. Direct teaching of classroom rules and procedures thus becomes essential at this level.

3. a   <u>Allocated time</u> is the time available for learning. Just because a certain amount of time is allocated, however, does not guarantee that students will be actively learning (engaged) for all or most of that period. Thus, allocated time provides a less useful indication of good management then does "academic learning time."

4. b   Class rules specify <u>appropriate and inappropriate actions</u> -- the "do's" and "don't's" of classroom life. They are more oriented toward general behaviors than are procedures, which deal with desired ways of completing specific tasks.

5. a   Elementary students may not be mature or responsible enough to "<u>bring all needed materials to class</u>." Secondary students, however, should generally be expected to have their materials with them. More essential rules for elementary students would appear to be respecting others' property, listening to others, and obeying all school rules.

6. b   During the first few weeks of the school year, effective managers will <u>explain and review rule</u>s. They <u>don't</u> spend time practicing non-essential routines such as fire drills. They also tend to use specific rather than vague criticisms when misbehavior occurs.

7. c   Mrs. Peeper is a "<u>with-it</u>" teacher. Kounin defined "withitness" as conveying to students an awareness of everything that is happening in the classroom. Mrs. Peeper is one of those teachers who seems to have "eyes in the back of their heads."

8. a   <u>Maintaining a group focus</u> means keeping as many students as possible involved inappropriate class activities and avoiding narrowing in on just one or two students. This is a way teachers can ensure that all students understand the material and are participating.

9. c   Your textbook suggests making eye contact or using some other <u>nonverbal signal</u> as a first step to dealing with a discipline problem. If the nonverbal signal does not work, more overt interventions, such as reminders and commands to stop, should be used.

10. b   Empathetic, or active, listening involves reflecting back to the student what you hear him or her saying. It should capture the emotions, intent, and meaning behind them. To do this, you must often block out external stimuli. Therefore, you should <u>not take account of all stimuli surrounding the speaker</u>.

PRACTICE TEST: Essay

A.   Effective teachers in the middle and upper elementary grades are those who are organized from the first day, giving children interesting tasks, monitoring behavior as a whole group, teaching rules, and consequating misbehavior immediately. The time spent monitoring and maintaining the management system is more time consuming than directly teaching rules. At the secondary level, time must be spent motivating students who are concerned with peer relations; teachers must channel challenges to authority into more productive pursuits. The curriculum must be tailored to student interests and abilities, and teachers must help students become more self-managing in learning.

B.   Students may become alienated because a whole group should not suffer for the misbehavior or mistakes of one individual. If the group has no real influence over that person, the consequences may be that the whole group turns against the offender.

12

Teachers and Teaching

Teaching Outline

I. What Do You Think?

II. The first step: Planning
   A. Planning determines what students will learn
   B. Teachers engage in various levels of planning
      1. Year, term, unit, week and day; experienced teachers find unit planning most important
      2. All levels must be coordinated
      3. Beginning of year planning very important
   C. Plans provide flexible framework for action; reduce uncertainty in teaching
   D. There is no one model for effective planning

III. Objectives for learning
   A. Instructional objective: Clear statement of what students are intended to learn through instruction
   B. Kinds of objectives
      1. Behavioral objectives use terms such as "list," "calculate"
      2. Cognitive objectives use terms like "recognize." "apply"; tend to be more general
      3. Mager: Start with the specific
         a. Verb phrase describing intended student behavior
         b. Conditions under which student performance will occur
         c. Criterion for acceptable performance
         d. Table 12-1: Mager's Three-Part System
      4. Gronlund: Start with the general
         a. State objective first in general terms
         b. List sample behaviors that would indicate student has attained general objective
         c. Fewer objectives, thus saving time; understanding is the purpose
         d. Recent research tends to favor this approach
         e. Table 12-2: Gronlund's Combined System of Writing Objectives
   C. Are objectives useful?
      1. Student achievement
         a. Most helpful with loosely organized and less structured activities, lectures and films
         b. Helps students focus on important information; may increase achievement
         c. Objectives may not be effective for cognitive skills such as transfer
      2. Criticisms of objectives
         a. Objectives that are too explicit may lead to limited focus on trivial things easily specified
         b. If only low-level abilities are specified as outcomes, it might hinder more subtle thinking such as student questions and exploration of the subject

        matter
    3. In defense of objectives, what are the advantages?
       a. Can humanize educational process by making students aware of what is expected
       b. Help to focus learning and set criteria
    4. Guidelines: Developing Instructional Objectives
  D. Taxonomy: classification system of educational objectives
    1. Types
       a. Cognitive, affective, and psychomotor domains
       b/ Behavior from different areas may occur simultaneously
    2. The cognitive domain
       a. Six levels of objectives: knowledge, comprehension, application, analysis, synthesis, and evaluation
       b Not necessarily a hierarchy
       c. Using cognitive objectives for evaluation
       d. Different types of test items are appropriate for objectives at various levels of Bloom's taxonomy
       e. Objective tests: measure knowledge, comprehension, application, and analysis levels if well constructed
       f Essay tests: more appropriate for measuring synthesis and evaluation levels; can work at the middle-level objectives
    3. The affective domain
       a. Objective range from least committed and emotionally involved to most committed
       b. Five basic objectives: receiving, responding, valuing, organization, and characterization by value
       c. Specific learning objectives: state what students will actually be doing when they are receiving, responding, and so on
       d. Evaluating affective objectives (Useful for diagnostic purposes: to see what values students bring to class
       e. Final evaluation: helps teacher gauge attitude or value changes
       f. Difficult to achieve valid self-reporting about values and beliefs; anonymous questionnaires may be useful
    4. The psychomotor domain
       a. Objectives range from lowest level of observable movements to highest
       b. Cangelosi: objectives in psychomotor domain
       c. Voluntary muscle capabilities that require endurance, strength, flexibility, agility, and speed
       d. Ability to perform a specific skill
       e. Methods of evaluating psychomotor objectives.
V. How to teach: Searching for the keys to success
  A. Do teachers make a difference?
    1. Coleman Report and Jencks' study: Teachers have very little impact on student learning
       a. Research failed to examine actual classroom activity
       b. Research looked only at groups of teachers instead of individual behavior

      c. Correlational research looked at teachers' verbal ability or social class, not at the effects of individual teacher's behavior

    2. Classroom studies that resulted from the challenge have profound implications for teaching

  B. Methods for studying effective teaching include direct observation, case studies, interviewing, questionnaires, association of achievement and teacher behavior, and other methods

VI. Characteristics of effective teachers

  A. Teachers' knowledge

    1. Knowing about knowing: How to transform their knowledge into curriculum

    2. Teachers must know the structure, functions, and development of the subject matter

    3.. Problems transforming knowledge

      a. Knowing the structure of the subject matter involves identifying concept relationships across subunits of the domain and being able to provide a knowledge framework

      b Knowing the function of the information taught means being able to teach how it is used or needed in everyday life; or when to use it

      c. Knowing how knowledge develops in individuals means being able to relate to alternative forms of levels of understanding, to deal with partial knowledge

  B. Organization and clarity

    1. Improves student learning and student rating of teachers

    2. Important connection between clarity, knowledge of the subject, and student learning

    3. Clarity is expressed in precise language, avoiding ambiguity

    4. Planning for clarity

      a. Possible student problems are anticipated

      b. Examples, definitions, and analogies are prepared

      c. Lesson is logically sequenced

      d. Introduction to the lesson, telling what is to be learned and how

      e. Explain the "how" of activities to be done

    5. Clarity during the lesson

      a. Important aspects of the lesson are emphasized

      b. Make sure one step is mastered before proceeding to the next

      c. Use models, examples, illustrations

      d. Pace smoothly, pausing to check for understanding by asking for summaries

      e. Reteach if necessary

      f. Transitions are signaled, with explanatory links used to connect ideas

      g. Outline topics or list key points

      h. Define new terms if necessary, being precise and specific

    6. After the lesson

      a. Spot-check student understanding as they do problems

      b. Correct misunderstanding quickly, including checking homework quickly

      c. Tape-record a lesson for a self-check

  C. Warmth and enthusiasm

1. Correlations between teacher warmth and student attitude, attentiveness and involvement
2. This trait is not necessarily related to student achievement
3. Warmth and enthusiasm are high-inference characteristics, difficult to define
   a. Behaviors may include animated delivery, demonstrative gestures, high energy level
   b. Easygoing acceptance of students' ideas and questions, use of descriptive words
4. Guidelines: Teaching Effectively

VII. Teaching methods: Direct instruction
   A. Lecturing and explaining
      1. Advantages
         a. Communicating large amount of information to many students in a short time
         b. Information can be integrated from many sources
         c. Good for introducing new topic and giving background information
         d. Promotes accurate critical student listening
         e. Appropriate for lower levels in cognitive and affective domains
      2. Disadvantages
         a. Students have trouble listening and tune out
         b. Students in a passive mode
         c. Does not accommodate varying learning rates
   B. Recitation and questioning
      1. Recitation format: Teacher questioning, student responding, and teacher feedback
         a. Structure (teacher setting framework)
         b. Solicitation (asking questions)
         c. Reaction (teacher praising, correcting, and expanding)
      2. Kinds of questions
         a. Categorizing according to Bloom's taxonomy
         b. Table 12-5: Classroom Questions for Objectives in the Cognitive Domain
         c. Convergent (asking for only one right answer) or divergent (asking for many possible right answers) questions
      3. Fitting the questions to the students
         a. One study showed that high-level questions negatively related to student achievement (grade level, socioeconomic background, and test type were factors)
         b. Low ability students: use simple questions that allow a high percentage of correct answers followed by help if needed, and praise
         c. High ability students: use harder questions at both higher- and lower-levels with more critical feedback
         d. Thought-provoking questions appropriate with all students
         e. Teachers need to provide support but allow students ample time to consider response - 5 seconds of silence (longer wait brings more thoughtful responses)
         f. Make effective use of silence by asking students to jot down their answers
         g. Calling upon students: use index cards or pull names from jar to ensure

fairness
    4. Responding to student answers:
       a. Correct responses: accept answer and move on
       b. Correct but hesitant response: give feedback to student why answer is correct
       c. Wrong answers; an honest attempt: provide clues and ask student to elaborate; probe, give clues, simplify, review, or reteach
       d. Wrong answers, careless and silly: supply the correct response and go on

C. Seatwork and homework
    1. Well designed homework may increase achievement; seatwork should not be main mode of instruction
    2. Alternatives to workbooks and ditto sheets
       a. Silent reading and partner reading
       b. Writing letters, journals, and transcribing conversations
       c. Making up projects, working on reports, solving puzzles, computer activities
    3. Effective seatwork
       a. Meaningful extensions of lessons
       b. Students must be actively involved
       c. Before starting, students should be checked for understanding the assignment
       d. Accountability for work should be maintained
    4. Being available to students doing seatwork is more effective than offering help before they ask for it
    5. Structure is important: need clear objectives and materials available

D. Putting it all together: Models of direct instruction
    1 Limitations
       a. Effectiveness defined as improvement on standardized tests
       b. Applies best to clearly structured knowledge and skills
       c. Tasks are unambiguous and can be taught step-by-step
       d. Step-by-step approach is less appropriate for creative writing or complex problem solving
    2. Rosenshine's six teaching functions:
       a. Review and check previous day's work
       b. Present new material
       c. Provide guided practice
       d. Give feedback and correctives
       e. Provide independent practice
       f. Review weekly and monthly
    3. Hunter's mastery teaching program:
       a. Emphasis on six teaching functions
       b. Emphasis on preparing students to learn and presenting material effectively
       c. Table 12.6 The Hunter Mastery Teaching Program: Selected Principles
    4. Good and Grouws' Missouri Mathematics Program:
       a. Resulted from study of effective math teachers
       b. Successful with elementary and middle school students

   c. Emphasizes meaning and understanding in presentation, rather than procedures and rules

   d. Demonstrations, illustrations, diagrams, and models are important

   e. Table 12.7: Missouri Math Program: Key Instructional Elements

 E. Adapting models to student abilities

  1. Aptitude-Treatment Interactions (ATI)

   a. Individual differences related to learning (aptitudes) interact with particular teaching methods (treatments)
interacted with ability to show variable effects of instructional type

   b. Teachers must be prepared to be flexible in meeting variable instructional needs of students: no single effective educational treatment

  2. Ability differences and prior knowledge

   a. Ability: readiness to profit from instruction

   b. The less students know, the more they need instructional support

   c. When students have little prior knowledge, reduce information processing demands; organize materials around clear objectives; include visual support; find ways to focus attention and relieve burden on memory

   d. Low achieving students often have poor attitudes, motivation, and discipline

  3. Lesson formats for low-ability classes:

   a. More than one cycle of content presentation and student seatwork in each period

   b. Suggestions for making students more responsible for own work: short daily assignments, students keep records of grades and averages, make class participation count, help students use learning and metacognitive strategies

   c. Class atmosphere should remain friendly and supportive

  Point/Counterpoint: What is the Best Way to Help Students at Risk of Failing?

  4. Teaching high achievers

   a. Wider range of methods can be effective

   b. More nurturing style less important; thrive on fast pace and challenging tasks

   c. More material can be covered; less review; shorter guided practice

VIII. Criticism of direct instruction

 A. Teacher-centered instruction is limited to lower-level objectives

   a. Discourages independent thinking

   b. Innovative models ignored

 B. Based on a behavioral or receptive model of learning

   a. Teachers transmit knowledge but do not develop it within students

   b. Knowledge is broken into small segments and taught with reinforcement

 C. Rosenshine's factors that support complex learning (see Table 12.8)

 D. Being sensible about teaching

IX. Summary

X. Key terms and concepts

XI. What would you do?

XII. Teachers' casebook

Key Points

The first step: Planning

- Coordinated planning is needed for the school year, term, unit, week, and day

    - Experienced teachers find unit planning most important

    - Plans provide flexible framework for action and reduce uncertainty in teaching

Objectives for Learning

- Instructional objective: Clear statement of what students are intended to learn through instruction

    - Objectives promote student achievement by giving students structured goals

    - Communication is improved as teachers communicate expectations more clearly and consistently to students

    - Students' prior knowledge of evaluation criteria leads to more efficient studying

    - General objectives: Global, but can be ambiguous and not clearly measurable

    - Specific objectives: Defined in measurable terms

    - Behavioral objective: Instructional objective that is stated in terms of observable behaviors

    - Cognitive objective: Instructional objective that is stated in terms of higher-level thinking operations

    - Mager's approach uses verb phrases, conditions for the behavior to occur, and criteria for acceptable performance

    - Gronlund starts with the general objective first, then lists sample behaviors that would indicate student has attained general objective

- Objectives that are too explicit may lead to limited focus on trivial things easily specified

- Objectives should also involve subtle thinking such as student questions and exploration of the subject matter

- Objectives can humanize educational process by making students aware of what is expected

- Taxonomy: Classification system of educational objectives

  - Behavior from cognitive, affective, and psychomotor domains may occur simultaneously

    - Cognitive domain includes memory and reasoning objectives

    - Affective domain (emotional objectives): Receiving, responding, valuing

      - Helps teacher gauge attitude or value changes, before/after instruction

    - Psychomotor domain involves physical ability objectives, or ability to perform a specific skill

How to teach: Searching for keys to success

- Correlational studies in the 1950's and 1960's concluded that social class and student ability had more to do with learning than did teachers

- Researchers set out to devise methods for studying effective teaching

Characteristics of effective teachers

- Teacher's knowledge of subject matter is necessary, but not sufficient for student learning

  - Teachers must know how to transform their knowledge into curriculum that is understandable to students

  - Teachers must know the structure, function, and development of the material they teach

    - Structure: Relations among concepts, procedures, applications

    - Function: What subject is used for, what problems it solves

    - Development: Sequence of learning complex ideas

- Knowledge must be presented with organization and clarity

    - Clarity during lesson: adequate transitions between ideas, sequence of ideas, specific vocabulary

- Warmth and enthusiasm keeps students attentive and involved

Teaching methods: Direct instruction

- <u>Lecturing</u>: Instructional strategy in which the teacher gives an organized explanation for a topic

    - Phrases: Entry, presentation, and closure

    - Helps to integrate information from many sources, introduce new topic and give background information

    - Students in a passive mode may tune out or not receive accommodation to varying learning rates

- <u>Recitation</u>: Format of consisting of teacher questioning, student responding, and teacher feedback

    - Kinds of questions include convergent (asking for only one right answer) or divergent (asking for many possible right answers)

        - Low ability students may require simple questions that allow a high percentage of correct answers followed by praise

            - High ability students can receive harder questions at both higher- and lower-levels with more critical feedback

            - Thought-provoking questions appropriate with all students

            - Teachers should respond to student answers by accepting correct answers and moving on, or giving feedback to student to provide clues

- Group discussion utilizes students' communication skills and allows teacher to assume less dominant role

    - Some students may be reluctant to participate and may become anxious; others may dominate

- <u>Seatwork</u>: Independent classroom work which can include silent reading and partner reading, writing letters and journals, transcribing conversations, making up projects, working on reports, solving puzzles, and computer activities

- Effective seatwork is a meaningful extension of the lesson, with students actively involved and accountable for work

- Models of direct teaching include such terms as active teaching, explicit teaching, basic skills teaching

  - Rosenshine's six teaching functions: Review and check previous day's work; present new material; provide guided practice; give feedback and correctives; provide independent practice; review weekly and monthly

  - Hunter's Mastery Teaching Program: Anticipatory set; presentation; checking for understanding; guided practice; independent practice; evaluation; follow-up

  - Good and Grouws' Missouri Math Program provides structured math lessons

- Adapting models to students' abilities means matching teaching methods with students of differing abilities; this can involve honors courses, vocational courses, performing arts experiences, cooperative work-study, independent study or tracking into ability levels

- Aptitude-Treatment Interactions (ATI): Individual differences related to learning (aptitudes) interact with particular teaching methods (treatments)

  - Teachers must be prepared to be flexible in meeting variable instructional needs of students; there is no single effective educational treatment

  - Research on ability differences and prior knowledge shows that the less students know, the more they need instructional support

  - Lesson formats for low-ability classes should make students more responsible for own work; shorten daily assignments; have students keep records of grades and averages, make class participation count, help students use learning and metacognitive strategies

  - With high achievers, a wider range of methods can be effective, with a faster pace and challenging tasks; less review, and shorter guided practice

  - Overall, students who are younger, of low ability, or high anxiety need more structure, support, and direction; older, higher ability need freedom and higher performance standards

- Conclusions: Classroom teacher must decide on organization of classroom instruction and consider effects of methods with particular subjects and students

- Criticisms of direct instruction: success is limited to lower-level objectives; may stifle innovative teaching methods; may discourage independent thinking

- Rosenshine's factors that support complex learning: scaffolds to help students learn (procedural facilitators); modeling use of facilitators; modeling thinking out loud; anticipating difficult areas; providing prompts; regulating difficulty; providing half-done examples; reciprocal teaching; providing checklists

Concept Map: DIRECT INSTRUCTION

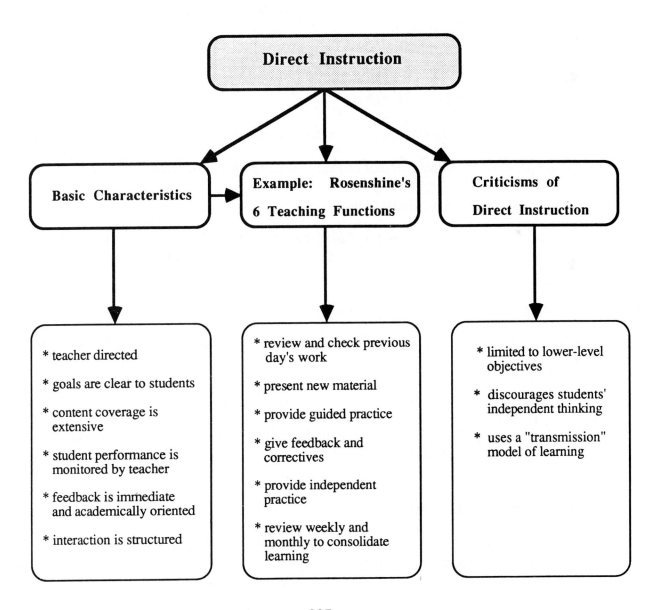

Do You Know This?

Answering these questions will help you to check yourself on your mastery of the chapter objectives.

The First Step: Planning

Can you describe a teacher's responsibility in planning: What is its function and what levels of plans are useful?

Objectives for Learning

Can you give several reasons for using instructional objectives?

Practice writing objectives for a lesson which you have observed. Use either Mager or Gronlund's approach.

Can you create objectives for cognitive, affective, and psychomotor learning?

Characteristics of Effective Teachers

Can you describe the characteristics that effective teachers seem to share?

Can you list steps of instruction that can insure clarity of presentation?

Teaching Methods: Direct Instruction

Describe situations in which each of the following formats would be most appropriate: Recitation and questioning, lecturing and explaining, group discussion, inquiry methods, seatwork, and individualized instruction, and computer-assisted instruction.

Can you plan a unit in your subject for a low-ability class?

Can you create a lesson in your subject area and make a plan for teaching it using direct instruction?

Models of Direct Instruction

Can you give examples of lessons based on direct instruction, on the Hunter model, and on the Missouri Mathematics Program?

Criticism of Direct Instruction

Can you summarize the criticisms of direct instruction and offer an alternative based on the cognitive/constructivist perspective?

Key Terms and Concepts

IDENTIFICATION: Domains of Objectives

Choose the domain which best describes each statement below (Cognitive, Affective, or Psychomotor). For answers, see Answer Key.

_____ 1. Catch a softball thrown from an outfielder in 8 out of 10 attempts.

_____ 2. Compare the battle readiness of Union and Confederate troops before the Battle of Manassas.

_____ 3. Determine the slope of a line given the coordinates of two points.

_____ 4. Show appreciation of a sonata by choosing a favorite movement after listening to a symphony recording.

_____ 5. Discover a general principle for the relation between pressure and temperature of a gas by performing a series of experiments.

_____ 6. Hold a stylus at the correct angle when carving a wood engraving.

_____ 7. Reinforce another student with appropriate praise after the contribution of a creative idea in a cooperative group.

_____ 8. Identify the turning point or climax of the plot in a short story.

APPLICATION: What is an Effective Teacher?

The following is a description of an ineffective teacher. For each category, supply the contrasting behaviors that would characterize an effective teacher.

After a busy weekend of skiing, Mr. Wilson came to school facing a new unit in mathematics on percentages and fractions for his sixth grade class. Since he had not taken the time to read the new chapter in the text, he was not familiar with the approach taken in presenting the material. He thought he could rely on his own previous knowledge, but when it came time to explain the material to the students, he did not include several important explanatory steps, apparently assuming that students could follow his lecture without the need for a careful sequence. He does not present the relationship between fractions and their corresponding percentages with a clear diagram or model, but rather he tries to teach students to memorize a series of formulas to convert fractions to percentages. This leaves students confused and unsure of when to apply which formula. Moreover, he cannot readily locate the worksheets he used with a similar unit last year and spends instructional time searching through his files for these materials. Consequently, the students begin talking among themselves, not focusing on the task at hand. Mr. Wilson becomes upset with the class, upbraiding them for misbehavior and penalizes them by withholding recess time. He reminds them that percentages are difficult and they cannot afford to fool around in class.

Knows subject matter _____

_____

Able to transform knowledge _____

_____

Organization and clarity _____

_____

Warmth and enthusiasm _____

_____

APPLICATION: Using Hunter's Lesson Plan Model

Ms. González is teaching her eighth grade English class a unit on poetry. The <u>haiku</u> form is the topic of today's class, a style of poetry which follows several other forms such as the lyric poem and the ballad. The <u>haiku</u> is a syllable-based non-rhyming poem which has three lines, with five syllables, seven syllables, and five syllables; it is based upon seasonal theme. Ms. González presents a series of such poems and will ask students to visualize an image and write their own <u>haiku</u>. Although the Hunter model is usually used with direct teaching of a basic skill, demonstrate how Ms. González could use the nine-step lesson plan outline below to generate a lesson which teaches <u>haiku</u>.

1. **Review** _____

_____

2. **Creating an anticipatory set** _____

_____

3. **Communicating lesson objectives** _____

_____

4. **Input of information** _____

_____

5. **Modeling** _____

_____

6. **Checking for understanding** _____

_____

7. **Guided practice** _____

_____

8. **Independent practice** _____

_____

9. **Evaluation** _____

_____

DEFINITIONS: Teaching Strategies

Write explanations for the following pairs of terms. Your explanations should clearly distinguish the two from one another. Check the text to make sure your explanations are equivalent.

Lecture/Recitation _____

_____

Individualized instruction/Team Assisted Individualization _____

_____

Computer tutorial/Computer simulation _____

_____

Convergent/Divergent questions _____

_____

Higher-order/Lower-order questions _____

_____

IDENTIFICATION: Higher and Lower Level Questioning

For each of the following questions, indicate whether it is higher-order (H) or lower-order (L). To check your answers, see Answer Key.

_____   1. What are the fifty states in the United States?

_____   2. What processes in the body are triggered by an histamine reaction?

_____   3. How can you show the speaker that you are a good listener?

_____   4. Who can tell me the name of the woman who founded the Red Cross?

_____   5. Did Macbeth and Lady Macbeth react differently to Duncan's murder?

_____   6. Let's review our colors. Which one is this one (points to red)?

_____   7. Describe the dwellings of the Sioux. How are these like other Plains Indians?

_____   8. Why were anti-trust laws necessary in the late nineteenth century?

_____   9. How many chromosomes do humans have?

_____   10. What are the nine positions on a baseball team?

APPLICATION: Writing Objectives

For each description of an activity given below, convert the statement into a behavioral objective using Mager's three components.

Ex.: Students will cut pictures out of magazines and paste them on cardboard to show the basic food groups.

Given magazines containing pictures of various foods (condition), students will group the foods into four basic food groups and create a collage on cardboard (behavior) which shows an arrangement of at least four different foods within each of the four groups (criterion).

1.   Students will play volleyball all period, using appropriate skills.

   Condition: _____

Behavior: _____

Criterion: _____

2.   Students will write a short ghost story for Halloween.

Condition: _____

Behavior: _____

Criterion: _____

3.   Students will plot an equation from a set of points.

Condition: _____

Behavior: _____

Criterion: _____

CASE STUDY: Matching Methods to Different Students' Abilities

Miss Rowlands has been assigned to a ninth grade low-ability group. The students seem to respond well to a highly structured, recitation model in a basic skills curriculum. However, Miss Rowlands wishes to incorporate teaching methods which she has used successfully in classes of higher ability students. In the areas given below, describe how Miss Rowlands could accomplish a transition in teaching methods for these students.

Expository teaching--> Cooperative learning_____

_____

Teacher-controlled learning --> Self-regulated learning _____

_____

Emphasis on basic skills --> Critical thinking skills _____

_____

CASE STUDY: Using Objectives

Mrs. Foster is teaching a unit called "Our Neighborhood." Today the second-grade students are drawing a map of their neighborhood. Mrs. Foster has noticed that several students have drawn only a few houses and then are ready to quit. Other students are drawing pictures of farm animals and rocket ships in their pictures, which are definitely <u>not</u> features of their neighborhood. Still other students have raised their hands several times, asking what needs to be included in their drawings.

When Mrs. Foster relates this experience to a peer in the teachers' lounge later that day, her colleague asks her what had been the objectives of that lesson. What might they have been? How might clarifying objectives before beginning have changed students' approach to the activity?

PRACTICE TEST: Multiple Choice

1. Which of the following is true regarding instructional planning?

    a. It is more critical at the beginning of the year than at any other time.
    b. Once plans are devised they should generally be followed without variation.
    c. It is more critical in elementary grades than in higher levels.
    d. For experienced teachers, daily planning is more important than unit or weekly planning.

2. The text defines an instructional objective as a

    a. broad and generalized description of instructional intent.
    b. clear and unambiguous description of instructional intent.
    c. specific listings of intended changes of behavior.
    d. summary of course content and intended activities.

3. Research indicates that announced instructional objectives increase learning

    a. only in isolated circumstances.
    b. in all common classroom situations.
    c. when instructional activities are less organized and structured.
    d. when instructional activities are more organized and structured.

4. Which of the verbs would be <u>least</u> desirable for use in a behavioral objective?

    a. Appreciates
    b. Lists
    c. Builds
    d. Isolates

5. Limitations and possible abuses of the use of objectives seem most likely to arise due to

a. current approaches to writing objectives having limited validity.
b. the failure by administrators to demand attention to quality in writing objectives.
c. trivial objectives being easier to specify than higher-level objectives.
d. students' using objectives as a basis for arguing about grades.

6. Psychologists generally agree that direct instruction is an effective system for teaching

   a. problem solving.
   b. creativity.
   c. abstract thinking.
   d. basic skills.

7. A student presents and defends her personal views on the desirability of having the current president nominate Supreme Court justices. The type of learning illustrated is

   a. evaluation.
   b. comprehension.
   c. application.
   d. synthesis.

8. All of the following are disadvantages of the lecture method of instruction <u>except</u>

   a. it reduces motivation for self-learning.
   b. some students may have trouble listening for more than a few minutes at a time.
   c. it does not allow for different paces in student learning.
   d. it puts students in a passive mode.

9. In identifying factors that support complex learning, what did Rosenshine mean by "procedural facilitators"?

   a. Devices that help students to check the quality of their responses
   b. Guides that prompt students to engage in certain learning activities while working on a task
   c. Half-done examples that leave out certain critical steps for students to complete
   d. Teachers' aides who can provide individual support to those experiencing difficulty

10. It is generally believed that teaching should become less direct as

    a. student ability decreases.
    b. student age decreases
    c. instructional goals become more affective in nature.
    d. teacher experience decreases.

PRACTICE TEST: Essay

A. Describe how a typical recitation lesson might be carried out in a class focusing on the writing of the Declaration of Independence. What are the advantages and disadvantages of using the recitation method in this content domain?

B. Hunter's Mastery Teaching Program and Rosenshine's six teaching functions present similar principles. Compare these models. What elements of effective instruction do they have in common?

Answer Key

IDENTIFICATION: Domains of Objectives

1. **Psychomotor**
2. **Cognitive**
3. **Cognitive**
4. **Affective**
5. **Cognitive**
6. **Psychomotor**
7. **Affective**
8. **Cognitive**

IDENTIFICATION: Higher and Lower Level Questioning

1. **L**
2. **H**
3. **H**
4. **L**
5. **H**
6. **L**
7. **H**
8. **H**
9. **L**
10. **L**

PRACTICE TEST: Multiple Choice

1. a Planning appears to <u>be more critical at the beginning of the year than at any</u> <u>other time</u> because many procedures, rules, and routines are established early. Plans should be flexible and initially concentrate on the unit level, followed by weekly and then daily planning.

2. b An instructional objective is a<u> clear and unambiguous description of your</u> <u>educational intentions</u> for your students.

3. c <u>Having instructional objectives seems to improve achievement </u>especially with activities such as lectures, films, and research projects that are <u>loosely</u> <u>organized and less structured</u>. With very structured materials like programmed instruction, objectives seem less important.

4. a. The verb "<u>appreciates</u>" would be the least desirable for use in behavioral objective because it is difficult to observe or operationally define. In contrast, verbs such as "list", "build," and "isolate" describe observable actions.

5. c The main cause of limitations and possible abuses of the use of objectives is that <u>trivial objectives are easier to specify than higher-level objectives</u>. Consequently, teachers might be inclined to emphasize instruction of lower-level skills and ignore new developments in their fields that do not fit well with present objectives.

6. d Direct instruction models have been proven to be effective in the teaching of <u>basic skills</u> involving tasks that are relatively unambiguous, which can be taught step-by-step and tested by standardized tests.

7. a The student is demonstrating <u>evaluation</u> skills by judging the desirability of having the President nominate Supreme Court justices. Evaluation is a high-order skill that involves forming an opinion on the worth or value of something.

8. a The lecture method puts students in a passive position and may prevent them from asking or thinking of questions. Also, students learn and comprehend at different paces, whereas a lecture established one pace. Students may become bored and "tune out." <u>There is no evidence that it reduces motivation for self-</u> <u>learning</u>.

9. b   Rosenshine defines procedural facilitators as scaffolding to help students learn implicit skills. More specifically, they serve as <u>guides that help to direct the individual into certain activities while engaged in learning</u> (e. g. a prompt to ask a question or reflect on something just read).

10. c   Teaching should become less direct as <u>instructional goals become more affective in nature</u>. As a teacher-centered and highly structured approach, direct instruction is less appropriate for developing affective goals than constructivist orientations such as discovery learning. Direct instruction would <u>not</u> be favored as students age and ability increase.

PRACTICE TEST: Essay

A. A recitation lesson in a class focusing on the writing of the Declaration of Independence would consist of the teachers' setting a framework, asking questions, and then praising, correcting, and expanding the students responses. For example, the teacher might ask a lower-order question such as "Where did the representatives meet to write the Declaration?" A student might answer, "Independence Hall." Then the teacher might react by praise/expansion: "And where is Independence Hall?" Alternatively, the teacher might ask a higher-order question such as, "What were the risks to the representatives as they met?" This question would then be followed by a student response, and teacher reaction. The advantages of the recitation method are that questions can be tailored to the ability of the students and students receive praise and feedback. Disadvantages of using the recitation method in this content domain may be that students are not given enough thinking time, or do not understand the question. Response opportunities may not be fairly distributed over all students.

B. **Rosenshine's Six Teaching Functions**	**The Hunter Mastery Teaching Program**
1. Review and check the previous day's work	Get students set to learn
2. Present new material	Provide information directly
3. Provide guided practice	Give guided practice

4. Give feedback and correctives	Check for understanding
5. Provide independent practice	Allow for independent practice
6. Review weekly and monthly to consolidate practice	Evaluation*
	Closure*

*Table 12.6 does not include these aspects of Hunter's model

Steps in common: Almost all, except Rosenshine's "Review weekly and monthly to consolidate practice." Hunter's "Evaluation" and "Closure" are a part of the "Seven-Step" lesson plan.

13

Rediscovering the Student in Teaching

Teaching Outline

I.   What Do You Think?
II. Perspectives on student-centered teaching
   A. The New Zealand studies: (Nuthall and Alton-Lee)
      1. What helps students to construct and remember accurate understandings
      2. Researchers record everything that happens in class, including presentations, handouts, assignments
      3. Detailed records are kept of students' activities
      4. Findings:
         a. Students learn different things from lessons; average scores are misleading
         b. Academic learning time is closely related to learning
         c. Information gained from demonstrations and charts is retained
         d. Students' prior knowledge shapes what they learn
      6. Conditions for learning from teaching
         a. Students must have opportunities to learn: sufficient time spent to clarify concepts and displace misconceptions
         b. Student must take advantage of these opportunities: pay attention, express orally or in writing what they are understanding
         c. Students must have resources to learn, including personal support, materials and equipment, relevant experiences
   B. APA's learner-centered psychological principles
      1.   Principle 1.   The nature of the learning process
      2.   Principle 2:   Goals of the learning process
      3.   Principle 3:   The construction of knowledge
      4.   Principle 4:   Higher-order thinking
      5.   Principle 5:   Motivational influences on learning
      6.   Principle 6:   Intrinsic motivation to learn
      7.   Principle 7:   Characteristics of motivation-enhancing learning tasks
      8.   Principle 8:   Developmental constraints and opportunities
      9.   Principle 9:   Social and cultural diversity
      10. Principle 10: Social acceptance, self-esteem, and learning
      11. Principle 11: Individual differences in learning
      12. Principle 12: Cognitive filters
III. Constructivist contributions
   A. The need for a constructivist approach
      1. Example: A student who had learned mathematics by memorizing an algorithm was unable to use this knowledge in problem solving
      2. A more effective way to utilize knowledge is needed
   B. Complex learning environments
      1. Students should deal with complex situations and ill-structured learning
      2. Students may need support as they work on complex problems

    C. Social negotiation
      1. Students should be able to establish and defend their own positions
      2. To facilitate this, students must talk and listen to one another
    D. Multiple representational content
      1. A variety of ways to present ideas and solve problems
      2. Use of different analogies, examples, and metaphors
    E. Understanding the knowledge construction process
      1. Differing assumptions about how knowledge is constructed, the role of the student in this process
      2. Different assumptions and experiences lead to different knowledges
IV. Student-centered instruction
    A. Planning from a constructivist perspective
      1. Students and teachers collaborate on goals of instruction, planning
      2. Learning environment respects students' individual interests and abilities
      3. Authentic assessment is used to help students demonstrate what they know
    B. Constructivist teaching practices
      1. See Table 13.1 Constructivist Teaching Practices
      2. Constructivist teaching includes a variety of learning methods
    C. Individualized instruction
      1. Students working with learning plans designed to meet their own individual needs, interests, and abilities
      2. Modifying lessons to fit individual needs:
        a. Pace of learning: students can set own pace
        b. Instructional objectives are tailored to needs and levels of students
        c. Students can use a variety of learning activities or materials
        d. Reading level: individualized units may need a wide range of materials
        e. Oral reports or diagrams can be used to demonstrate learning
      3. Research on individualized instruction
        a. Not superior to traditional forms if only form of instruction
        b. Depends on self-direction of students (a function of grade level)
        c. Elements of method can be incorporated into regular lesson
    D. Group discussion
      1. Students ask and respond to each other's questions
      2. Teacher becomes the moderator
      3. Advantages
        a. Direct involvement of students
        b. Utilizes students' communication skills, teaching how to justify and tolerate opinions
        c. Students can ask for clarification and information
        d. Students are given additional responsibility by sharing group leadership
      4. Disadvantages
        a. Unpredictable course; may easily digress
        b. Some students reluctant to participate and may become anxious; others may dominate
        c. Common background knowledge for each student required
        d. Large groups are unwieldy
      5. Guidelines: Leading Class Discussions

    E. Inquiry methods
       1. Format
          a. Presenting a puzzling event or problem
          b. Forming an explanatory hypothesis
          c. Collecting data to test hypothesis
          d. Drawing conclusions and reflecting on the problem
       2. Enable students to learn content and process at the same time
    F. Reciprocal teaching
       1. The process
          a. Summarizing passage content
          b. Questioning central point
          c. Clarifying difficult parts
          d. Predicting the next point
       2. An example of reciprocal teaching
       3. Applying reciprocal teaching
          a. Teacher models approach and students imitate behavior; gradual shift to student responsibility, matching task demands to abilities and using technique to diagnose students' thinking
    G. Humanistic education
       1. Includes the belief that each person constructs a unique reality
       2. Humanistic approaches stress the importance of feelings, open communication, and the worth of the individual
       3. Open schools group students by project and activity
       4. Learning involves hands-on, manipulatives
       5. Teachers use observation and work samples to guide further teaching
       6. These settings encourage creativity, cooperation, self-esteem, social adjustment, but academic learning is often no greater than in traditional classrooms
    H. Computers, videodiscs, and beyond
       1. Technology allows students to access resources and explore a wide variety of different worlds
       2. Much information is available at students' fingertips
       3. Interglobal connections and networks connect students around the world
       4. Computers can be used as learning environments, as tools, or as tutees
          a. Computer tutorials teach new materials with individualized pacing
          b. Simulations create situations in which students must apply learning
          c. Microworlds contain simplified but complete models of working systems
          d. Integrated information systems manage and pace student learning (also called integrated learning systems)
       5. Computers and learning: Some guidelines
          a. Take advantage of the capacity to individualize
          b. Involve students in decisions about hardware and software for the class
          c. Give students experience with technology as a tool
          d. Use computers as tools for your own work
  V. Constructivist teaching for different ages
    A. Early childhood/elementary
       1. Develop abilities in many areas while maintaining curiosity, zest for learning
       2. Emphasis should be on understanding, not just memorizing

    3. Constructing an understanding of numbers: Students can use mathematics to make sense of the world

    4. Children's museums are rich worlds in which children can develop multiple intelligences

B. Middle childhood

    1. Whole language

        a. Key to language development is students' using language by talking, listening, reading, and writing

        b. Whole-language teaching and learning are reciprocal and collaborative

        c. A whole-language approach integrates curriculum

        d. Most of the varied whole-language approaches share emphasis on authentic tasks and integrated curricula (Table 13.4)

Point/Counterpoint: Whole Language Versus Phonics in Learning to Read

    2. Cognitive apprenticeships

        a. Students learn from experts in various fields how thinking takes place

        b. Projects are tackled that challenge expert learning

C. High school and beyond

    1. Constructing mathematics: See Table 13.5

    2. Conducting research

        a. Students use actual research resources to learn to use authentic information

        b. They learn to use various types of information representation

    3. Christopherian encounters (Gardner)

        a. Students must learn to confront their intuitively based misconceptions

        b. Microworld formats present self-contained worlds based on assumptions that can be systematically challenged

VI.   Integrations

A. Can direct instruction encourage understanding?

    1. Well organized presentations help students construct accurate understandings and perceive links among main ideas

    2. Reviews activate prior knowledge

    3. Clear presentations and guided practice avoid overloading students' information processing systems

    4. Examples and explanations build multiple pathways for building networks of concepts

    5. Guided practice gives teacher a snapshot of students' thinking processes

    6. Weakest part of direct teaching is students' ownership of learning

B. Matching methods to learning goals

    1. Teacher-centered instruction leads to better achievement test performance

    2. Discovery learning leads to more creativity, abstract thinking, and problem solving

    3. Open learning improves attitudes toward school, stimulates curiosity, cooperation among students, and attendance rates

    4. With younger students, direct instruction works better for teaching math and English than questioning and discussion methods

    5. For older students, discussion, questioning, independent work, in-depth analysis was better for teaching English

    6. Each subject has skills better taught through direct instruction, with guidance,

                  modeling, and practice

7. Teaching should become less direct as students mature and when goals involve affective learning, problem solving, and critical thinking

VII.   Summary

VIII. Key terms and concepts

IX.   What would you do?

X.   Teachers' casebook

Key Points

Perspectives on student-centered learning

- The New Zealand studies (Nuthall and Alton-Lee) researched the conditions that encourage effective student learning: how and what students learn, what helps students to construct and remember accurate understandings

- Findings are that students learn different things from lessons; information gained from demonstrations and charts is retained; sufficient time is needed to clarify concepts and displace misconceptions

- Students must take advantage of their opportunities, and have the opportunity to express what they know

- Resources are necessary, including equipment, support, and relevant experiences

APA's learner-centered psychological principles

- The nature and goals of the learning process: Learning is active, meaningful, volitional, and should be tied to student responsibility to learn

- The construction of knowledge and use of higher-order thinking: Students try to link new learning with old. Metacognition and self-controlled learning are keys to creative and critical thinking

- Motivational influences, intrinsic motivation, and characteristics of motivation-enhancing tasks: Personal emotional, goals, and expectations influence what is learned. Learning should be personal, authentic, real-world

- Developmental constraints and opportunities due to genetic and environment factors, as well as individual differences, influence readiness for learning

- Social and cultural diversity should be respected in adapting instruction to meet a variety of contexts

- Self-esteem and social acceptance reinforce learning by exposing students to caring, individualized relationships

- Cognitive filters built up of personal beliefs and prior learning influence the ongoing construction of meaning

Constructivist contributions

- <u>Constructivist view of learning</u>: Emphasis on the active role of the learner in building understanding and making sense of information

- Students need a complex learning environment to learn how to solve ill-structured problems, using a variety of ways of representation

- Students learn to use social negotiation to work together to solve problems

- Students also benefit by understanding their own cognitive processes

Student-centered teaching methods

- Students and teachers collaborate to plan lessons and set goals

- Constructivist practices include individualized instruction, group discussion, inquiry methods, reciprocal teaching, humanistic education, and use of computer assisted instruction

- Constructivist teaching may also feature authentic forms of assessment

- <u>Individualized instruction</u>: Approach designed to meet individual students' needs, interests, abilities, and work pace

  - Instructional objectives, pace of instruction, content, activities, materials, reading level, and/or methods are tailored to the needs and ability levels of students

  - Much depends on self-direction of students (a function of grade level)

  - Team-assisted individualization: students work together but at own levels

- Group discussion are a way to directly involve students

  - Students are helped to evaluate ideas and synthesize personal viewpoints, assimilate complex ideas

- Group members may have widely differing abilities and willingness to participate; large groups may be unwieldy

- Inquiry methods: Teaching approaches in which teacher presents a puzzling situation and students solve the problem by gathering data and testing conclusions

  - Students learn content and process at the same time

  - Similar to guided discovery learning

- Reciprocal teaching is a set of strategies that help students to think about what they are reading

  - Strategies include summarizing content, asking a central question, clarifying difficult points, and predicting what comes next

  - Teachers can use the technique to look for clues about what and how students are thinking

- Humanistic education stresses the importance of feelings, open communication, and the worth of the individual

  - Learning involves use of hands-on, manipulatives in projects and open-ended learning involving creativity, cooperation, self-esteem, and social adjustment

  - Academic learning is often no greater than in traditional classrooms

- Computers technology allows students to access resources and explore a wide variety of different worlds and information

  - Interglobal connections and networks connect students from around the world

  - Computers can be used as learning environments, as tools, or as tutees

  - Computer simulations and microworlds create situations in which students must apply learning

  - Integrated information systems manage and pace student learning (also called integrated learning systems)

  - Computers increase the capacity to individualize instruction

Constructivist teaching for different ages

- Develop abilities in many areas in early childhood while maintaining curiosity, zest for learning; emphasis should be on understanding, not just memorizing

- In middle childhood, use whole language instruction to integrate curriculum and develop authentic language ability

    - Cognitive apprenticeships help students to learn from experts in various fields how thinking takes place, using projects that challenge expert learning

- In high school and beyond, students use actual research resources to learn to use authentic information and various types of information representation

    - Christopherian encounters (Gardner) challenges students to learn to confront their intuitively based misconceptions

Integrations

- Direct instruction can be interpreted cognitively

    - Well-organized presentation helps students construct accurate understandings and perceive links among main ideas and activate prior knowledge

    - Clear presentations and guided practice avoid overloading students' information processing systems and build multiple pathways for concept networks

    - Weakest part of direct teaching is students' ownership of learning

- Teaching methods should be matched to the goals of instruction

    - Use teacher-centered instruction to better achievement test performance

    - Use discovery learning to foster creativity, abstract thinking, and problem solving

    - Open learning improves attitudes toward school, stimulates curiosity, cooperation among students, and attendance rates

    - Teaching should become less direct as students mature and when goals involve affective learning, problem solving, and critical thinking

    - Each subject has skills better taught through direct instruction, with guidance, modeling, and practice

Concept Map: SELF-REGULATED LEARNING

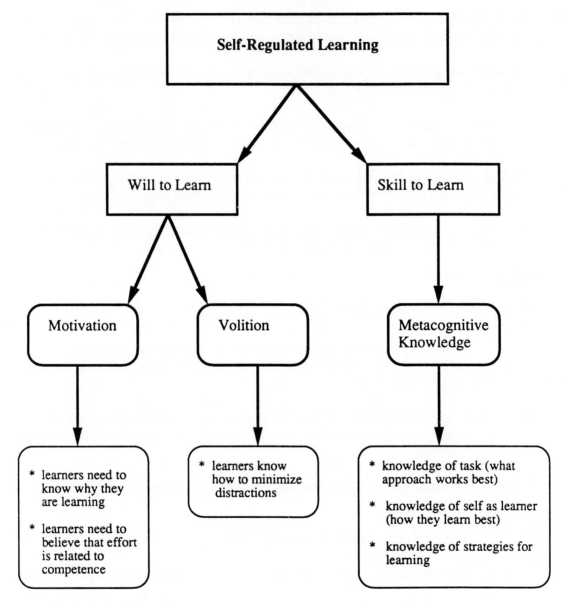

Do You Know This?

Answering these questions will help you to check yourself on your mastery of the chapter objectives.

Perspectives on Student-Centered Teaching

Can you describe methods for studying the links between classroom teaching and student learning?

What are the APA's 12 learner-centered psychological principles?

Constructivist Contributions

Can you describe the characteristics that are shared by many constructivist approaches to teaching?

Student-Centered Instruction

Can you give situations in which the following formats would be most appropriate: Individualized instruction, group discussion, inquiry, reciprocal teaching, humanistic education?

Can you explain how you will evaluate computer packages and microworld simulations for use with your classes?

How will you incorporate student-centered approaches into your teaching?

Constructivist Teaching for Different Ages

Can you compare how student-centered teaching differs at various levels of schooling?

Integrations

Choose one lesson in your own area and explain how you would go about presenting this to students you will be teaching in two ways: using teacher-centered instruction and using student-centered methods.

Key Terms and Concepts

DEFINITIONS: Concepts of Computer Learning

Write explanations for the following pairs of terms. Your explanations should clearly distinguish the two from one another. Check the text to make sure your explanations are equivalent.

Word processing/information processing _____

_____

Computer simulation/microworld _____

_____

Videodisc/CD-ROM disc _____

_____

Tutorial/Integrated information system _____

_____

APPLICATION: What makes an effective class discussion?

The following is a description of a class discussion that never got off the ground. For each category, supply an example what the teacher could do to create a contrasting behavior that would characterize an effective discussion.

The eighth grade United States history class taught by Mr. Olmez was studying the process of making laws under the Constitution. To engage students in active learning, Mr. Olmez introduced the idea that the neighbors near the local elementary school were interested in having a stop sign installed at a busy intersection near the school. He asked the class as a whole to discuss how this might be carried out. After a long silence, two students raised their hand. Mr. Olmez called on one student, who suggested that the neighbors call the city police headquarters. Another student suggested a letter to a state congressional representative. Mr. Olmez called on two more students who did not have their hands raised, but who were whispering to one another. Most students averted their eyes, not wishing to be called upon. After several more attempts to have students volunteer ideas, Mr. Olmez gave up, frustrated. No one knew anything about local government!

Teacher acts as central mediator, controlling turn-taking _____

_____

Some students reluctant to speak_____

_____

Large, unwieldy group _____

_____

Students lack common background knowledge _____

_____

APPLICATION: Critique of Direct Instruction

How would you incorporate basic principles of the cognitivist model within a direct instruction lesson? Refer to Table 12.6 to review the basics of Hunter's Mastery Teaching Program. For each of the main principles of cognitivist teaching given below, discuss where it might be included in Hunter's model.

Promote student autonomy and goal-setting _____

_____

Develop students' reflective processes _____

Emphasize authentic tasks and integrated curriculum _____

Incorporate questioning and discussion _____

Use problem solving to stimulate inquiry _____

CASE STUDY: Defending the Inquiry Model

Mr. Zaharopoulous was able to practice inquiry teaching methods as a student teacher, and upon being hired as a first-year teacher in a fifth grade class, incorporated these methods into the science curriculum. However, the school district had adopted a policy of evaluating teachers on the basis of their use of a popular direct instruction model. His principal has scheduled a series of new-teacher performance reviews. Mr. Zaharopoulous desires to gain the support of the principal in the use of inquiry methods in science. Give arguments that would assist Mr. Zaharopoulous in presenting the advantages of the inquiry method as opposed to direct instruction. You may wish to refer to Chapter 8 of the text to review the fundamentals of the inquiry method of teaching.

CHARTING: COMPARING CONSTRUCTIVIST AND DIRECT INSTRUCTION

In the clarifying circles below, area A represents a constructivist view of learning. Area C represents a direct instruction teaching model, and area B represents views common to both. Choose A, B, or C for each of the following statements. For answers, check Answer Key.

1. ____ Teacher uses questions to focus student learning.
2. ____ Student is responsible for creating individual meaning.
3. ____ The teacher transmits knowledge.
4. ____ The teacher transforms knowledge into a manageable curriculum.
5. ____ Students see the teacher as the source of information.
6. ____ Students take responsibility for generating questions.
7. ____ Teacher generates questions and controls discussion.
8. ____ Student actively involved in planning learning.
9. ____ The teacher's directions are

precise and specific.

PRACTICE TEST: Multiple Choice

1. Group discussions are most appropriate when

    a. questions require convergent answers.
    b. the class is well-prepared to evaluate and synthesize.
    c. the students have difficulty expressing themselves.
    d. all of the above.

2. Which of the following procedures is recommended for teachers using the discussion method?

    a. Let shy children decide to participate when they're ready.
    b. If uncertain about what a student has said, ask another student to summarize the first student's response.
    c. Discourage students from mentally rehearsing or writing responses before speaking.
    d. All of the above.

3. Ms. French would like her science students to discover some key principles of gravity by experimenting on their own with structured materials. Which of the following teaching methods should be most appropriate for this purpose?

    a. Mastery learning
    b. Lecture
    c. Inquiry
    d. Discussion

4. The simplest form of individualized instruction is

    a. variations in reading level.
    b. tailored learning activities.
    c. self-pacing.
    d. programmed instruction frames.

5. Research reported in your text suggests that completely individualized instructional systems seem best suited for

    a. elementary students.
    b. special education students.
    c. poorly motivated students.
    d. college students.

6. A component of team-assisted individualization is having students

    a. work in mixed-ability groups on materials matched to their needs.
    b. compete against one another in end-of-week tournaments
    c. work in same-ability dyads and tutor one another in reading
    d. earn incentives for tutoring low-ability students in lower grades.

7. Which of the following is not one of the factors that Nuthall and Alton-Lee view as necessary for meaningful learning?

    a. Opportunities to learn
    b. Being able to take advantage of learning opportunities
    c. An anticipatory set for learning
    d. Resources to learn

8. Which of the following examples of mathematics learning is compatible with a constructivist view?

    a. Using flash cards to teach math facts
    b. Using a drill-and-practice computer program dealing with factoring
    c. Simplifying an equation by following the steps listed in the textbook
    d. Learning to convert Fahrenheit to Celsius temperatures by experimenting with actual thermometer readings

9. Based on research findings on effective uses of different teaching orientations, in which of the following situations would constructivist models be least applicable?

    a. Teaching English to eleventh graders
    b. Developing fourth graders' appreciation of science methods
    c. Teaching math facts to fourth graders
    d. Teaching students to perform experiments in science

10. Which of the following teaching methods would be most compatible with a constructivist teaching perspective?

    a. Recitation
    b. Guided discovery
    c. Direct instruction
    d. Hunter's Mastery Teaching Program

PRACTICE TEST: Essay

A. In a physical science class, the teacher proposes to use the inquiry method to have students understand a principle of soil acidity. The teacher poses the following problem: "Do pine needles make the soil more or less acidic?" Detail the subsequent steps which the student will follow.

B. Describe the process of helping your class learn a reciprocal teaching procedure.

Answer Key

CHARTING: Comparing Constructivist and Direct Instruction

1. **B**
2. **A**

3. **C**
4. **B**
5. **C**
6. **A**
7. **C**
8. **A**
9. **B**

PRACTICE TEST: Multiple Choice

1. b   Discussions are most appropriate when students are able and <u>prepared to</u> evaluate and synthesize. They would not be a good choice for answering lower-level questions that have convergent answers or when a lot of material needs to be covered in a limited time.

2. b   The only correct procedure of those listed is to ask students to summarize other students' responses, especially when the initial responses are not clear.   Shy children should be directly invited to participate, and it is generally desirable for students to be given time to rehearse mentally or write down their ideas before responding.

3. c   The <u>inquiry approach</u> would be the best choice for Ms. French. It would involve her students in questioning how growth works, and in actively experimenting and gathering data to test their hypotheses.

4. c   Clearly, the simplest form of individualization is to allow students to <u>work at their own pace</u> on the same assignment. While the teacher should organize the task into a series of objectives, new material or methods to accommodate individual differences would not be needed.

5. d   Completely individualized instruction is most effective for <u>college students.</u> It is likely that elementary, special education, or poorly motivated students would LACKthe self-discipline and maturity to handle completely unsupervised work.

6. a   A primary component of Team Assisted Individualization is having students work in mixed ability groups on materials matched to their needs. This orientation differs from many other forms of cooperative learning because each student's assignments are individualized as opposed to having the entire team help each other with the same assignment.

7. c   An <u>anticipatory set</u> is <u>not</u> one of Nuthall and Alton-Lee's three factors. In fact, it is a component of Hunter's Mastery Teaching Model and involves capturing students' attention at the beginning of a lesson.

8. d   A constructivist approach to teaching mathematics uses real-life events

as a basis for making the concepts understandable and interesting. An example would be learning temperature conversion formulas by <u>experimenting with actual thermometer readings</u>. This approach contrasts with memorizing math facts through drill-and-practice exercises.

9.   c   <u>Constructivist approaches would generally be least applicable to teaching math facts</u>. Such approaches become more effective when objectives stress meaningful learning and affective outcomes.

10. b   Constructivist teaching perspectives stress students' construction of personal knowledge by actively working with instructional materials to "discover" ideas and concepts. <u>Guided discovery</u> would be very compatible with this philosophy, while direct instructional methods would not be as a result of being teacher-centered rather than learner-centered.

PRACTICE TEST: Essay

A.   To use the inquiry method, first the teacher presents a puzzling question: "Do pine needles make the soil more or less acidic?" Next, students propose hypotheses to solve the problem (hypotheses: 1. "More acidic" 2. "Less acidic" 3. "No change."). Students then collect data to test the hypotheses, by composting pine needles into soil samples that been previously tested with litmus paper. Lastly, students draw conclusions by retesting the soil. They then reflect on the original problem and on the thinking processes they used to solve it.

B.   First, reciprocal teaching involves learning to summarize the content of a passage and pinpoint the main ideas(s). Next, students learn to formulate their own questions about the main idea(s). They can learn to clarify the difficult parts of the material to make sure they have understood. Lastly, they can learn to predict what will come next. Lessons move from teacher-directed to student-led as students gain experience and knowledge.

14

Standardized Testing

Teaching Outline

I. What Do You Think?

II. Measurement and evaluation
- A. Evaluation: Comparing information to criteria and then making judgments; always involved in teaching
- B. Measurement
  1. Applying a set of rules to describe events or characteristics with numbers
  2. Allows comparison of one student's performance with a standard or with the performance of other students
  3. Evaluation may involve more than measurement, but measurement can be a source of unbiased data
- C. Norm-referenced tests
  1. Performance of others as basis for interpreting a persons' raw score (actual number of correct test items)
  2. Three types of norm groups (comparison groups): Class or school, school district, national
  3. Score: Reflects general knowledge of subject rather than mastery of specific skills and information
  4. Uses of norm-referenced tests: Measuring overall achievement and choosing a few top candidates
  5. Limitations
     - a. Do not indicate if prerequisite knowledge for more advanced material has been mastered
     - b. Less appropriate for measuring affective and psychomotor objectives
     - c. Tend to encourage competition and comparison of scores
- D. Criterion-referenced tests: Comparisons with fixed standard
  1. Example: Driver's license
  2. Uses: Measuring the mastery of specific objectives when goal is to achieved set standard
  3. Limitations:
     - a. Absolute standards difficult to set in some areas
     - b. Standards tend to be arbitrary
     - c. Not appropriate comparison when others is valuable

III. What do test scores mean?
- A. Basic concepts
  1. Standardized tests
     - a. Standard methods of administration, scoring, and reporting
     - b. Test items and instructions have been tried out; final version has been administered to a norming sample (a comparison group)
  2. Frequency distributions: Listings of the number of people who obtain each

score on a test

3. Measurements of central tendency and standard deviation
   a. Measures of central tendency: Mean (arithmetical average groups of scores); median (middle score); and mode (score that occurs most often)
   b. Bimodal distribution: Two modes
   c. Standard deviation: Measure of how wide the scores vary from the mean (degree of variability among scores)
   d. Knowing the mean and standard deviation gives meaning to a individual score (Figure 14.2)
4. The normal distribution: The bell-shaped curve (Figure 14.3)
   a. Mean, median, and mode are same point
   b. Percentage of scores for each area under the curve are known

B. Types of scores
   1. Percentile rank scores
      a. Show the percentage of students in the norming sample who scored at or below a particular raw score
      b. Interpretation problem: Greater difference in raw score points to make difference in percentile rank at the extreme ends of the scale
   2. Grade-equivalent scores
      a. Averages obtained from norming samples for each grade level
      b. Interpretation problem: Different forms of test often used for different grades
      c. High score indicates superior mastery of material at that grade level rather than capacity for doing advanced work
      d. Often misleading; should not be used
   3. Standard scores
      a. Differences in raw scores are the same at every point on the scale
      b. Based on the standard deviation: Z-score tells how many SDs above or below the average a raw score is; T-score has mean of 50 and SD of 10 (eliminates negative numbers)
      c. Stanine scores combine some of the properties of percentile ranks and standard scores; nine possible units (1 though 9) have a mean of 5 and a SD of 2; each unit contains a specific range of percentile scores

C. Interpreting test scores
   1. No test provides a perfect picture of a person's abilities
   2. Reliability
      a. Test-retest reliability: Consistency of scores on two separate administrations of the same test
      b. Alternate-form reliability: Consistency of scores on two equivalent versions of a test
      c. Split-half reliability: Degree to which all the test items measure the same abilities
   3. True score
      a. Hypothetical mean of all scores if student took test many times
      b. Standard error of measurement: Standard deviation of scores from hypothetical true score; the smaller the standard error the more reliable the test

4. Confidence interval or "standard error bank": Raw score plus or minus the standard error; provides a range within which true score might be found
5. Validity
   a. A test is valid if it measures what it is suppose to specifically measure
   b. Ways to determine validity: Content, criterion and construct evidence
   c. Factors that interfere with validity: Lack of relation to curriculum; mismatch with students' test-taking skills
   d. To be valid, a test must be reliable
   e. Guidelines: Increasing Test Reliability and Validity

IV. Types of standardized tests
   A. Achievement tests: What has the student learned?
      1. Intention: Measure how much student has learned in specific content areas
      2. Frequently used achievement tests
         a. Group tests for identifying students who need more testing or for grouping students
         b. Individual tests for determination of academic level or diagnosis of learning problems
      3. Using information from a norm-referenced achievement test: Individual profiles (Figure 4.6)
      4. Interpreting achievement test scores: Norm-referenced and criterion-referenced interpretations
   B. Diagnostic tests: What are the student's strengths and weaknesses?
      1. Given individually by a trained professional, usually to elementary students
      2. Intention: Identify students' specific problems and weaknesses
   C. Aptitude tests: How well the student does in the future?
      1. Intention: Measures abilities developed over years, predict how well a student will do in learning new material in the future
      2. Scholastic aptitude (SAT, ACT, etc.): Achievement or aptitude?
         a. SATs used as predictors of future achievement (less subject to teacher bias and grade inflation than grades)
         b. Controversy continues over fairness and validity
      3. IQ and scholastic aptitude tests: Small differences in scores not important
      4. Vocational aptitude and interest
         a. Vocational aptitude: Differential Aptitude Test (DAT) matches student's aptitude to average scores for people in different occupations
         b. Vocational interest tests: Ask students to rate activities and identify interest
         c. Test should be used to motivate, not to close off career options

V. Issues in standardized testing: The ethics of "high-stakes testing"
   A. The uses of testing in American society
      1. Readiness testing: Used to determine if a child is ready for first grade or developmental kindergarten
      2. National testing: Same test administered across United States
      3. Minimum competency testing: Proposed as solution to adult literacy; still controversial

   Point/Counterpoint: To Test or Not to Test
      4. Testing teachers: Teacher assessment designed to test basic skills,

professional skills and academic knowledge
  B. Advantage in taking tests--fair and unfair
    1. Bias in testing: Factors that put low SES and minority students at a disadvantage
      a. Most standardized tests predict school achievement equally well for all groups
      b. Caution: Some tests' content and procedures believed to put minorities at a disadvantage (e.g. language, achievement orientation)
      c. Culture fair-tests: Making assessment more appropriate for minorities
  C. Coaching and test-taking skills: Popular test preparation technique
    1. Special training courses usually result in only a 10 to 50-point gain
    2. Familiarity with the procedures of standardized tests appear to help
    3. Instruction in general cognitive skills (metacognitive and study skills) appears helpful
    4. Guidelines: Taking a Test
VI. New directions in standardized testing
  A. Assessing learning potential: Learning Potential Assessment Device looks at process of learning, rather than product, to gauge potential for future learning
  B. Authentic assessment: Problem of how to assess complex, important, real life outcomes
    1. Some states developing authentic assessment procedures
    2. "Constructed-response formats'" have students create, rather than select, responses; demand more thoughtful scoring
  C. Changes in the SAT: New SATs will have tests of verbal and mathematical reasoning, and subject matter; will use constructed-response format and essay questions
VII.   Summary
VIII.   Key terms and concepts
IX.   What would you do?
X.   Teachers' casebook

Key Points

Measurement and evaluation

- Measurement: The evaluation expressed in quantitative (numerical) terms

- Evaluation: Decision making about student performance and appropriate teaching strategies

- Norm-referenced testing: Testing in which scores are compared with the average performance of others

  - Norm group: A group whose average score serves as a standard for evaluating any student's score on that test (Ex.: class, school, district, nation)

- The score on norm-referenced test reflects general knowledge of subject rather than mastery of specific skills and information

- Useful for measuring overall achievement or choosing a few top candidates

- Limitations are that there is no way to know if prerequisite knowledge for more advanced material has been mastered

- Norm-referenced tests are less appropriate for measuring affective and psychomotor objectives

- Tend to encourage competition and comparison of scores

- <u>Criterion-referenced tests</u>: Testing in which scores are compared to a set performance standard

  - Useful for measuring the mastery of very specific objectives

  - Limitations are in measuring areas where absolute standards difficult to set and standards tend to be arbitrary

What do test scores mean?

- <u>Standardized test</u>: Test given, usually nationwide, under uniform conditions and scored according to uniform procedures

  - <u>Norming sample</u>: Large sample of students serving as a comparison group for scoring standardized test

  - <u>Frequency distribution</u>: Record showing how many scores fall into set groups

    - <u>Histogram</u>: Bar graph of a frequency distribution

- Measurements of central tendency include mean, mode, median

  - <u>Central tendency</u>: A typical score for a group of scores

  - <u>Mean</u>: Arithmetical average

  - <u>Median</u>: Middle score in a group of scores

  - <u>Mode</u>: Most frequently occurring score

- Bimodal distribution: Distribution with two modes

- Standard deviation: Measure of the spread of scores around the mean (degree of variability among scores)

- Variability: Degree of difference or deviation from the mean

- The normal distribution: The most commonly-occurring distribution in which scores are distributed evenly around the mean

  - In normal distribution, the percentage of scores for each area under the curve is known

- Types of scores are percentile ranks, grade-equivalent scores, and standard scores

  - Percentile rank score: Percentage of those in the norming sample who scored at, or below, an individual score

  - Grade-equivalent score: Measure of grade level based on comparison with norming samples from each grade

    - Different forms of test often used for different grades

    - High score indicates superior mastery of material at that grade level rather than capacity for doing advanced work

  - Standard scores: Scores based on the standard deviation

    - z-score: A standard score indicating number of standard deviations above or below the mean

    - T-score: A standard score with a mean of 50 and standard deviation of 10

    - Stanine scores: Whole-number scores from 1 to 9, each representing a wide range of raw scores

- Two factors in interpreting test scores are reliability and validity

  - Reliability: Consistency of test results

    - Test-retest reliability: Consistency of scores on two separate administrations of the same test

    - Alternate-form reliability: Consistency of scores on two equivalent versions of a test

- Split-half reliability: Comparing performance on half of the test questions with performance on the other half

- True score: Hypothetical average of all scores if repeated testing under ideal conditions were possible

- Standard error of measurement: Hypothetical estimate of variation in scores if testing were repeated

- Confidence interval: Range of scores within which a particular score is likely to fall

- Validity: Degree to which a test measures what it is intended to measure

Types of standardized tests

- Achievement test: A standardized test measuring how much students have learned in a given content area

  - Results are meaningless unless test is administered according to the instructions

  - Frequently used achievement tests are group tests and individual tests

- Diagnostic test: Individually administered test to identify special learning problems

  - Used to identify specific problems and weaknesses in the student's learning process

  - Some diagnostic tests: Woodcock-Johnson, Detroit Test of Learning Aptitude, Bender-Gestalt Test

- Aptitude test: Test for predicting future performance, how well a student will do in learning unfamiliar material in the future

  - Scholastic aptitude: Predicts how well you will do in college

  - Vocational aptitude test matches student's aptitude to average scores for people in different occupations

  - Vocational interest test: Test indicating possible areas of career interest

Issues in standardized testing

- The role of testing has been increasing yearly in the U.S.

  - High-stakes testing: Standardized test whose results have powerful influences on students and teachers and those results are used by school administrators, employers, or other officials to make decisions

  - Readiness testing: Testing procedures that are meant to determine if an individual is ready to proceed to the next level of education or training; especially to determine if a child is ready for first grade or developmental kindergarten

  - Minimum competency testing: Standardized tests or school-district-made that are meant to determine if students meet minimum requirements to graduate or to proceed in school

    - Functional literacy: A level of reading, writing, and communication ability that allows the individual to function independently in society

  - Standardized tests are also used for testing teachers for basic skills, professional skills, and academic knowledge

- Are standardized tests biased against minority students?

  - Bias in testing include content and testing procedures that put minority students at a disadvantage (e.g. the language used and values reflected)

    - Most standardized tests predict school achievement equally well for all groups

- Coaching and test-taking skills include gaining familiarity with the procedures of standardized tests and instruction in general cognitive skills (metacognitive and study skills)

New directions in standardized testing

- Learning Potential Assessment Device: An innovative method for testing the student's ability to benefit from teaching

- Authentic assessment evaluates complex, important, real life outcomes

  - Constructed-response format: Test questions and other assessment procedures that require the student to create an answer instead of simply selecting the answer from a set of choices

    - New SATs will have tests of verbal and mathematical reasoning and subject matter

Concept Map: TYPES OF TEST SCORES

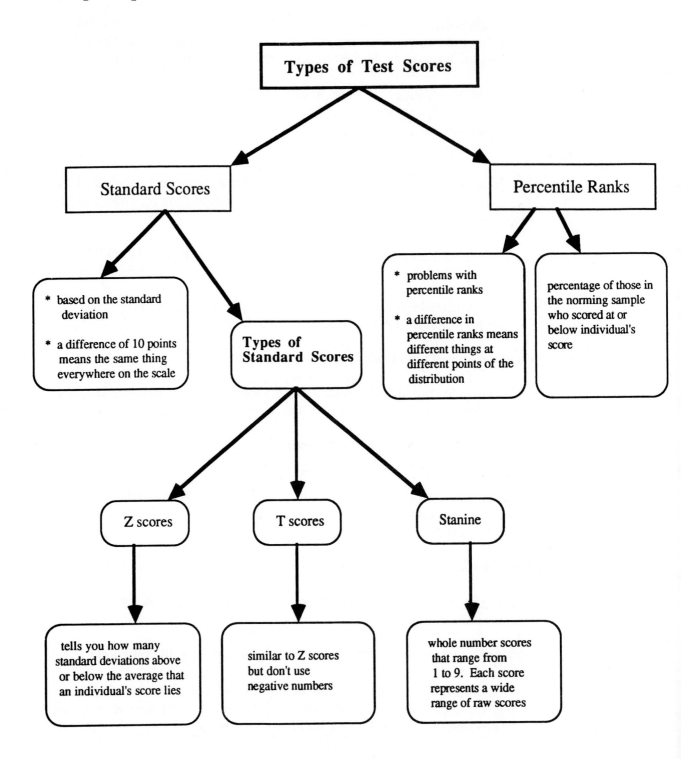

Do You Know This?

Answering these questions will help you to check yourself on the mastery of the chapter objectives.

What Do Test Scores Mean?

Can you calculate mean, median, mode, and standard deviation?

Can you define percentile ranks, standard deviations, z-scores, T-scores, and stanine scores?

Can you explain how to improve validity and reliability in testing?

Types of Standardized Tests

Could you interpret the results of achievement, aptitude, and diagnostic tests in a realistic manner?

Issues in Standardized Testing

Define your position on the testing issue and defend your position.

Can you describe how to prepare your students (and yourself) for taking standardized tests?

New Directions in Standardized Testing

What are the strengths and weaknesses of alternative forms of assessment such as portfolios?

Key Terms and Concepts

IDENTIFICATION: Norm-Referenced and Criterion-Based Testing

For each situation below, choose Norm-referenced (N) or Criterion-referenced (C) as best fits. For answer, see Answer Key.

_____ 1. Friendly Hill School wants to predict how well their elementary students will perform when they transfer to the high school.

_____ 2. Friendly Hill School wants to ensure that each elementary school student will leave sixth grade having mastered the basic skills.

_____ 3. The sixth grade teachers assess each student at the beginning of the year to evaluate upon what aspect of the curriculum that student needs to concentrate in order to graduate with a basic competency in all areas.

_____ 4. Friendly Hill School wants to assure the parent community that their students are achieving at a par with peers nationwide.

_____ 5. Friendly Hill School administers a vocational interest test to seniors to assist them with career planning.

_____ 6. Friendly Hill School teachers use the last end-of-year math module that a student has completed to place the student in next year's math program.

MATCHING: Concepts in Testing

Match the letters of the descriptions on the right to the corresponding items on the left. Use each definition only once. For answers, see Answer Key.

_____	1.	Central tendency	a.	Most frequently occurring score
_____	2.	Mean		
_____	3.	Frequency distribution	b.	Measure of the spread of around the mean
_____	4.	Median		
_____	5.	Mode	c.	Large sample which serves as comparison group for scoring standardized test
_____	6.	Bimodal distribution		
_____	7.	Standard deviation		
_____	8.	Variability	d.	A typical score for a group of scores
_____	9.	Normal distribution		
_____	10.	Norming sample	e.	Middle score in a group of scores

f. Degree of difference or deviation from the mean

g. The most commonly occurring distribution, in which scores are distributed evenly around the mean in a bell shape

h. Arithmetical average

i. Distribution with two peaks

j. Record showing how many scores fall into set groups

DEFINITIONS: Interpreting Test Scores

See if you can define the following terms. Then check your definitions with the Glossary.

Learning Potential Assessment Device _____

_____

Authentic Assessment _____

_____

Constructed-Response Format _____

_____

APPLICATION: Measures of Central Tendency

Students in a math make-up examination received the scores below. Calculate the mean of these scores. Then find the median score. Compare these measures. In this case, which is the most effective measure of central tendency? What, if any, useful information for teachers is added by each measure of central tendency?

95, 92, 92, 88, 87, 86, 79, 78, 19, 13, 0

APPLICATION: Interpreting Standardized Tests

The following is part of the Individual Test Record of a student. Using these data, answer the questions below. For answers, see Answer Key.

Student: Susy Quinlin   **Grade:** 8.2 **Age:** 13   **Test date:** 10/04/92

Subtest	GE	NP	Stanine	Confidence Interval for NP
Vocabulary	8.4	48	4.8	40-59
Comprehension	9.4	64	6.1	57-76
Total Reading Score	8.9	55	5.9	47-67
Math Computation	10.1	68	6.9	61-79
Total Battery	9.6	62	5	58-72

[Key: GE = Grade Equivalent   NP = National Percentile Equivalent]

_____   1.   Compared to her peers, in which area does Susy score higher?

_____   2.   Compared to her peers, is Susy better in Comprehension or Total Battery?

_____   3.   Susy received an NP of 62 on her Total Battery and an NP of 48 on Vocabulary. It would appear that Susy did somewhat better on the Total Battery compared to Vocabulary. How would explain the stanine of about 5 on both subtests?

_____   4.   Susy's friend Janine scored at the level of NP = 50 on Vocabulary. Examine the confidence interval on this subtest. Is the score difference an important one between Susy and Janine's Vocabulary ability?

CASE STUDY: Readiness Testing

Although Joey's age of 5-5 qualifies him for entrance into kindergarten, Mrs. Slovasky, the kindergarten teacher, has observed that he seems to lack the gross and fine motor skills which he needs for success in kindergarten. She believes that kindergarten students should be able to write clearly and sit quietly to perform seatwork. She has asked Dr. Kleinfelt, the school psychologist, to determine Joey's readiness. Dr. Klienfelt's report subsequently indicates that although Joey appears awkward when writing or drawing with crayon or pencil, he has adequate fine motor control when using scissors. His gross motor movements are within a normal range for a child of this age. Comment on Joey's potential for success in kindergarten. Does this reflect on Mrs. Slovasky's teaching approach?

CASE STUDY: Authentic Assessment

Mr. Amir's eighth graders will take a minimum competency examination before they can enter ninth grade. He has argued that this nationally normed exam does not help the eighth grade teaching staff to plan effectively for giving weak students additional aid in improving their writing. This feedback could be incorporated into a summer school curriculum for those students who must pass the competency exam at the end of the summer before they can enter ninth grade. What type of authentic assessment device would perform this function?

PRACTICE TEST: Multiple Choice

1.　A histogram is used to show

　　a.　the reliability of standardized test.
　　b.　students' performances on a standardized test over time.
　　c.　the scores obtained by a group on a test.
　　d.　the difficulty level of individual test items.

2.　The Algebra I class mean and standard deviation are 80 and 10, respectively. The Biology II class mean and standard deviation are 79 and 2, respectively. Tina scored 90 in Algebra I and 86 in Biology II. Which of the following is true?

　　a.　She did better relative to her class in Biology II than in Algebra I.
　　b.　She did better relative to her class in Algebra I than in Biology II.
　　c.　She should earn an A in Algebra I and B in Biology II.
　　d.　She would be better served by criterion-referenced grading than by norm-referenced grading in both classes.

3.　IQ scores are normally distributed with a mean of 100 and a standard deviation of 15. Based on normal curve properties, which of the following is true?

　　a.　There are more scores above 130 than below 85.

   b. A score of 70 is equally probable as one of 130.
   c. About 90% of the scores fall between 85 and 115.
   d. All of the above.

4. Martina's score of 75% on a district reading test surpasses 88 out of the 100 students in the sample. Her score is at the

   a. 8.8 percentile.
   b. 75th percentile.
   c. 88th percentile.
   d. can't be determined without the norming sample mean.

5. Grade equivalent scores should be avoided because they

   a. are unreliable measures.
   b. are easily misinterpreted.
   c. give no criterion for evaluation.
   d. may change drastically from year to year.

6. When individual's scores on a test remain consistent from one testing to the next, the test is said to have high

   a. construct validity.
   b. reliability.
   c. confidence.
   d. predictive validity.

7. Which of the following is true?

   a. A test that is reliable has a high confidence interval around scores?
   b. A test must have validity to be reliable.
   c. A useful test can have low validity as long it has high reliability.
   d. A valid test must be reliable.

8. On a norm-referenced achievement test, the "anticipated achievement grade-equivalent score" indicates the

   a. projected score for an examinee based on past performances.
   b. the examinee's own estimate of how he/she is likely to achieve.
   c. the average grade-equivalent score for a national norming sample at the same grade level as the examinee.
   d. the level at which test experts and curriculum experts feel that students at certain grade levels should perform.

9. Which of the following is not true of diagnostic tests?

   a. Given by trained specialists
   b. Usually given to groups of students
   c. Given to find weaknesses in learning processes
   d. Generally aimed at younger students

10. Which of the following is most likely to directly improve standardized test scores?

    a. Drills of vocabulary words
    b. Familiarity with the test-taking procedures
    c. Practice in quick computation
    d. Mnemonic memory aids

PRACTICE TEST: Essay

A. The Scholastic Aptitude Test was originally developed by the College Board to promote an equal opportunity for access to selected Ivy League colleges despite applicants' having graduated from other than prestigious preparatory schools. Argue the pros and cons of today's use of standardized testing to predict success in college. Discuss the issue of test bias toward minorities.

B. What are the implications of having a national minimum competency examination? Give possible positive and negative ramifications.

Answer Key

IDENTIFICATION: Norm-Referenced and Criterion-Based Testing

1. N
2. C
3. C
4. N
5. N
6. C

MATCHING: Concepts in Testing

1.	d	6.	i
2.	h	7.	b
3.	j	8.	f
4.	e	9.	g
5.	a	10.	c

APPLICATION: Measures of Central Tendency

Mean: 66.3
Median: 86
Mode: 92

Discussion: In this case, the mean score does not reflect how the majority of the students performed on the make-up examination. The median is a better indication of how most of the students did. The mode is not useful in this case. This set of results might reflect, for example, test results in which the best students in the class missed the original test administration due to a honor society meeting, while the lowest scoring students in the class may have missed the original test due to chronic absences.

APPLICATION: Interpreting Standardized Tests

1. **Math Computation**
2. **Scores on Comprehension and Total battery are not significantly different.**
3. **The comparison group's score distribution on these subtests may be very different.**
4. **Not important: The confidence interval is broad enough that a 2-point difference may be within the range of test error.**

PRACTICE TEST: Multiple Choice

1. c   A histogram is a graphical representation of a frequency distribution. It shows the <u>scores obtained by a group on a particular test</u>. It is sometimes called a bar graph.

2. a   Tina did <u>better relative to her class in Biology than in Algebra II</u>. This conclusion is supported by the fact that Tina's z-score in Biology is +3 (indicating that she is 3 standard deviations above the mean) while it is only +1 in Algebra II. Note: To determine the z-score, (a) subtract the class mean from the student's score and (b) divide the result by the class standard deviation.

3. b   Given the properties of the normal curve, a score of 70 <u>would be equally probable as one of 130</u>. Both are 30 points from the mean (100). Because the normal curve is symmetrical, scores at the identical positions above and below the mean occur with the same frequency.

4. c   Martina's score is at the <u>88th percentile</u>. Percentiles represent the percentage of scores at or below a given score. Martina has tied or surpassed 88 out of 100 or 88% of the total.

5. b   The main problem with grade equivalent scores is that <u>they are easily misinterpreted</u>. A common error is to believe that the student can actually perform at the same level as the grade indicated. For example, a sixth grader who scores 8.3 cannot necessarily do eight grade work.

6. b   <u>Reliability</u> is a measure of the consistency of scores from one testing to the next. Validity, which requires reliability, is whether the test measures what it is supposed to.

7. d   <u>A valid test must be reliable</u> because validity means that a test is measuring what it is supposed to. If students' scores fluctuated widely from testing to testing (without cause), it would be difficult to justify that the test is assessing a stable construct.

8. c   The anticipated achievement grade-equivalent score (AAGE) represents the <u>average grade-equivalent score for a national norming sample at the same grade level as the examinee</u>. Thus, in the textbook figure, the national norming sample to which Susie Park is being compared has an average grade equivalent of 8.4 in vocabulary.

9. b   Diagnostic tests are given by trained specialists to individual students, <u>not groups of students</u>, to identify weaknesses in academic content areas.

10. b   One type of training that appears likely to directly improve standardized test scores is <u>familiarization with the procedures of the testing</u>. Much of the advantage may be due to greater confidence and practice with the answering procedures.

PRACTICE TEST: Essay

A. The SAT seems to be a good predictor of college achievement. The SAT scores, unlike high schools grades, are not influenced by grade inflation or teacher bias. Therefore, a minority candidate from a school in which pre-college preparation is weak may still compete successfully for admission to a highly competitive college. However, possible biasing factors may be that the test reflects middle-class bias; students may lack familiarity with, or fluency in, the language of the test; and minorities may be more anxious in test-taking situations or may be less motivated for achievement in school.

B. A national minimum competency exam may provide a basis for comparing students irrespective of their academic backgrounds. It may increase the attention paid in the schools to proficiency in basic skills. However, the pressure to succeed on such an examination might reduce a teacher's freedom in interpreting the curriculum. Moreover, teachers might have a tendency to teach to the "middle" rather than attending to the high or low achieving students. Such testing might discriminate against minority students.

15

Classroom Evaluation and Grading

Teaching Outline

I. What Do You Think?
II. Formative and summative assessment
    A. Formative assessment: Before and during instruction
        1. Has two basic purposes: Guiding teacher in planning and helping students identify problem areas
        2. Helps form instruction
            a. Pretests identify what students already know
            b. Diagnostic tests identifies strengths and weaknesses in content areas
            c. Data-based instruction or curriculum-based assessment (CBA) uses daily "probes" to get precise picture of current performance
    B. Summativeassessment: Summary of accomplishment at end of instruction
III. Getting the most from traditional assessment approaches
    A. Planning for testing
        1. Using a behavior-content matrix as a guide for constructing a unit test
        2. When to test? Frequent testing encourages greater retention of information; cumulative questions are key
        3. Judging textbook tests: Teacher must consider objectives, the way the material was taught
    B. Objective testing
        1. Definition: Multiple-choice, matching, true/false, and short-answer items; Gronlund suggests using multiple-choice unless other format is needed
        2. Using multiple-choice tests
            a. Can be used for factual and higher-level objectives
            b. Most difficult part is making up the tests
        3. Writing multiple choice questions
            a. Items should be designed to measure knowledge rather than test-taking skills or guessing
            b. Items consist of stem (part that asks the question) and alternative answers; "distractors" are plausible wrong answers
            c. Guidelines: Writing Objective Test Items
        4. Evaluating objective test items
    C. Essay testing
        1. Constructing essay tests
            a. Essay tests sample a small number of learning outcomes; require more time to answer; use should be limited to complex learning objectives
            b. Present a clear and precise task
            c. Ample time for answering should be provided
            d. Should include only a few questions

    2. Evaluating essays: Dangers
       a. Graders' individual standards and unreliable scoring procedures produce wide variability of scores
       b. Research: Jargon-filled verbose essays that are neatly written with few grammatical errors seem to be given better grades
    3. Evaluating essays: Methods
       a. Construct model and assign points
       b. Assign grades and sort
       c. Skim pile for consistency within grades
       d. Grade all answers to one question then all answers to next, etc.
       e. Consider having another teacher grade tests as a cross-check

IV. Innovations in assessment
  A. Authentic classroom tests: Tests that ask students to write, speak, create, think, solve, and apply
  B. Performance in context: Portfolios and exhibitions
    1. Portfolios
       a. Definition: Purposeful collections of student work that exhibit effort, progress, and achievement in one or more areas
       b. Guidelines: Creating Portfolios
    2. Exhibitions: Public performance tests that require hours of preparation; culmination of a whole program of study
  C. Evaluating portfolios and performances:
Point/Counterpoint: To Test or Not to Test, Part II

V. Effects of grades and grading on students
  A. There are many different effects of grades on students
    1. High standards and competitive atmosphere associated with increased absenteeism, dropout rates; hard on anxious or low-self-confidence students
    2. Failure can have both negative and positive effects
       a. Helpful if students can see connections between hard work and improvement
       b. May help students to learn to take risks, cope with failure
       c. Being held back results in lowered self-esteem; positive effects unclear
  B. Effects of feedback
    1. Helpful if reason for mistake is explained so same mistake is not repeated
    2. For older students, encouraging personalized written comments can lead to improved performance
    3. For younger students, oral feedback and brief written comments appropriate
  C. Grades and motivation
    1. Grades can motivate real learning appropriate objectives are key
    2. Grades should reflect learning, so working for a grade and working to learn will be the same
    3. Guidelines: Minimizing the Detrimental Effects of Grading

VI. Grading and reporting: Nuts and bolts
  A. Criterion-referenced versus norm-referenced grading
    1. Criterion-referenced systems reflect achievement according to preset criteria for each grade
       a. Motivation to succeed and academic improvement can be enhanced

   b. Clearly defined instructional objectives govern judgments about students

  2. Norm-referenced systems reflect students' standing in comparison with others who took the same course

   a. "Grading on a curve": Grading relative to "average grade" assigned to group's average level of performance

   b. Flexible use of curve is usually more appropriate: Depends on actual distribution of scores and characteristics of particular group

 B. Preparing report cards

  1. Criterion-referenced grading: Report level or proficiency for objectives listed on the report card

  2. Norm-referenced grading: Merge all scores based on a common scale

 C. The point system

  1. System for combining grades from many assignments

  2. Points assigned according to importance of assignments and student's performance

 D. Percentage grading

  1. Grading symbols A to F commonly used to represent some percentage categories

  2. System assumes we can accurately measure what percentage of a body of knowledge each student should attain

  3. Grades are influenced by the level of difficulty of the test and concerns of the individual teacher

 E. The contract system

  1. Specifies type, quantity, and quality of work required for number or letter grade; students "contract" to work for a grade

  2. Can overemphasize quantity of work at expense of quality

  3. The revise option: revise and improve work

 F. Grading on effort and improvement

  1. Question underlying many grading systems: Should grades be based on how much a student improves, or on the final level of learning

  2. Using improvement as a standard penalizes the best students, who naturally improve the least

  3. Individual learning expectation (ILE) system allows everyone to earn improvement points based on personal average score

  4. Dual marking system is a way to include effort in grade

 G. Cautions: Being fair

  1. The halo effect: Tendency for a general impression of a person to influence teacher in grading student's work

  2. Guidelines: Using any grading system

VII. Beyond grading: Communication

 A. Conference with students and parents

  1. Individual student conferences can make judgments of nonacademic achievements and attitudes more accurate and valuable

  2. Teachers need skill in interpersonal communication, especially listening and problem-solving skills

 B. The Buckley amendment

  1. Information in student's records available to students and/or parents

2. Information in cumulative folders must be based on firm, defensible evidence
VIII.   Summary
IX.   Key terms and concepts
X.   What would you do?
XI.   Teachers' casebook

Key Points

Formative and summative assessment

- Formative assessment: Ungraded testing used before or during instruction to aid in planning and diagnosis

  - Guides teacher in planning and helps students identify areas needing work

  - Pretest: Assesses student knowledge readiness and abilities

  - Diagnostic test: Determines students' strengths and weaknesses in content areas

  - Data-based instruction: Method using daily probes of specific-skill mastery

- Summative assessment: Testing that follows instruction and assesses achievement

Getting the most from traditional assessment approaches

- Planning for testing helps instruction and evaluation

  - Using a behavior-content matrix can help you plan for evaluation

  - Immediate testing after the learning is more effective with retestings spaced farther and farther apart and using cumulative questions that ask students to apply information learned

  - It is important to judge textbook tests and decide whether they are appropriate for students and teacher objectives

- Objective testing: Multiple-choice, matching, true/false, short- answer, and fill-in terms; scoring answers does not require interpretations

  - Multiple-choice tests are appropriate for factual and higher-level objectives

- Stem: The question part of a multiple-choice item

- Distractors: Wrong answers offered as choices in multiple-choice item

- Items in a multiple choice test should be designed to measure knowledge rather than test-taking skills or guessing

- Discrimination index tells how well each test item discriminated between those who did well and poorly on the test

- Essay tests require students to create answers on their own

- Essay test: Sample a small number of learning outcomes; require

- Scoring essays: Dangers are that individual standards of the grader and unreliable scoring procedures produce a wide variance in grades

- Methods of evaluating: Construct model and assign points; assign grades and sort; skim pile for consistency, grade all answers to one question before going to next, and remove names from papers

- Holistic scoring: Evaluation of a piece of written work as a whole, without separate grades for individual elements

Innovations in assessment

- Authentic testing: Assessment procedures that test skills and abilities as they would be applied in real-life situations, for example, testing ability to use fractions by having students enlarge or reduce recipes

- Performance in context includes portfolios and exhibitions

- Portfolio: A purposeful collection of student work that exhibits students' effort, progress, and achievements in one or more areas

- Exhibition: Performance test that is public and requires hours of preparation because it is the culminating experience of a whole program of study

Effects of grades and grading on students

- Failure can have both positive and negative effects on students

- Teachers should help students make connection between hard work and

- Whether promoted or retained, students should receive the help they need to maintain performance

- Feedback is helpful if students not only know if they are wrong but why they are wrong

  - With older students, personalized comments are most helpful

- Grades and motivation are often intertwined because students are more likely to do assignments that influence their grade

  - Receiving external rewards for something they already enjoy may diminish motivation

  - Required but ungraded assignments can be returned with critical feedback

  - Grades should reflect meaningful learning so that working for a grade and working to learn are the same

Grading and reporting: Nuts and bolts

- Criterion-referenced grading: Assessment of a student's mastery of course objectives

  - Criteria for each grade is given in advance

  - Motivation to succeed and academic improvement can be greater

  - Judgments about students related to clearly defined instructional objectives

- Norm-referenced grading: Assessment of students' achievement in relation to one another

  - Grade reflects student's standing in comparison with others who took the same course

  - "Grading on a curve": Average performance (defined by mean of the group) given average grade

  - Flexible use of curve is usually more appropriate and depends on actual distribution of scores and characteristics of particular group

- Report cards can feature norm- or criterion-referenced grading

  - Using criterion-referenced grading, level or proficiency which student has gained, is listed on the report card

- Using norm-referenced grading, all scores are based on a common scale

- The point system combines grades from many assignments

- Percentage grading: Converting class performances to percentage scores and assigning grades based on predetermined cutoff points

- Contract system: System in which each student agrees to work for a particular grade according to agreed-upon standards

- Grading on effort and improvement is an alternative to grading on achievement alone

  - Using improvement as a standard penalizes the best students who naturally improve the least

  - Individual learning expectation system: Allows everyone to earn improvement points based on personal average score

  - Revise option: Chance to revise and improve work in a contract system

- Teachers should guard against unfair influences on grading practices: The effects of attributions of causes of success/failure

  - Halo effect: Tendency for a general impression of a person to influence perception of any aspect of that person

Beyond Grading: Communication

- Conferences with students and parents can assist in communicating feedback

- Teachers need skill in interpersonal communication, especially listening and problem- solving skills

- The Buckley Amendment protects students' and families' rights to privacy and access

  - Information in students' records is available to students and/or parents

  - Information in cumulative folders must be based on firm, defensible evidence

Concept Map: ALTERNATIVES FOR ASSESSMENT

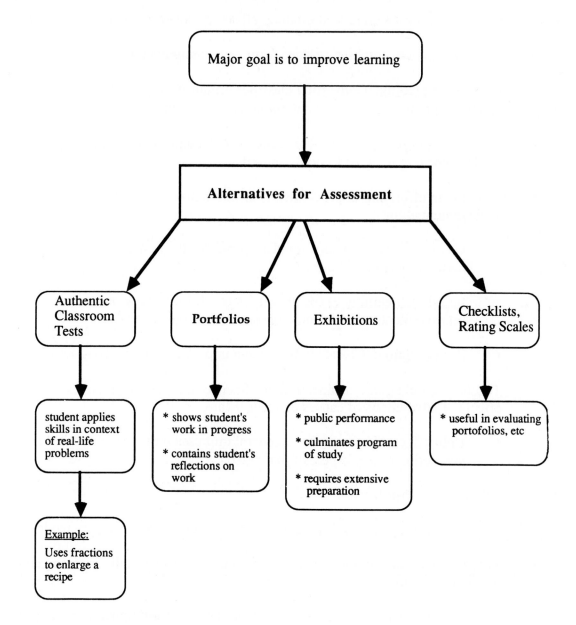

Do You Know This?

Answering these questions will help you check yourself on the mastery of the chapter objectives:

Formative and Summative Assessment

Can you make a plan for testing students on a unit of work?

Getting the Most from Traditional Assessment Approaches

How can you evaluate tests that accompany textbooks and teacher's manuals?

Could you create multiple-choice and essay test items for a given unit of your subject area?

Innovations in Assessment

Can you describe authentic assessment approaches, including portfolios, performances, and exhibitions?

Effects of Grades and Grading on Students

What are the potential positive and negative effects of grades on students?

Can you give examples of criterion-referenced and norm-referenced grading systems?

Grading and Reporting: Nuts and bolts

Assign grades to a hypothetical group of students.   Could you defend your decisions in a class debate?

Beyond Grading: Communication

Could you role-play a conference with parents who do not understand your grading system or their child's grades?

DEFINITIONS: Concepts in Assessment

Write explanations for the following pairs of terms. Your explanations should clearly distinguish one from the other. Check the text to see if your explanations are equivalent.

Formative/Summative Assessment _____

_____

Pretest/Diagnostic test _____

_____

Stem/Distracter _____

_____

Objective testing/Authentic testing _____

_____

COMPLETION: Concepts in Assessment

Fill in the blanks with the following concepts. Each term is used only once. To check answers, see Answer Key.

Holistic scoring	**Criterion-referenced grading**	**Dual marking system**
Authentic testing	**Norm-referenced grading**	**Grading "on a curve"**
Exhibition	**Percentage grading**	**Contract system**
Halo effect	**Individual learning expectation system**	**Portfolio**

1. As a teacher, you wish to assess if the students have accomplished the learning objectives. You will use _____.

2. Each student agrees to work for a particular grade according to pre-agreed-upon standards. This is called a (an)¨_____."

3. A collection of the student's work in an area, showing growth, self-reflection, and achievement is a(n) _____.

4. A general impression of a person influences the evaluation he or she receives. This is a(n) _____.

5. Students compete against their own personal average score. This is an example of _____.

6. In a(n) _____, students' grades reflect both achievement and effort.

7. You have given your students a test that was, apparently, too difficult for them. The students' scores are very much below their usual performance. You still assign average grades to the students in the middle of the score distribution, low grades to the lower scores, and high grades to the high scores. This is an example of

    _____.

8. Converting class performances to percentage scores and assigning grades based on pre-determined cutoff points is called _____.

9. A performance test that is public is called a(n) _____.

10. Assessment of students' achievement compared against a national sample can be considered _____.

11. Testing skills using real-work applications is called _____.

12. You give students a grade for their essays based on a point value which does not detail small errors. This may be considered an example of _____.

APPLICATION: Parent Conferencing on Grading

Often teachers are in the position of explaining and justifying educational practices to parents. Imagine that have a fourth-grade class in the school's Gifted and Talented program. The class is graded on a "curve," and students who in the past were high achievers in relation to their peers, when grouped in a class of high achievers may now find their grades are now "average." You are conducting a conference with a parent whose child did not receive as "A" grade in your class, whereas in past years the child's achievement has consistently been rewarded with this grade. For each parent comment below, defend the practice of "grading on a curve." (In the dialogue below, the opening introductions, etc., have been deleted. This segment represents an interchange which assumes you have communicated some preliminary information about the classroom procedures and the student's progress).

Parent: Now, my chief concern is that Deborah is unhappy with her grade in reading. She feels that it is unfair to compare her with her classmates. Her teacher last year let her work at her own pace. The students worked under contracts and students could set their own goals and work at their own pace.

(Your sample answer explains whole-class norm-referenced grading):
Because this class is composed of gifted students who all achieve within a fairly consistent and narrow range, I am able to keep the class working together on activities and skills that I feel benefits them. The class is moving at a fast pace and most students are able to keep up. It is important for them to be judged against high standards.

Parent: So you are using a competitive structure to evaluate achievement. Do you think this is a fair way to motivate students?

Your answer (A1): _____

Parent: Yet a contract system would allow students to set individual goals, which I think increases their ability to take responsibility for their own learning. Aren't you encouraging students to depend on y<u>our</u> setting their performance standards through this kind of competition?

Your answer (A2): _____

Parent: But I feel that your standards of performance are unreasonable for students of this age. This is causing Deborah unneeded anxiety.

Your answer (A3): _____

Parent: If you tell students what they need to do succeed and let them work at their own pace, it teaches them to manage their own learning wisely. In this way, they also are encouraged to cooperate with one another rather than suffer such cutthroat competition.

Your answer (A4): _____

Discussion: Compare criterion-referenced measurement with norm-referenced measurement? Which is most consistent with cooperative learning? (Were you comfortable defending a norm-referenced, competitive environment? Do you believe this is the ambiance that gifted students need?

CHARTING: Selecting a Textbook

The text offers key points to consider when judging whether a textbook test is appropriate for a group of students. Choose a textbook from any content area that includes a suggested test. Using the Decision-Making Frame below, list the criteria that would lead you to either use this test or choose not to use it for a given group of students.

Question:	Is this textbook appropriate for my students?	
Important Information:		
Decision:	YES	NO

CASE STUDY: Giving Feedback to Students

To encourage students to write more effectively, Mrs. Chang uses portfolio assessment. In designing writing samples that will be included in the portfolio, Mrs. Chang attempts to utilize a wide variety of genres that reflect authentic language use, such as essays, creative writing, letter writing, and personal journal writing. (She also includes student self-evaluations and anecdotal entries written by the teacher.) How can Mrs. Chang give students feedback on their writing which encourages accuracy in mastering writing conventions such as grammar and punctuation, but at the same time promotes fluency and enjoyment in writing? Compare the role and purpose of several kinds of feedback, such as holistic scoring versus a skill-diagnostic approach.

CASE STUDY: Criterion-Referenced Evaluation

Each year, students in grades six, seven, and eight have the opportunity to enter a school-wide competition that culminates in a city-wide spelling contest. Preparation for this is time-intensive, with about 1000 possible words that the contestants must master. Mr. Hawkins is concerned that each year, preparation for this contest takes time away from other class activities. Describe how a criterion-referenced, self-paced instructional system could help students to prepare for this competition without taking extensive time away from other activities.

PRACTICE TEST: Multiple Choice

1. Summative tests are used to assess students'

    a. readiness for instruction.
    b. knowledge during an individual lesson.
    c. specific skills over the course of an instructional unit.
    d. level of achievement following instruction.

2. When you write multiple-choice items, you should favor

    a. stems that present a single problem.
    b. distractors that require five discriminations.
    c. using as much wording as possible in the distractors relative to the stem.
    d. "none of the above" over "all of the above."

3. Which of the following is a disadvantage of objective tests?

    a. Student can obtain answer by guesswork
    b. Cannot measure higher-order learning
    c. Difficult to grade
    d. Difficult to prepare

4. As part of a general test plan, it is recommended that tests be

    a. frequent.
    b. limited to one or two item forms.
    c. unit-specific rather than cumulative.
    d. all of the above.

5. With regard to the practice of retaining or "holding back" students with failing grades, your textbook's general recommendation is

    a. promote the student if at all possible, but provide extra help.
    b. retention is generally better for self-esteem and performance.

  c. promotion should include resource assignments.

  d. promotion underscores the idea that poor performance brings negative consequences.

6. Which grading system would be <u>least</u> likely to involve the computation of an average or mean performance in determining grades?

  a. Norm-referenced
  b. Criterion-referenced
  c. Normal curve grading
  d. Point system

7. A grading system in which score of 90-100 earns an "A," 80-89 earns a "B," etc., is _____ grading.

  a. point
  b. criterion-referenced
  c. norm-referenced
  d. percentage

8. Contract systems seem to have beneficial effects in
  a. improving learning.
  b. increasing the objectivity of grading.
  c. reducing student anxiety.
  d. reducing grade inflation.

9. The Buckley Amendment of 1974 provides that

  a. certain information in school records must be kept confidential.
  b. parents may review or challenge material in school records.
  c. no federal monies may be used for testing minority students.
  d. placement tests given to minorities must be culture-fair.

PRACTICE TEST: Essay

A. You are teaching a senior high school economics course and you wish to construct an essay test that assesses students' understanding of such concepts as the law of supply and demand. How would you proceed with scoring such an essay test?

B. You are teaching a class in which half of the students are classified as having limited English proficiency, including several students who have just entered the United States from Southeast Asia. At the end of the first grading period, you are faced with a dilemma: Do you grade the students according to the reading level they have achieved, or do you grade them on their improvement on reading proficiency? Discuss the pros and cons of grading for achievement vs. improvement.

Answer Key

COMPLETION: Concepts in Assessment

1. **Criterion-referenced grading**
2. **Contract system**
3. **Portfolio**
4. **Halo effect**
5. **Individual learning expectation system**
6. **Dual marking system**
7. **"Grading on a curve"**
8. **Percentage grading**
9. **Exhibition**
10. **Norm-referenced grading**
11. **Authentic testing**
12. **Holistic scoring**

PRACTICE TEST: Multiple Choice

1. d Summative tests are used to assess students' <u>level of achievement following instruction</u>. They are used for determining the final accomplishment attained in a course.

2. a The stems in multiple-choice questions <u>should present a single problem</u>. Also, nonessential details should be left out. The result is a clearer and more readable question. It is advisable not to repeat words in the alternatives that would be included in the stem and not to overuse "all of the above" and "none of the above."

3. d Objective tests are typically <u>difficult to prepare</u> due to having to develop a large number of items having the appropriate style and structure.

4. a Dempster found in a review of the literature that <u>frequent</u> testing encourages the retention of information. Tests should also use cumulative questions and varied item forms and be given soon after material has been learned.

5. a. Research suggests that retraining students in grades is usually detrimental and certainly not advantageous. It is therefore recommended that, if at all possible <u>students be promoted and given extra support to help them succeed</u>.

6. b Computing a class mean would be least valuable under a <u>criterion-referenced grading system</u>. The focus of criterion-referenced grading is what objectives the student has and has not mastered, regardless of how others perform.

7. d   A <u>percentage grading</u> system assigns grades based on established percentage scores, such as 90-100 earns A, 80-89 earns B, and so on.

8. c   A beneficial effect of contract systems is <u>reducing student anxiety about grades</u>. The possible reason is that contracts give the student more control over the grades they earn than occurs with other systems.

9. b   The Buckley Amendment of 1974 provides that <u>parents may review or challenge material in school records</u>. This means that teachers and schools must be careful about the grades given to students because they can be held accountable for their accuracy and validity.

PRACTICE TEST: Essay

A.   For each question, construct a model answer that contains the desired content. Assign points to each feature of the desired answer. Read the essays and assign points. Double- check the scores for consistency. Grade all answers to one question before going on to the next question. For additional fairness, score "blindly," removing names from papers.

B.   Equating the reading grades of students with limited English proficiency and English-only students is fair to neither group, for it does not recognize progress in English as a second language; nor does it fairly reward English only students whose rate of improvement may not be as dramatic. It would be best to use a dual marking system.

NOTES

NOTES

NOTES

NOTES

NOTES